FROM PUPPET TO CYBORG
PINOCCHIO'S POSTHUMAN JOURNEY

LEGENDA

LEGENDA is the Modern Humanities Research Association's book imprint for new research in the Humanities. Founded in 1995 by Malcolm Bowie and others within the University of Oxford, Legenda has always been a collaborative publishing enterprise, directly governed by scholars. The Modern Humanities Research Association (MHRA) joined this collaboration in 1998, became half-owner in 2004, in partnership with Maney Publishing and then Routledge, and has since 2016 been sole owner. Titles range from medieval texts to contemporary cinema and form a widely comparative view of the modern humanities, including works on Arabic, Catalan, English, French, German, Greek, Italian, Portuguese, Russian, Spanish, and Yiddish literature. Editorial boards and committees of more than 60 leading academic specialists work in collaboration with bodies such as the Society for French Studies, the British Comparative Literature Association and the Association of Hispanists of Great Britain & Ireland.

The MHRA encourages and promotes advanced study and research in the field of the modern humanities, especially modern European languages and literature, including English, and also cinema. It aims to break down the barriers between scholars working in different disciplines and to maintain the unity of humanistic scholarship. The Association fulfils this purpose through the publication of journals, bibliographies, monographs, critical editions, and the MHRA Style Guide, and by making grants in support of research. Membership is open to all who work in the Humanities, whether independent or in a University post, and the participation of younger colleagues entering the field is especially welcomed.

STUDIES IN COMPARATIVE LITERATURE

Studies in Comparative Literature are produced in close collaboration with the British Comparative Literature Association, and range widely across comparative and theoretical topics in literary and translation studies, accommodating research at the interface between different artistic media and between the humanities and the sciences.

ALSO PUBLISHED IN THIS SERIES

From Puppet to Cyborg

Pinocchio's Posthuman Journey

❖

Georgia Panteli

l

LEGENDA

Studies in Comparative Literature 40
Modern Humanities Research Association
2022

Published by Legenda
an imprint of the Modern Humanities Research Association
Salisbury House, Station Road, Cambridge CB1 2LA

ISBN 978-1-78188-712-7 (HB)
ISBN 978-1-78188-417-1 (PB)

First published 2022

Copy-Editor: Charlotte Brown

CONTENTS

❖

To Phileas,
for the many adventures
we have shared together

ACKNOWLEDGEMENTS

❖

This book comes from my PhD thesis and I would therefore like to thank my PhD supervisors, Dr Katia Pizzi and Professor Florian Mussgnug, for their insightful supervision. I would also like to thank my examiners, Professor Enrico Palandri, Professor Elinor Shaffer for her encouragement, as well as Professor Timothy Mathews for his ongoing support. Special thanks go to my friends Sarah de Sanctis and Dr Paola di Gennaro for their help with the Italian translations and Dr Noëmie Duhaut with the French translations. Thanks are also due to the artists Ausonia and Winshluss for granting permissions to reproduce their art for this book, including the cover image. Finally I would like to thank my parents, Stratos and Maria Panteli, as well as Alexandra Panteli and Dr Gerald Kössl for their practical support and their belief in me.

Part of Chapter 7 appeared, in a different form, as 'The Satirical Tradition of Collodi and Pinocchio's Nose', in *The Rhetoric of Topics and Forms*, ed. by Gianna Zocco (Berlin & Boston, MA: Walter de Gruyter, 2021), pp. 381–90.

All translations are my own unless otherwise stated. For excerpts from *The Adventures of Pinocchio*, I am using the translation of Nicolas Perella throughout the book.

ABBREVIATIONS

❖

The following abbreviations are used for in-text references to frequently-cited works:

AP   Carlo Collodi, *The Adventures of Pinocchio*, trans. by Nicolas Perella (Berkley & London: University of California Press, 1986)

PN   Jerome Charyn, *Pinocchio's Nose* (New York: Arbor House, 1983)

PV   Robert Coover, *Pinocchio in Venice* (New York: Linden Press/ Simon & Schuster, 1991)

LIST OF ILLUSTRATIONS

❖

INTRODUCTION

❖

Carlo Collodi's *Le avventure di Pinocchio: storia di un burattino* (hereafter *Pinocchio*) is one of the most famous texts in the world.[1] Daniela Marcheschi refers to the book's popularity in relation both to the size of the audience the book reached, and to the impact it had on authors all over the world:

> Il capolavoro la cui grazia e forza non solo hanno tanto colpito da farne il libro più letto e venduto nel mondo, dopo la Bibbia e il Corano, ma anche animato la fantasia, mosso lo stile e la creatività di molti altri autori italiani e stranieri, che, con il burattino Pinocchio, hanno ripetutamente sentito il bisogno di misurarsi.[2]

> [The masterpiece whose grace and power have not only managed to make it the most widely read and best-selling book in the world, after the Bible and the Koran, but also inspired the imagination and influenced the style and creativity of many other authors, both Italian and foreign, who have constantly felt the need to measure themselves against the puppet Pinocchio.]

Twenty years after Marcheschi's statement, the book remains 'il libro non religioso più tradotto al mondo' [the most translated non-religious book in the world], according to Massimo Rollino.[3] The popularity of Collodi's novel has contributed substantially to the creation and distribution of the Pinocchio myth through numerous adaptations and retellings. The most significant adaptation with regard to popularity was Walt Disney's film *Pinocchio* of 1940, which had a major impact on the formation of the Pinocchio myth.[4]

After presenting the context of Collodi's novel, I explain how it was adapted and retold until it came into the hands of Disney. In order to clarify the context further, I demonstrate why and how Collodi's work falls within the fairy-tale tradition. The focus will be on the ways in which the story of *Pinocchio* — mythicised and reinstated in the fairy-tale world — has been used in contemporary texts and in popular culture in order to either represent or critique the prevailing culture. This is followed by an outline of the main themes of the Pinocchio myth, which are revisited, reinterpreted, or deconstructed in the retellings that will form the case studies in the following chapters. More specifically, Part I is a revisiting of the Pinocchio myth, while Part II mostly deconstructs it, and Part III consists both of reinterpretation and deconstruction.

Part I. Film and Television

Lying at the heart of the Pinocchio myth is the desire to become human. Part I considers examples of films and television series in which Pinocchio is a robot or cyborg that craves humanity. The main case studies are Ridley Scott's *Blade Runner* (1982) in Chapter 1, Steven Spielberg's *A.I. Artificial Intelligence* (2001) in Chapter 2, and the 2004 television series *Battlestar Galactica* in Chapter 3.[5] Chapter 4 focuses on the different endings of the three case studies and their significance within the context of imagining the future. Part I shows how the Pinocchio myth is used in the context of 'posthumanism' to reflect anxieties and hopes for humanity's technological progress. 'Posthumanism' is a term that has been used in various contexts and can include different theoretical approaches, as I explain in detail. My approach refers to 'transhumanism' which, as Nick Bostrom emphasises, 'embraces technological progress while strongly defending human rights and individual choice'.[6] I demonstrate how the desire for humanity perpetuates the Pinocchio myth by resonating with transhumanist ideas of self-enhancement, and how science-fiction films provide the ideal showcase for portraying the perpetuation of the Pinocchio myth.

Part II. Metafiction

In Part II the case studies will be two metafictional novels, both belonging to the genre of postmodernist fiction: Jerome Charyn's *Pinocchio's Nose* (1983) and Robert Coover's *Pinocchio in Venice* (1991).[7] Both novels deconstruct the Pinocchio myth and the original text as much as the process of writing itself. Chronologically the case studies in this part span about the same time as those of the first. In this case, however, the Pinocchio myth is not perpetuated but dissected. The first two parts of the book therefore function as a chronological bifurcation, with each path following a different theoretical direction. While science-fiction films are very successful at portraying popular culture, the ideal field for deconstructing popular myths is that of postmodern literature because of its subversive nature. Both novels question the idea of becoming human, as both protagonists turn from flesh to wood. Their post-humanity is very different from that of the previous examples. Not only the relation to the body but every theme of the Pinocchio myth is broken down into its components and then scrutinised: the Blue Fairy, the colour blue, the growing of Pinocchio's nose. All these elements have great significance in the formation of the Pinocchio myth, and looking at each one of them separately will serve to expose and deconstruct the myth of Pinocchio. Chapter 5 focuses on the role of the author and how the process of writing and autobiographical elements are used in metafiction. Chapter 6 analyses the function of the Blue Fairy, with careful examination of the cultural context of the use of the colour blue. In Chapter 7 the focus is on the metaphor of the nose in Collodi's text and in its retellings.

Part III. Graphic Novels

The third part of the book combines posthumanism and postmodernism to expose the Pinocchio myth and the ways in which it has been used so far and suggests an alternative reading and use of the myth. This will be shown by analysis of two graphic novels, Winshluss's *Pinocchio* and Ausonia's *Pinocchio*.[8] These two artists are very subversive and, with their texts, they challenge conventional interpretations of the Pinocchio myth that tend to portray capitalist dreams and aspirations. Moreover, the significance and role of the genre of graphic novels and *fumetti* is not irrelevant to the way in which the Pinocchio myth is addressed. While the first two parts focus more on the individual, Part III focuses on a strong critique of society's consumerist values. In Chapter 8, I show how both authors challenge and deconstruct the Pinocchio myth by examining the role of desire. Chapter 9 focuses on the role of the cricket as a failed conscience.

The case studies of Part I were chosen because they all contain robots or cyborgs, in which the desire for humanity plays a vital role in the plot and therefore allows for close analysis of the perpetuation of the Pinocchio myth. The novels of Part II are both examples of postmodernist, fictional retellings of Pinocchio. In both novels, Pinocchio's relation to his body is a major theme, and both texts refer substantially to the process of writing and the role of the author, which is very relevant to my analysis. Finally, the texts that I have chosen for Part III bring all the previous points together: they are graphic novels with postmodernist elements. Stylistically, therefore, they combine the visual and textual aspects of the previous chapters. This time posthumanism is combined with postmodernism and, moreover, the cricket character in Winshluss is an author with writer's block. The thematic elements of the chapters are connected and even though each chapter has case studies in a different medium, they are all both theoretically and thematically interrelated.

The concept of 'becoming' will be explored throughout the book and challenged in the last two parts. By 'becoming' I refer to the ontological quest of the individual to change his or herself, whether this reflects a desire or aspiration, as in Parts I and II, or it functions in contrast with 'being', as in Part III, all the while within the frame of the Pinocchio myth. This will be further explored through the autobiographical references of the two authors in Part II, and also through the references to the process of writing in Parts II and III.

The theories I use as methodological tools in my analysis approach the concept of becoming from different angles. One such angle will be that of posthumanism. In Part I, I define the particular framework of posthumanist theory I will be working with. All three parts relate to the posthuman, whether it is in relation to technological advancement and human enhancement, as in Part I, or in relation to body politics, as in Part II, or with regard to both, as in Part III.

Psychoanalysis is another theoretical approach used throughout this study. More specifically, Freudian psychoanalysis as a tool of literary analysis is particularly relevant. The authors of most of my texts (and especially those of Part II) are very aware of Freudian psychoanalytic theory and they use it either playfully or subversively. For example, even though Charyn's protagonist is portrayed in a way that invites Freudian analysis and interpretation, when he tries to cure himself by using psychoanalysis, his condition worsens. Such types of 'inside joke' within the text are also found in Coover's novel. Both authors are aware that Freud's theory, applied in literary and film analysis, had become widely popularised, and in the style of self-referential fiction consistent to the texts under discussion, they refer to it mostly in a humoristic way, quite unlike the approach of the case studies in Part I. The popularity of Freudian psychoanalysis in literary theory is particularly relevant to this study, as it is related to the popularity of myths and how they are used. My focus therefore is not on the latest developments in psychoanalytic studies, but on the way its popularised form is applied in my case studies. Another way to illustrate this is by using a model of Freud's definition of the human psyche in the structure of the chapters. More specifically, the division of the psyche into id, ego, and super-ego, according to Freud, will be applied in all three parts in order to emphasise the effect of the different constituents of the Pinocchio myth in relation to the thematic focus of each part.[9]

Part I focuses on Pinocchio and his desire for humanity, reflecting the ego, the part of the psyche that tries to balance its lower instincts and the societal demands it is exposed to in order to belong and feel stabilised. The thematic focus of Part II is the Blue Fairy. As will be explained in detail, the Fairy's role challenges the function of the id, as the Fairy is the one who activates Pinocchio's desire to become something different from his initial impulses and instincts, which were oriented to the desire for a carefree life full of pleasures. The id corresponds to the pleasure principle and this is what the Fairy tries successfully to control. The battle between the pleasure principle and the reality principle is further explored in Part III, which focuses thematically on the Talking Cricket, which represents the super-ego, as, in Collodi's novel, and throughout the different *Pinocchio* retellings, it has represented Pinocchio's conscience. In Freudian terms, the conscience corresponds to the super-ego, as it is the part of the psyche that has internalised the rules imposed by society on the individual in order for him/her to be accepted and to co-exist functionally within human society.

Such is the power of the Pinocchio myth, that it has a significant effect on the reader when it is dissected into its different components and each of them exposed and re-defined. Due to its plasticity, the myth readjusts to contemporary values and is used anew to criticise and turn the reader's attention in a different direction, as will be shown by the end of this book.

Carlo Collodi's *Pinocchio*

Pinocchio tells the story of an animate puppet, carved by Geppetto from a talking log. Pinocchio is a puppet-boy who is supposed to go to school but he is side-tracked by the Fox and the Cat, who deceive and almost kill him. He is saved by the Blue Fairy, but he has more adventures in which he faces enemies and is helped by friends and by the Fairy, until he is finally transformed into a human boy with her help and reunited with his 'father', Geppetto. The story has been given many characterisations, from rite-of-passage novel to *Bildungsroman* and picaresque novel.[10]

It started as a series of stories for the children's magazine *Giornale per i bambini*, and due to its great success grew from what was originally fifteen to thirty-six chapters. As Collodi had written educational texts before, it has been widely argued that with Pinocchio he wanted to educate young children in the newly-unified Italy with the values that would keep the consolidated country strong and render it prosperous.[11] This is one of the reasons that *Pinocchio*, with its great success and numerous retellings within and beyond Italy, has often been connected with Italian identity. Besides, as Amy Boylan suggests, *Pinocchio* was written 'during a time when the task of creating an Italian national identity was being passionately discussed by politicians, writers, and socially engaged citizens'.[12] As she argues further, the clear language of the Tuscan dialect that most Italians could understand, together with the middle-class values that were promoted at that time, were some of the reasons that Pinocchio was turned into a symbol of the Italian national character.

Numerous *Pinocchiate* have been written, both as critical analyses and as re-narrations of Collodi's text. Many of these focus on the desire of the puppet to become human and the mystery of his growing nose. However, what Collodi had originally planned to be the story of Pinocchio would have finished in Chapter xv, and up to that chapter the themes of telling lies and the desire to become human had not been yet included. His young readers, however, insisted that the story continue and the magazine's editor, convinced by the financial possibilities, asked Collodi to keep writing. He revived the dead Pinocchio and added more episodes to his adventures and thus lying was invented as part of Pinocchio's naughty and disobedient character. His desire to become a real boy appeared only in Chapter xxv. However, what is truly his heart's desire, often neglected by the writers who have retold or revised the story, is epitomised by the answer he gives to the Talking Cricket early on in the story (in Chapter iv) describing the only trade that is to his liking as 'that of eating, drinking, sleeping, having fun, and living the life of a vagabond from morning to night' (*AP*, p. 109). It is this desire that clashes all the time with Pinocchio's efforts to be obedient. Even when he has come very close to being transformed into a real boy (having been good, obedient, and attended school) and the Fairy prepares a breakfast party for him and his friends to celebrate his upcoming metamorphosis, he regresses to his pleasure instinct and turns his back on the Fairy and on being human. He escapes to the 'Paese dei Balocchi', a land with no school, no teachers, and only fun, where he can fulfil his wildest dream, the life of a vagabond. This, however, cannot be fulfilled in Collodi's book. In fact, as Carl Ipsen points out, 'the 1859 Piedmontese/Italian criminal code allowed for the institutionalization of child vagabonds'.[13] Therefore Pinocchio's desire and tendency towards something illegal (i.e. a vagabond's life), is used by Collodi as a bad example in order to educate his young readers and satisfy their middle-class parents. However, Pinocchio remains ambiguous throughout the story: even though he and his wild instincts are 'tamed' in the end, the amiable puppet has managed to raise doubts in the audience's minds.

Geppetto pushes Pinocchio towards the virtuous path of school and education (according to the Fairy and her middle-class values), yet it is noteworthy that he had similar desires to Pinocchio, as he reveals to Maestro Ciliegia early on:

> I thought of making myself a fine wooden puppet, but a wonderful puppet
> who can dance, and fence, and make daredevil leaps. I intend to travel around
> the world with this puppet so as to earn my crust of bread and a glass of wine.
> (*AP*, p. 89)

Geppetto, an old unmarried man, is inspired by wanderlust and a desire for
adventure and this desire brings him the creativity to carve a puppet: this desire
makes him creator and artist at the same time. With this paternal attitude towards
his work of art, he carves his desires into his son, as he is carving Pinocchio's
characteristics on that piece of wood.

Desire is a concept that will be further discussed in the book. In Part I, the
desire to be human is applied within the context of the cyborg, using, as examples,
posthuman retellings of Pinocchio. In Part II Pinocchio's desire to become human
will be interpreted and examined as one of the Fairy's tricks to keep him close to
her. Giorgio Manganelli in *Pinocchio: un libro parallelo*, his famous parallel text to
Collodi's original — a unique retelling, a blend of novel and critical analysis —
suggests that the Fairy needs Pinocchio as much as he needs her. The Fairy's nature
is dark and ambiguous: she needs Pinocchio's sacrifice and death in order to be
saved from her own death and become the powerful Fata who will then save him
in return: 'essa ha bisogno di Pinocchio, non meno che Pinocchio ha bisogno di lei'
[she needs Pinocchio no less than he needs her]. And further on: 'E Pinocchio vuole
ignorare che, in realtà, non ha una mamma, ma un mostro amoroso e sapiente'
[And Pinocchio wants to ignore the fact that, in reality, he does not have a mother,
but a loving and wise monster].[14] By tempting Pinocchio with the possibility of
transforming him into a real boy if he behaves well, she keeps him under control
and close to her. As Manganelli suggests, since he has to go to school, he has to
stay in the town of the Busy Bees at the Fairy's house, with her, keeping her strong
and keeping away the spells that weaken her. One of the conditions for becoming
a proper boy is, as she says, obedience: 'You'll obey me and always do as I tell you'
(*AP*, p. 287). This is how she offers to be his mother; so Pinocchio faces a dilemma
because even though he enjoys the vagabond life, like every child, he cherishes the
care and protection that his parents give him.

Another point worth clarifying is that Pinocchio perceives himself as a child.
There are many instances in the book where he refers to himself as 'ragazzo' [boy]
and some others where he opts for 'burattino' [puppet], but it seems that for him
one does not exclude the other. He has human emotions and needs like hunger,
fear, and joy. Pinocchio wants to become a grown-up man with the excitement
and haste that all children have for growing up. This is how the Fairy tricks him
into blind obedience: in order to become a man, he has to be a proper boy, not
a puppet. However, by 'proper', the Fairy means obedient, tamed, fitting in with
the morals of the society that she represents. Nicolas Perella categorises her (in her
form as Pinocchio's mother in the town of the Busy Bees) as 'somewhere between
a lady of the middle class and a woman of the rural popular class'. In fact, as he
argues further on, 'there was never any real chance of Pinocchio's continuing in
school while living with Geppetto', as 'education was the kind of luxury that poor

Geppetto could not have offered his son for long'.[15] In accordance with Perella's view, Pinocchio's transformation in the end is more significant for portraying his social advancement, having internalised the work ethic of the middle class; he has been transformed into a 'proper' human boy, who finds himself in a proper middle-class house.

Collodi suggests that the chances for those who struggle for food and a proper education are very limited, and that it is more important that they are fed first. By being ambiguous, he is managing to make his point and, at the same time, please his middle-class readers. For example, we can assume that Pinocchio actually learns his lessons 'on the road', rather than at school. Life and the road have taught him and matured him so that he can save himself and his father. Therefore, the life of a vagabond, Pinocchio's original (and perhaps unchanged) desire, teaches him what he needs to know in order to survive.

From Tuscany to Disney and Beyond

Collodi's novel went through several transformations, through translations and adaptations, until it reached the studio of Walt Disney. Disney's *Pinocchio* contributed substantially to the creation of the Pinocchio myth, as Umberto Eco points out.[16] I will therefore firstly show how Disney found out about the book which he subsequently transformed into his famous film. Richard Wunderlich and Thomas J. Morrissey's *Pinocchio Goes Postmodern: Perils of a Puppet in the United States* gives an extensive account of the first translations and adaptations of Collodi's novel outside Italy and in particular in North America.[17] Wunderlich and Morrissey's book focuses on the various phases of reception that Collodi's text underwent from when it was first translated into English in 1892, including different translations, abridgements, theatre and film adaptations, as well as retellings.

Starting with the first translation of Collodi's book, which entered the American market in 1892, there were numerous translations in the years to follow. These often came with alterations, especially once Pinocchio was used in school classrooms as a text. One such example is Walter S. Cramp's first American translation in 1904, which omitted all the violent episodes, to discourage juvenile delinquency, a major issue at the time. Another victim of censorship were the scenes that ridiculed adults (e.g. Master Cherry and Geppetto fighting or Pinocchio sticking his tongue out and disrespecting Geppetto). As Wunderlich and Morrissey suggest, 'the stress on industrial moralism, favored by business interests predominant on school boards, clearly is evident in the text revision', and further on, 'these revisions, which also teach the proper relation between subordinates and superiors, provide guidance not only for the child's future work role, but also for the way the child's parents are supposed to act toward their own employers'.[18] It is not unusual, however, for *Pinocchio* to be adapted to the different historical and cultural contexts of the country into whose language it was translated. Examples from different translations demonstrate this. Salvador Bartolozzi's Spanish translation added quixotic values to *Pinocchio*, as is described by G. J. Manila.[19] Dieter Richter explains in detail how the first German translation of *Pinocchio* by Otto Julius Bierbaum in 1905 was deliberately rendered into a German version of the story — not only through its translation choices for names, but also by adapting the cultural context (replacing grapes with apples) and adding entire episodes in order to parody contemporary German politics.[20] Natalia Kaloh Vid points out how *The Golden Key or the Adventures of Buratino*, Alexej Tolstoi's famous translation-adaptation of *Pinocchio* into Russian in 1935, went through several ideological changes in order to depict Soviet values, such as the abolition of private property and the importance of collective labour.[21] It is therefore only to be expected that similar cultural adaptations occurred in the US as well.

In the decade following the first American translation, Pinocchio became increasingly popular as numerous translations were released every year, often with different illustrations, or even abridged editions for school use. The first sequels of the puppet's adventures appeared as well: *Pinocchio in Africa* by Cherubini,[22] in translation from Italian, was a colonial, racist text, resonating with Italy's unsuccessful attempt to invade Ethiopia and therefore serving to heal a recent wound in national pride.[23] Given the strong racist context in the US, with the spread of the Ku Klux Klan, it is not surprising that the book survived in print for more than forty years. More adventures of Pinocchio included *Pinocchio Under the Sea*, published as an educational tour of ocean life in 1913 by Macmillan, and *The Heart of Pinocchio: New Adventures of the Celebrated Little Puppet*.[24] In this tale by 'Collodi Nipote' (Paolo Lorenzini), Collodi's nephew, Pinocchio is a soldier in World War One defending Italy against the Austrians.

Emily Gray's play, *The Adventures of Pinocchio, a Marionette*, was even more didactic than Cramp's translation; it was representative of the multiple pedagogically-driven renditions of the time: 'Written didactically, almost every scene concludes with a recital of what Pinocchio learned or should have learned'.[25] The 1920s, the 'Golden Age for children's literature', embraced Pinocchio with particular enthusiasm.[26] Luxurious editions with new illustrations and colour plates were published. Angelo Patri, the child of Italian immigrants in America and translator of *Pinocchio in Africa*, wrote *Pinocchio in America* in 1928.[27] This time the adventures of the puppet brought him to New York, in a context of growing anti-Italian and anti-immigrant prejudice. All goes better for him, though, as soon as he embraces his new American identity. Susan Honeyman claims that Patri's work 'seems to have been the inspiration for Ned Washington's lyric "When you wish upon a star" ', the song that Jiminy Cricket sings in Disney's *Pinocchio* and the words of which 'have become the Disney anthem and spell out a consumerist ideal of permitted passivity'.[28] Josef Marino's *Hi! Ho! Pinocchio* dealt with the same topic a decade later, but by that time Italian Americans had been identified with organised crime and Marino's text aimed to restore their reputation by presenting the puppet as getting help from his honest and honourable relatives in Chicago.[29]

The 1920s was the decade that also opened the stage door for Pinocchio. At least five theatre adaptations are known from that time; these brought about more alterations to the Pinocchio myth, but at the same time they etched it more deeply in the audience's consciousness. A very characteristic example is the stage adaptation of Remo Bufano, an Italian immigrant in the US, who rewrote Pinocchio for American audiences, including children from rough city streets.[30] Even though he followed Collodi's text closely, he was the first to spare the life of the Talking Cricket and so started a tradition that Disney embraced later.

The 1930s was a triumphant time for Pinocchio, despite the Great Depression. New editions, abridgements, and retellings appeared together with stage adaptations for actors as well as puppets, operettas, pantomime performances, ballets and radio broadcasts. During this golden age for Pinocchio some of the major alterations to its storyline occurred. Yasha Frank's stage adaptation, *Pinocchio*, which premiered in June 1937, was a great success.[31] However, Pinocchio in this case was not the familiar mischievous puppet, but a meek, innocent, obedient one, and Geppetto was a loving old man who needed a son. The focus turned to the happiness of family life. As Wunderlich and Morrissey note, Walt Disney and his technical staff attended several performances of Yasha Frank's play.[32]

Obviously influenced by Frank's successful play, Walt Disney created a Pinocchio who is naively innocent and brought into this world by Geppetto's 'wish upon a star' for a child. The wish is granted by the Blue Fairy who will make Pinocchio a 'real boy' if he behaves well and listens to his father and his conscience, Jiminy Cricket. Therefore, Pinocchio already has a task from the beginning of his animated life, whose obscure origin in Collodi's text is here eradicated and simplified. Disney portrays Geppetto as an old, lovable clockmaker who longs to have a son and not be lonely. Poverty is completely wiped out of the story as this was something that would upset post-Depression audiences. Moreover, to add to the claustrophobia of that post-Depression era, Disney presented a world where the only safety was within the family. Collodi's Pinocchio is street-smart and learns how to become responsible through his exposure to the road: he encounters thugs but also helpers. In Disney, all external encounters are dangers and the message is that the only safe place for the child is the family:

> The new Pinocchio espoused a political message peculiarly appropriate to help calm any unrest provoked by the long, wearying Depression. [...] Just as the child should be in harmony with the family, so should the citizen be in harmony with the state and its leader, for that is the natural order.[33]

New renditions and plays were created during the 1940s and '50s. In Brian Way's 1954 interactive stage version, *Pinocchio: A New Version of the Story by Carlo Collodi*, Collodi's world is turned upside down.[34] Pinocchio has no wish to become a real boy; that is Geppetto's wish instead. The Judge imprisons the Fox and the Cat, but not Pinocchio, and returns Pinocchio's coins to him: 'The world is well ordered, the civil authorities do just what they are supposed to do'; 'This is no longer a story about growing up; it is a story about being comfortable, sheltered, and having fun in a world of make-believe'.[35]

During the subsequent decades, more translations and adaptations were done but not as many as during the 1930s, Pinocchio's golden age. The interest in Pinocchio increased again during the 1980s, when the puppet's centenary was celebrated.

New translations and beautifully illustrated volumes appeared. In 1986, Nicolas J. Perella made a new translation, published by the University of California Press. Lou Scheimer's 1987 animated film *Pinocchio and the Emperor of the Night* starts with Pinocchio's first birthday as a real boy.[36] Here he has to retain his free will or he will turn into a puppet again. In this Manichaean worldview, very well suited to the mentality of the Cold War, Pinocchio is a representation of the good American boy, born in the land of the free. He needs to fight Evil (alluding to the alleged communist danger of the time) and prevent it from stealing his freedom away. Apart from the obvious political message, this is a captivating film with quite audacious images for children. In this rendition Pinocchio is not supposed to go to the carnival: an evil place, the domain of the Emperor of the Night. Puppetino, the Emperor's servant, convinces Pinocchio to dance and then with his evil magic turns him into a puppet again, in an extremely frightening scene that received a lot of criticism as inappropriate for children. The magic instrument that Puppetino plays forces Pinocchio to dance and, as he dances out of control, against his will, every part of his body turns into wood while he is screaming, begging Puppetino to stop. Puppetino finally attaches strings to his body and Pinocchio becomes a lifeless puppet, like all the others around him — puppets that had presumably been children before Puppetino inflicted this horrible transformation upon them. The scene has been described as suggesting child rape by a paedophilic Puppetino and therefore it was removed when the film was aired on television. It is relevant both to Pinocchio's transformation into a donkey in Collodi's text and to Winshluss's retelling, as I will show in Part III. It is also revisited in the animation film, *Pinocchio 3000*, a disturbing retelling in which children are turned into robots.[37]

In the next two decades, Pinocchio's popularity decreased. At the same time, the renditions or retellings that appeared were of a more subversive nature. Postmodernism was a useful tool to question the established consumerist culture. Charyn's *Pinocchio's Nose* (1983) and Coover's *Pinocchio in Venice* (1991) are two such texts, as I explain in detail in Part II.

In recent years more and more authors from different genres, as well as film-makers and artists, have taken an interest in reinterpreting Pinocchio. A new English translation by Geoffrey Brock was published in 2008, with an introduction by Umberto Eco. In 2011 the Folio Society, famous for its illustrated editions, published a now-collectible edition of Pinocchio with new illustrations by Grahame Baker-Smith.[38] The plasticity of the Pinocchio myth allows for its application in all different contexts. Graphic novels such as the case studies in Part III, *Pinocchio* by Ausonia, *Pinocchio* by Winshluss, and also the series *Pinocchio Vampire Slayer*, are some of the best examples of the genre.[39] Michael Morpurgo's *Pinocchio* is a modern adaptation adjusted to address contemporary children's problems: Pinocchio decides to run away from school because he is bullied.[40] Silvio Donà's *Pinocchio 2112* is a cyberpunk novel describing a social dystopia set in a not so distant future.[41] In 2008 American pop artist Jim Dine built a nine-metre-high bronze Pinocchio in the Swedish town of Borås.[42] In film, *A.I. Artificial Intelligence* is one example of reinterpreting Pinocchio, as I will show in Part I. Another type of Pinocchio film retelling is to present him among fairy-tale characters. The filmic examples are numerous and include the South Korean 2014 television series *Pinocchio*,[43] and also upcoming productions such as Guillermo del Toro's stop-motion adaptation, which he has been 'slowly co-developing' with the Jim Henson Company since 2008.[44] Finally, Walt Disney studios have decided to come back to *Pinocchio*, this time as a live-action feature film.[45] The story is expected to focus on the relationship between father and son and, since the latest Disney productions have moved away from the naive stereotypes they reproduced in previous decades, it is not entirely unexpected that Disney's second attempt to reinterpret *Pinocchio* may prove closer to the original than the famous adaptation of 1940.

Fairy Tales and Pinocchio

The connection of Pinocchio to fairy tales plays an important role throughout this book. Carlo Collodi had translated the fairy tales of Madame d'Aulnoy, Madame Leprince de Beaumont, and Charles Perrault from French and was consequently influenced by the genre. Apart from the historical indications, there are also formalistic ones that demonstrate the similarity of Collodi's novel to a fairy tale. Finally, in many contemporary retellings of fairy tales, where different fairy-tale characters appear together, Pinocchio often appears, as will be shown presently.

Formalistic characteristics of the fairy-tale genre can be observed throughout Collodi's text. First of all, the story starts in the unspecified chrono-topos of fairy tales ('C'era una volta' [Once upon a time]). Throughout the novel, there is not a single mention of a real place or a specific time, a common characteristic of fairy tales. Even the elements that might signify some particular time reference, such as the *carabinieri*, are mingled and assimilated in the story so that it might have taken place anywhere in a mythical fairy-tale time. Collodi uses such specific elements as the *carabinieri* and the marionette theatre so that his audience can relate to it better, but at the same time he blends these characters with fairy-tale ones: the ogre Mangiafuoco, the magical carriage, the live piece of wood, metamorphoses (into animal/donkey or human), and the Fairy ('Bambina coi capelli turchini' [Little girl with blue hair]/ Fata). Talking animals are another typical fairy-tale element and in Collodi's novel there are nineteen such examples if we include the Fairy's metamorphosis into a Blue Goat; if we also add the Poodle Coachman, even though he does not speak, he brings the number of anthropomorphic animals to twenty.

In her work *Pinocchio e Collodi*, Rossana Dedola highlights how important the influence of Collodi's translated fairy tales was in the creation of Pinocchio: 'Gli studiosi italiani tendono in sostanza a sottovalutare il ruolo che ha avuto per Collodi l' ingresso nel regno delle fate' [Italian scholars essentially tend to underestimate the role played by Collodi's entry into the kingdom of the fairies].[46] Jack Zipes also supports this view: 'Collodi's fairy-tale translations and textbooks prepared the way for his writing of *Pinocchio*'.[47] Dedola goes on to explain how motifs from the various fairy tales Collodi translated may have influenced *Pinocchio* — for example, the afore-mentioned talking animals or other elements from 'The White

Cat', 'Beauty and the Beast', 'Prince Désir', and 'Little Red Riding Hood': 'Ma altri segnali, se non addirittura veri e propri sintomi, si sposteranno dalle fiabe francesi per prender posto nel testo delle *Avventure*' [But other elements, if not even exact parts, are transferred from French fairy tales into the text of *The Adventures of Pinocchio*].[48] In addition to Dedola's examples, there are more fairy tales that show similarities with Pinocchio or even different aspects of the tales that Dedola mentions. For example, if we consider the tale of 'Little Red Riding Hood', Pinocchio seems like a male version of her: a child before or in early adolescence straying from the path and not going to school and punished for this with his death as an example to others. 'L'Oiseau bleu' by Madame d'Aulnoy is another story that strongly influenced Collodi, as I will show in Part II. Dedola looks at the fairy tales that Collodi translated, yet Collodi's translations were only of a selection from the fairy tales to which he had been exposed. It is therefore easy to observe influences and inspiration from other fairy tales as well, such as 'Hansel and Gretel'. This is a fairy tale that has the motif of the land of Cockaigne which turns out to be a trap — the same motif that is found in Collodi's Funland, as I will show in Part III.

Most of all, Collodi's novel has a very characteristic fairy-tale structure. In *Morphology of the Folktale*, Vladimir Propp explained how all fairy tales have a similar structure, with a number of variations that can be classified.[49] His theory is still respected in fairy-tale studies and Alberto Asor Rosa refers to him in relation to Collodi's text.[50] *Pinocchio* shares that structure, together with the functions of the dramatis personae as Propp describes them. This can be illustrated by the following transcription of the different narrative themes and functions that appear in *The Adventures of Pinocchio* into the coding system that Propp introduced, and according to which he classified all fairy tales and their structure:

$$[\alpha\gamma^2\beta^3\delta\eta^I\theta^I A^6 F^9\beta^3\gamma^I\delta\eta^I\theta^I A_5{}^{15}D^I E^I{\uparrow}D^I E^I F^9 G^I\gamma^2\delta A^{17}F^9\gamma^2\delta A^{11}F^9 K F^5{\downarrow}M T^I w^0]$$

The synthesis of the above formula, which represents the narrative functions of *The Adventures of Pinocchio*, can be seen in detail in the short Appendix at the end of this book.

Not every novel can be transcribed into such a formula and this proves what an integral part the fairy-tale structure plays in Collodi's novel. This can also be seen by the inclusion of Pinocchio's character in many contemporary retellings of fairy tales, where all fairy-tale characters co-exist. The animated film series *Shrek* (2001–10) is a story that combines many fairy-tale characters interacting in a modern retelling of the classic fairy tales.[51] Pinocchio is one of them — part of the fairy-tale realm in the cultural conscience. Disney's adaptation contributed to the establishment of Pinocchio in popular culture as a fairy-tale character, since the effect was similar with other children's novels such as *Peter Pan* or *Alice in Wonderland*, after they were adapted in Disney's films. The graphic novel series *Fables* (2002–15) is another such example: fairy-tale characters live in disguise in New York City, after they have been forced out of their homelands by the big Adversary, who is Geppetto.[52] Pinocchio plays a major part in the series, as do Geppetto and the Blue Fairy, belonging in the same realm as Little Red Riding Hood, Snow White, and all the other fairy-tale personae. The most recent example of Pinocchio's place within the fairy-tale realm is the ABC television series *Once Upon a Time* (2011–18).[53] Largely inspired by the aforementioned graphic novels, the series portrays all the fairy-tale heroes doomed by the Evil Queen's curse to live oblivious to their real nature in a contemporary Maine town called Storybrooke. Pinocchio, Geppetto, and Jiminy Cricket are part of the fairy-tale world here as well.

The Myth of Pinocchio

'The nature and functioning of myth are among the longest standing topics of speculation in the history of Western thought,' as Phillip Stambovsky points out.[54] Myth scholar Robert Segal, agreeing on the difficulty of the definition of myth, proposes that it should be broken down into very small and simple components: 'a story about something significant'.[55] As acknowledged by theorists in the field, myth has been given different definitions and there is no universal one upon which everyone agrees. As Segal explains, myth is used differently by different disciplines in order to showcase their applications. It is therefore important to clarify how myth and the concept of the Pinocchio myth will be used in this study. Rather than agreeing with one or other theorist, I suggest that combining elements from different schools of mythology studies is the most constructive approach to defining and utilising the Pinocchio myth. I referred earlier to Propp's structuralist approach. Another approach that I discuss is that of Jungian archetypes that connect myth with psychoanalysis. My research is informed by other theoretical approaches too, such as religious and political interpretations of myth, as for example that of Roland Barthes, which will be discussed in Part III. As I show throughout the book, myth is interdisciplinary by nature, as it combines approaches in literary criticism, depth psychology, psychoanalysis, anthropology, and structuralism. It is at the same time both an approach and an analytical tool. Rachel Bowlby points out that 'the word "mythologies" implies a narrative movement of telling and retelling that at once sustains and changes the likely or fabulous ideas and stories in circulation'.[56] This study focuses on the elements of the Pinocchio myth that are sustained and those that are challenged through the retellings under examination. As Bowlby adds, 'myths also alter their possible or likely meanings according to the changing cultural contexts in which they are retold'.[57] My analysis investigates the reasons for and illustrates the context of these changes.

To use Segal's definition of myth, Pinocchio's story is about something significant. His magical transformation from puppet to human boy is the result of hard work: he desires it so strongly that he manages to make the impossible possible. There is something heroic in the core of this story and this is one reason why it acquires mythic dimensions. The Pinocchio myth is not related to classical mythology; it is a modern myth, yet rich in symbolism and archetypes that evoke connections to older myths and religious motifs. Such archetypes are those of the trickster and of the animate/inanimate, as revealed in Part I. Collodi's symbolism has been interpreted in various ways. The biblical reference to Jonah and the whale allowed for theological and Christological interpretations, the most famous being that of the Catholic cardinal Giacomo Biffi.[58] Other interpretations of Collodi's text have included ones that point to freemason symbolism, as explained in Part II. This variety of approaches highlights the ease with which the Pinocchio myth can be applied to different contexts.

Pinocchio's strong fairy-tale background adds to the myth as well. Segal argues that 'classical Freudians tend to see myths and fairy tales as akin', yet it is not only classical Freudians who are interested in the relations between myths and fairy tales.[59] Jack Zipes sees the two genres as being so close that he claims that 'the fairy tale is myth. That is, the classical fairy tale has undergone a process of mythicization'. He goes on to explain how this process reflects the ideology of the middle classes, i.e. by pretending to be apolitical, fairy tales that have been mythified into popular culture through numerous adaptations 'represent and maintain the hegemonic interests of the bourgeoisie'.[60] Another connection between myths and fairy tales can be seen in the way both are classified: in the same way that myths are classified into hero myths, creation myths, flood myths, and so on, fairy tales are classified by their thematic references.[61] A good example of the close relationship between myths and fairy tales is their linguistic connection in Greek, from which the word 'myth' originates in most Western languages. As David Leeming points out, 'in the case of the word "myth", etymology, or the tracing of roots, can be useful in pointing toward the meaning of a complex concept'.[62] 'Myth' comes from the ancient Greek word μῦθος (mythos), which had multiple meanings, mainly that of 'word' and of 'story'. The Greek word for 'fairy tale' is παραμύθι (paramythi). The first compound, παρα- (para-) means 'beside'. Therefore, the Greek word for 'fairy tale' includes the word 'myth', placing it conceptually close to myth. G. S. Kirk wonders if it is 'really feasible to separate myths from folktales', whereby he considers fairy tales as a variety of folk tales.[63] Indeed the meaning of the word paramythi in Greek includes both fairy tales and folk tales.

In his essay, 'Myths and Fairy Tales', Mircea Eliade describes how closely connected myths and fairy tales are.[64] He suggests that fairy tales are secularised myths that still portray old initiation rites, but in a more hidden way and with the religious elements smoothed out. However, the fallen gods still retain their functions in the form of helpers, donors, and so on. A very good example of this is the story of Cupid and Psyche as narrated in Lucius Apuleius's The Golden Ass.[65] The structure and form of the tale within the story is much more similar to the written European fairy tale of the sixteenth to nineteenth centuries than the epic myths which are chronologically closer. One need only replace the ancient Greek gods in the Cupid and Psyche story with witches, evil stepmothers, and heroes and the tale is clearly recognisable as a fairy tale. In fact, Zipes confirms Eliade's approach and also considers the story of Cupid and Psyche in The Golden Ass as an early form of fairy tale.[66] In the same tone as Eliade and Zipes, Marina Warner, in her British Academy lecture, 'Into the Woods', points out that one of the differences between myths and fairy tales is that myths have more religious aspects, such as cosmological references.[67] In fact, she finds many elements in fairy tales that stem from myths, such as metamorphoses and the motif of the enchanter/enchantress.[68] Even though

I agree with all the aforementioned theorists, the focus of this study is not on the connection between the myth of Pinocchio and possible religious elements in the origin of the story. It is, however, important to be aware of this background of myth studies, as at times it will resonate in my analysis, in particular in Part I.

Salvatore Consolo considers the story of Pinocchio as a myth mainly because of the heroic traits that Pinocchio bears: his unusual birth which resembles theophany, the obstacles he overcomes through metamorphoses that resonate with the heroic motif of birth-loss-rebirth, and the wisdom he acquires after his adventures end.[69] Building on Consolo's views, I regard Pinocchio's heroic journey as an example of a monomyth — as I will show further on — but while for Consolo the quest for the father is the main aspect of the Pinocchio myth, I consider this to be the quest for humanity. The term 'monomyth' was a concept that Joseph Campbell developed after he first encountered it in James Joyce's *Finnegans Wake*, of which he was one of the first literary critics to publish a thorough analysis.[70]

Mythologist Joseph Campbell, largely influenced by Jung's psychoanalytic theory, defines the 'nuclear unit of the monomyth, or the standard path of the mythological adventure of the hero', as 'a magnification of the formula represented in the rites of passage: *separation — initiation — return*'.[71] This formula applies to numerous myths and religious texts and it applies to *The Adventures of Pinocchio* as well. Campbell introduces some further stages in these three phases of the hero's journey. In the same way that I showed earlier how *Pinocchio* fits Propp's structure of fairy tales, I will now show how it also fits Campbell's structure of the monomyth. First of all, the circumstances of the hero's birth are extraordinary and unusual, as is Pinocchio's birth from a piece of wood. 'The Call to Adventure' comes for Pinocchio when he is distracted by the puppet theatre from going to school. Followed by the 'refusal of the call' when he hesitates because he is thinking about his father and then accepts the call, this is a motif that is repeated several times in Collodi's text, every time Pinocchio faces a new adventure and has second thoughts when thinking of his father or the Fairy. 'Supernatural aid' is the next phase according to Campbell, and this is the kind of help that Pinocchio receives repeatedly throughout his adventures, whether in the form of advice from the ghost of the cricket, the pigeon that carries him to his father, or even the Blue Fairy, in her various forms. 'The Crossing of the First Threshold' happens for Pinocchio when he sells his spelling book in order to go to the theatre, as this is the point of no return from his original purpose, which was to go to school. The first stage of the hero's journey, that of separation, ends with what Campbell symbolically names 'Entering the Belly of the Whale', which will happen literally later on for Pinocchio, but at that first stage means confronting danger, which is the encounter with Mangiafuoco.

The second stage of the hero's journey is that of initiation and it starts with the 'Road of Trials'. This is when Pinocchio overcomes his entrapment in Mangiafuoco's theatre but then falls into another dangerous adventure when he encounters the Fox and the Cat. 'The Meeting with the Goddess' takes place when the hero receives help from a female agent, here the Blue Fairy, one of the major figures of the text. She appears again in the role of the 'Woman as Temptress' when on the island of the Busy Bees she tests Pinocchio before letting him into her house. The 'Atonement with the Father' comes symbolically, when Pinocchio decides to accept his father's values and go to school again. His progress at school brings him to the level of 'Apotheosis', as he has finally learnt to be hardworking and obedient. 'The Ultimate Boon' is the present the Blue Fairy intends to give him as a reward: she will turn him into a human boy and to celebrate this she organises a party.

The final stage of the hero's journey, his return, starts with his 'Refusal of the Return': in a last regressive impulse Pinocchio turns his back on the humanity he has so long desired and escapes with Lucignolo to the 'Paese dei Balocchi', only to realise that it was a trap, after he is turned into a donkey. After his unfortunate adventures as a donkey, he escapes again and with the help of the Fairy he is restored to puppet form. However, this 'Magic Flight' from his last digression ends with the encounter with a final danger, when he is swallowed by the whale and reunited with his father. The 'Rescue from Without' appears in the form of the tuna fish that helps Pinocchio and Geppetto escape and reach the shore in safety. 'Crossing of the Return Threshold' usually finds the hero back in safety where he still needs to go through a final task. Pinocchio is back safe with his father and his final task is the hard work he undertakes day and night to earn their living. He has earned wisdom after all his adventures and he is now 'Master of the Two Worlds', that is, both street-smart and hard-working: the Fairy finally rewards him by turning him into a human boy. 'Freedom to Live' is the stage where the hero's journey ends and Pinocchio can now live his new life as a human boy, exactly as he had long wished and desired.

As seen from the above examples, Pinocchio's mythification is a result of many factors, all present in the original text: the elements that the text shares with the genre of fairy tales, but also the elements of the story that resonate with heroic and even religious motifs, render the story of Pinocchio into a monomyth. The fact that it is the most translated non-religious book, together with its numerous adaptations and retellings reflecting the ongoing popularity of the story, only confirms its mythic dimensions.

Simply put, the core of the Pinocchio myth is the story of a puppet who desires to become human. There are more elements or parallel themes to it than that — such as desire, becoming, and the transformation of an inanimate to an animate being — and I refer to these as well throughout the book. The Pinocchio myth lives and is transformed beyond Collodi's tale, but the original novel is inseparable from it. The references by critics to the myth of Pinocchio are the result of the vast popularity of the text, its multiple-layered symbolism and its ability to be adapted to almost any context. According to Gilbert Bosetti:

> Ogni epoca aggiorna il mito e lo interpreta secondo l'ideologia dominante. [...] Ma è proprio del mito autorizzare tali letture plurime e sopravvivere così all'arbitrio della Storia. Il burattino di legno è una figura archetipica dell'infanzia che si presta a riletture incessanti.
>
> Il mito ricomincia inesausto: Pinocchio non è ancora pronto a finire in cantina. E quando da gran tempo nessuno leggerà più Collodi, la sua creatura abiterà ancora le memorie: la si ritroverà in formati multimediali — così come

la si è potuta vedere nei film o nei fumetti — e i bambini, un po' preoccupati, si toccheranno il naso caso mai si allungasse.[72]

[Every age updates the myth and interprets it according to the dominant ideology. [...] But it is precisely part of the myth to allow for such multiple readings and thus survive the arbitrariness of history. The wooden puppet is an archetypal figure of childhood that lends itself to endless interpretations.

The myth starts again tirelessly: Pinocchio is not yet ready to end up in the attic. And even when no one has read Collodi for a long time, his creation will still live on in people's memories: he will be found in multimedia formats — as he can now be seen in films and comics — and children, a bit worried, will still touch their noses to check if they have grown longer.]

Notes to the Introduction

1. Carlo Collodi, *Le avventure di Pinocchio: storia di un burattino* (Florence: Felice Paggi, 1883); *The Adventures of Pinocchio/ Le avventure di Pinocchio*, parallel text, trans. by Nicolas Perella (Berkley & London: University of California Press, 1986) (this translation hereafter referenced as *AP*).

2. Daniela Marcheschi, 'Introduzione', in Carlo Collodi, *Opere*, ed. by Daniela Marcheschi (Milan: Arnoldo Mondadori, 1995), p. xi.

3. Massimo Rollino, 'Presentazione', in Giuseppe Garbarino, *Pinocchio svelato: i luoghi, il bestiario e le curiosità nella favola del Collodi* (Florence: AB, 2014), p. 5.

4. *Pinocchio* (USA: Walt Disney Productions, 1940).

5. *Blade Runner,* dir. by Ridley Scott (USA & Hong Kong: The Ladd Company, 1982); *A.I. Artificial Intelligence*, dir. by Steven Spielberg (USA: Warner Bros. Pictures, 2001); *Battlestar Galactica* (USA & UK: British Sky Broadcasting, 2004–09).

6. Nick Bostrom, 'In Defense of Posthuman Dignity', *Bioethics*, 19.3 (2005), 202–14 (p. 203).

7. Jerome Charyn, *Pinocchio's Nose* (New York: Arbor House, 1983) (hereafter referenced as *PN*); Robert Coover, *Pinocchio in Venice* (New York: Linden Press/ Simon & Schuster, 1991) (hereafter referenced as *PV*).

8. Winshluss, *Pinocchio* (Albi: Les Requins Marteaux, 2008); Ausonia, *Pinocchio: storia di un bambino* (Turin: Pavesio, 2006).

9. See Sigmund Freud, *The Ego and the Id*, in *The Standard Edition of the Complete Psychological Works of Sigmund Freud*, ed. and trans. by James Strachey, 24 vols (London: Hogarth Press, 1953–74), XIX (1961).

10. See Jean-Marie Apostolidès, 'Pinocchio, or a Masculine Upbringing', *Merveilles & Contes*, 2.2 (1988), 75–86; Umberto Eco, 'Introduction', in Carlo Collodi, *Pinocchio: The Tale of a Puppet*, trans. by Geoffrey Brock (New York: New York Review, 2008); and Thomas J. Morrissey, and R. Wunderlich, 'Death and Rebirth in Pinocchio', *Children's Literature*, 11 (1983), 64–75.

11. See Alberto Asor Rosa, 'Le avventure di Pinocchio', in *Letteratura italiana: le opere*, ed. by Alberto Asor Rosa, 4 vols (Turin: Einaudi, 1992–95), III, 879–950; and Carl Ipsen, *Italy in the Age of Pinocchio: Children and Danger in the Liberal Era* (New York: Palgrave Macmillan, 2006).

12. Amy Boylan, 'Carving a National Identity: Collodi, Pinocchio, and Post-unification Italy', in *Approaches to Teaching Collodi's 'Pinocchio' and its Adaptations,* ed. by Michael Sherberg (New York: Modern Language Association of America, 2006), pp. 16–20 (p. 18).

13. Ipsen, *Italy in the Age of Pinocchio*, p. 2.

14. Giorgio Manganelli, *Pinocchio: un libro parallelo* (Milan: Adelphi, 2002), pp. 103, 140.

15. Nicolas Perella, 'An Essay on *Pinocchio*', in *AP*, pp. 1–69 (pp. 28, 29).

16. Eco, 'Introduction', in Collodi, *Pinocchio*.

17. Richard Wunderlich and Thomas J. Morrissey, *Pinocchio Goes Postmodern: Perils of a Puppet in the United States* (New York: Routledge, 2002).

18. Ibid., p. 38.

19. Gabriel Janer Manila, 'Tres infancias soñadas: Pinocchio, Alicia y el Pequeño Príncipe', in

Infancia y escolarización en la modernidad tardía, ed. by J. Carlos González Faraco (Madrid: AKAL, 2002), pp. 201–31 (p. 207).

20. Dieter Richter, *Carlo Collodi und sein Pinocchio: ein weitgereister Holzbengel und seine toskanische Geschichte* (Berlin: Klaus Wagenbach, 2004), pp. 88–96.

21. Natalia Kaloh Vid, 'Translation of Children's Literature in the Soviet Union: How Pinocchio Got a Golden Key', *International Research in Children's Literature*, 6.1 (July 2013), 90–103.

22. Eugenio Cherubini, *Pinocchio in Africa*, trans. by Angelo Patri (Boston & New York: Ginn, 1911).

23. As Morrissey explains in Chapter 6 of Wunderlich and Morrissey, *Pinocchio Goes Postmodern*.

24. Gemma Mongiardini-Rembadi, *Pinocchio Under the Sea* (New York: Macmillan, 1913); Nipote Collodi (Paolo Lorenzini), *Il cuore di Pinocchio: nuove avventure del celebre burattino* (Florence: Bemporad, 1917); *The Heart of Pinocchio: New Adventures of the Celebrated Little Puppet by Nipote Collodi (Paolo Lorenzini), Adapted From the Italian by Virginia Watson* (New York & London: Harper & Brothers, 1919).

25. Emily Gray, *The Adventures of Pinocchio, a Marionette* (Chicago: A. Flannagan, 1912). Wunderlich and Morrissey, *Pinocchio Goes Postmodern*, p. 45.

26. Wunderlich & Morrissey, *Pinocchio Goes Postmodern*, p. 59.

27. Angelo Patri, *Pinocchio in America* (Garden City, NY: Doubleday, Doran, 1930).

28. Susan Honeyman, *Consuming Agency in Fairy Tales, Childlore, and Folkliterature* (New York: Routledge, 2010), p. 29.

29. Josef Marino, *Hi! Ho! Pinocchio* (Chicago: Reilly & Lee, 1940).

30. Remo Bufano, *Pinocchio for the Stage in Four Short Plays* (New York: Alfred Knopf, 1929).

31. Yasha Frank, *Pinocchio (a Musical Legend)* (New York: Edward B. Marks Music, 1939).

32. Wunderlich and Morrissey, *Pinocchio Goes Postmodern*, p. 87.

33. Ibid., p. 109.

34. Brian Way, *Pinocchio: A New Version of the Story by Carlo Collodi* (London: Dennis Dobson, 1954).

35. Wunderlich and Morrissey, *Pinocchio Goes Postmodern*, pp. 124, 126.

36. *Pinocchio and the Emperor of the Night*, dir. by Hal Sutherland (USA: Filmation Associates, 1987).

37. *Pinocchio 3000*, or *Pinocchio le Robot* (Canada, France, Spain: CinéGroupe, Filmax, Anima Kids, 2004). This children's film is a technophobic retelling of Pinocchio where Pinocchio is a little robot brought to life with the help of electricity in a futuristic steampunk imagery. The film's main theme is the conflict between nature and technology. There are similarities between this film and Winshluss's *Pinocchio*, which suggest this as a possible influence on Winshluss, as I will show in Chapter 3. The transformation scene (of the children into wolves in Winshluss) is one such example.

38. Carlo Collodi, *Pinocchio: The Story of a Puppet*, trans. by Mary Alice Murray, intro. by David Almond, illus. by Grahame Baker-Smith (London: Folio Society, 2011).

39. Van Jensen and Dustin Higgins, *Pinocchio: Vampire Slayer* (San Jose, CA: SLG, 2009); *Pinocchio, Vampire Slayer Vol. 2: The Great Puppet Theater* (San Jose, CA: SLG, 2010).

40. Michael Morpurgo, *Pinocchio, by Pinocchio* (London: Harper Collins, 2013).

41. Silvio Donà, *Pinocchio 2112: romanzo di fantascienza* (Milan: Leone, 2009).

42. Jim Dine, 'Walking to Borås', sculpture, 2008.

43. *Pinocchio* (South Korea: Seoul Broadcasting System, 2014–15).

44. Sandy Schaefer, 'Guillermo Del Toro's Stop-motion Pinocchio Adaptation Still Moving Forward', *Screen Rant*, 2 January 2013 <http://screenrant.com/guillermo-del-toro-pinocchio-not-postponed/> [accessed 21 March 2019].

45. Anita Busch, '"Pinocchio"-inspired Live-action Film Being Developed at Disney', *Deadline Hollywood*, 8 April 2015 <http://deadline.com/2015/04/pinocchio-inspired-live-action-film-being-developed-at-disney-1201406564/> [accessed 21 March 2019].

46. Rossana Dedola, *Pinocchio e Collodi* (Milan: Bruno Mondadori, 2002), p. 116.

47. Jack Zipes, *Happily Ever After* (New York: Routledge, 1997), p. 76.

48. Dedola, *Pinocchio e Collodi*, p. 132.

49. Vladimir Propp, *Morphology of the Folktale* (Austin: University of Texas Press, 1968).

50. Asor Rosa, 'Le avventure di Pinocchio', p. 901.

51. *Shrek*, dir. by Andrew Adamson and Vicky Jenson (USA: Dreamworks, 2001); *Shrek 2*, dir. by Andrew Adamson & others (USA: Dreamworks, 2004); *Shrek the Third*, dir. by Chris Miller & Raman Hui (USA: Dreamworks, 2007); *Shrek Forever After*, dir. by Mike Mitchell (USA: Dreamworks, 2010).
52. Bill Willingham, *Fables: Legends in Exile*, illus. by Lan Medina (New York: Vertigo, DC Comics, 2002).
53. *Once Upon a Time* (USA: Kitsis/Horowitz, ABC Studios, 2011–18).
54. Phillip Stambovsky, *Myth and the Limits of Reason* (Amsterdam & Atlanta, GA: Rodopi, 1996), p. 23.
55. Robert A. Segal, *Myth: A Very Short Introduction* (Oxford: Oxford University Press, 2004), p. 5.
56. Rachel Bowlby, *Freudian Mythologies: Greek Tragedy and Modern Identities* (Oxford: Oxford University Press, 2007), p. 8.
57. Ibid., p. 9.
58. Giacomo Biffi, *Contro maestro Ciliegia: commento teologico a 'Le avventure di Pinocchio'* (Milan: Jaca Book, 1977).
59. Segal, *Myth*, p. 99.
60. Jack Zipes, *Fairy Tale as Myth — Myth as Fairy Tale* (Lexington: University Press of Kentucky, 1994), pp. 5, 6.
61. The most acknowledged classification system of fairy tales and folktales is that of the Aarne-Thompson tale type and motif index, despite its imperfections. See Alan Dundes, 'The Motif-index and the Tale Type Index: A Critique', *Journal of Folklore Research*, 34.3 (1997), 195–202.
62. David Leeming, *The Oxford Companion to World Mythology* (Oxford: Oxford University Press, 2005), p. 127.
63. Geoffrey S. Kirk, *Myth: Its Meaning and Functions in Ancient and Other Cultures* (Cambridge: Cambridge University Press, 1983), p. 34.
64. Mircea Eliade, *Myth and Reality* (London: Allen & Unwin, 1964) pp. 195–202.
65. Lucius Apuleius, *The Golden Ass or Metamorphoses*, trans. by E. J. Kenney (London: Penguin, 1998), pp. 58–88.
66. Zipes, *Happily Ever After*, pp. 63–64.
67. Marina Warner, 'Into the Woods', The British Academy Lecture, 11 May 2015 <http://www.britac.ac.uk/events/2015/Into_the_Woods.cfm> [accessed 30 June 2015].
68. Marina Warner, *Once Upon a Time: A Short History of Fairy Tale* (Oxford: Oxford University Press, 2014), p. 34.
69. Salvatore Consolo, 'The Myth of Pinocchio: Metamorphosis of a Puppet from Collodi's Pages to the Screen', in *Pinocchio, Puppets and Modernity: The Mechanical Body*, ed. by Katia Pizzi (London & New York: Routledge, 2012), pp. 163–74.
70. I refer to Joseph Campbell and Henry Morton Robinson, *A Skeleton Key to Finnegans Wake* (New York: Harcourt Brace, 1944).
71. Joseph Campbell, *The Hero with a Thousand Faces*, Bollingen Series, 17 (Novato, CA: New World Library, 2008), p. 23.
72. Gilbert Bosetti, 'Pinocchio, perennità del mito', in *Pinocchio esportazione: il burattino di Collodi nella critica straniera*, ed. by Giorgio Cusatelli (Pescia: Armando, 2002), pp. 117–28 (pp. 126–27).

PART I

❖

Film

Posthuman Retellings of the Pinocchio Myth

Science Fiction

The three examples of posthuman retellings of the Pinocchio myth that will be analysed here are Scott's *Blade Runner*, Spielberg's *A.I. Artificial Intelligence* (hereafter *A.I.*), and the television series *Battlestar Galactica* (hereafter *BSG*). All three refer to a possible future when humanoid robots have acquired artificial intelligence and human emotions. The concept of creating artificial life dates back to antiquity. In the *Iliad*, Homer refers to female, intelligent, humanlike servants that the god Hephaestus had created in order to serve himself:

> ἔλε δὲ σκῆπτρον παχύ, βῆ δὲ θύραζε
> χωλεύων· ὑπὸ δ᾽ ἀμφίπολοι ῥώοντο ἄνακτι
> χρύσειαι ζωῇσι νεήνισιν εἰοικυῖαι.
> τῇς ἐν μὲν νόος ἐστὶ μετὰ φρεσίν, ἐν δὲ καὶ αὐδὴ
> καὶ σθένος, ἀθανάτων δὲ θεῶν ἄπο ἔργα ἴσασιν.
> αἵ μὲν ὕπαιθα ἄνακτος ἐποίπνυον.

> [Hephaestus] grasped a stout staff, and went forth halting;
> but there moved swiftly to support their lord
> handmaidens wrought of gold in the semblance of living maids.
> In them is understanding in their hearts, and in them speech and strength,
> and they know cunning handiwork by gift of the immortal gods.
> These busily moved to support their lord.[1]

There are more examples of robot-like characters in ancient Greek literature, such as the giant automaton Talos that the Argonauts meet in Crete, yet Hephaestus's womanoid servants have intelligence and their physical appearance resembles that of young women, a very early precursor to womanoid cyborgs.[2]

Even though such themes have existed since antiquity, it is only since the 1920s, when the term 'science fiction' was coined, that they have been classified as such.[3] Darko Suvin defines science fiction as the 'literature of cognitive estrangement'; he explains how 'the effect of [...] factual reporting of fictions is one of confronting a set normative system — a Ptolemaic-type closed world picture — with a point of view or glance implying a new set of norms'.[4] Science fiction often addresses the fear or excitement caused by technological advances. Luckhurst describes how electricity affected everyday life and consequently the imagination of science-fiction authors:

> Indeed, the extension of these technologies into the domestic sphere produced an updated, electrified version of the uncanny. The phonograph preserved the living voice beyond death; the telephone crackled with spooky echoes and unearthly noises that some interpreted as spiritual or interstellar messages; telegraphy, hailed in Britain as the Empire's nervous system, was commonly used by Spiritualists as an analogy for contacting the dead.[5]

A similar response has been observed and reflected in science-fiction literature after the introduction of computers to everyday life, as well as in response to current technological advancement in artificial intelligence, robotics, and biotechnology.

In an attempt to identify what all science-fiction films have visually in common, cinema and media theorist Vivian Sobchack concludes that

> The visual connection between all SF films lies in the consistent and repetitious use not of *specific* images, but of *types* of images which function in the same way from film to film to create an imaginatively realized world which is always removed from the world we know or know of. The visual surface of all SF film presents us with a confrontation between and mixture of those images to which we respond as 'alien' and those we know to be familiar.[6]

Sobchack points out that, unlike film genres such as the western or gangster film, the references of science-fiction film's iconography have no constant basis. She gives the example of the railway as it appears in western films and how it contains a common topos, having the same historical references and invoking specific emotions across all films of the genre. She goes on to explain how the spaceship or the robot cannot function similarly in the science-fiction film, since they have been used for entirely different settings and ideological references, either as negative or positive symbols, or even as entirely neutral and unimportant in the film's plot. However, what I consider important in the science-fiction film genre is that such iconographic references invoke in the viewer's memory all the moral debates that have been raised regarding technological progress and technophobia in earlier films. This thus defines their own position in the debate in the current instance, even when the choice of using them is based in an unwillingness to express a direct opinion by using these symbols in a neutral way, merely as film props. Katherine Hayles considers 'the locus classicus for reframing transhumanist questions to be science fiction and speculative fiction'.[7] In the science-fiction film, it is through visual references such as aliens, spaceships, robots, androids etc., that different filmmakers choose to present their political and ideological tendencies. These visual references stand for the battlefield on which the battles between technophilia and technophobia take place. Moreover, one more visual connection between science-fiction films and technological progress (and therefore indirectly to transhumanism too) is the consistent use of special effects: 'the genre's reliance on special effects is itself an enactment of science fiction's thematic concern with technology'.[8]

Narratives that include androids or robots have been classified as 'posthuman science fiction', a subgenre of science fiction. According to M. Keith Booker and Anne-Marie Thomas, posthuman science fiction 'imagines a future in which technological changes have brought about dramatic physical and intellectual changes in the human species itself — or even rendered that species irrelevant through the rise of superior artificial intelligence (AI) technologies'.[9] This classification is much more accurate than that of Mark Bould and Sherryl Vint, who describe this subgenre as 'embodiment'.[10] The concept of embodiment limits the subgenre to mind uploading and human body enhancement, whereas the earlier definition includes all robot and cyborg literature, which is firmly intertwined with embodiment. Booker and Thomas define the subgenre of cyberpunk as a precursor to posthuman science fiction, which is closely related to and influenced by postmodernism. This will be particularly relevant to Parts II and III, where postmodernism is part of the analysis of most texts. The case studies in this part belong to the subgenre of posthuman science fiction. One of them, *Blade Runner*, a genre-bending film mixing elements of noir, crime, and science fiction, has been classified by Booker and Thomas as a 'proto-cyberpunk' film, a categorisation with which I agree insofar as it does not exclude it from posthuman science fiction.

As Hayles has suggested, posthuman science fiction is a subgenre that offers the ideal ground for debate on transhumanism. To add to Hayles, one reason why science fiction frequently deals with posthumanist and transhumanist topics is due, as Suvin suggests, to the challenging approach that science fiction has to normative values.

The three case studies that will be examined in this part focus on the comparison between Pinocchio's desire to become human, which is one of the main elements of the Pinocchio myth (as explained in the Introduction) and the desire for humanity, or lack thereof, in the different examples of sentient androids. All three of them become aware of their non-human nature in what I have defined as the 'confrontation scene', which will be analysed in detail further on and which is first encountered in Collodi's novel.

The Animate/ Inanimate Archetype

The story of Pinocchio is one of the literary manifestations of the animate/ inanimate archetype. As such, it is loaded with different connotations and sub-layers of meaning, many of which reveal hidden fears and desires. According to C. G. Jung's definition of archetypes, since a concept reappears in various forms of artistic creativity, mythology and religion, it does not reflect only an individual's feelings and experiences, but it is also connected to the collective unconscious:

> Jung envisions a great psycho-physical mystery to which the alchemists of old gave the name of *unus mundus* (one world). At the root of all being, so he intimates, there is a state wherein physicality and spirituality meet in a transgressive union'.[11]

Archetypes are therefore significant, as they portray primal fears and desires that can have variations in their many manifestations but are at the same time universal.

Pinocchio is an archetypal story because of all its mythical, fairy-tale, and religious references. It is not only the animate/ inanimate archetype that resonates through it, but also the child archetype, that of the trickster, and most importantly that of metamorphosis/ rebirth.[12] There are several transformations that Pinocchio goes through: from piece of wood to puppet, from puppet to donkey and back to puppet, and finally to human boy. These transformations have similarities to Greek myths or texts such as Apuleius's *The Golden Ass* or Ovid's *Metamorphoses* or even the numerous transformations that occur in fairy tales, as explained in the Introduction. However, there is a crucial element to Collodi's story that connects Pinocchio to the animate/ inanimate archetype as well: the puppet's desire to become human. This is what triggers the final metamorphosis and turns the wooden puppet into a human being.

Even though Pinocchio is not inanimate as a puppet or as a piece of wood, the importance of his transformation, intensified by his desire for humanity, perfectly connects Pinocchio's example to the literary tradition of the animate/ inanimate archetype. This is because a very prominent element in most of the literary examples of the animate/ inanimate archetype is desire. Most frequently, it is the maker's desire that animates their creation or the inanimate object. Similarly, it is Pinocchio's desire that triggers and brings about his final transformation.

To put the myth of Pinocchio into the context of the literary tradition of the animate/ inanimate archetype, I will give a brief overview of a few such examples. One of the first examples of the archetype of inanimate matter that comes to life is the Greek myth of Pygmalion, King of Cyprus, who falls in love with his creation, the beautiful statue of Galatea, as told by Ovid in Book x of his *Metamorphoses*.[13] The Goddess Aphrodite hears Pygmalion's prayers and brings Galatea to life. Many centuries later, in medieval times, alchemists tried to transform base metals into gold — a metal considered divine — during which procedure they were also transformed to a higher level of gnosis. 'This dual resurrection of the body (of the metal and of the human operator) culminated in a material-spiritual event variously concretized as a stone statue or "Philosopher's Stone" or a child/homunculus ("little man", as also manikin)'.[14] This metaphysical desire is depicted in post-Enlightenment literature as something wrong or forbidden. Lois Rostow Kuznets points out that 'among the many illicit desires of Faust, according to Goethe in the second part of his tragedy [...] is that of creating a homunculus'.[15]

In the fairy-tale tradition, 'Pinto Smalto' is the tale of a woman who bakes the man of her dreams with flour and sugar and brings him to life with care and special rituals. It was written by Giambattista Basile in the Neapolitan dialect and published in 1634 in *Lo cunto de li cunti*.[16] Basile was one of the first authors to transcribe tales from the oral tradition and 'Pinto Smalto' is the first story in the animate/ inanimate tradition with a woman as creator. Sometime later, in 1875, the popular tale of 'The Gingerbread Boy' was published anonymously for the first time in the American children's magazine, *St Nicholas Magazine*. In this tale, a childless woman wishing to have a child bakes a little man-shaped gingerbread biscuit which comes to life and runs away from everyone but the sly fox, who finally eats it.[17] It is noteworthy that in both fairy tales, it is the wish for a husband or a child that animates matter originally meant to be eaten as food, and also that in both cases the creator is a woman. Given that fairy tales reflect archetypal fears and desires, both these examples portray the feminine power of creativity together with the fear this power inspires: the fear of a woman-devourer, a 'vagina dentata', as both creatures that the women-creators have brought to life are edible.[18]

The archetype of animating the inanimate does not only portray the primal desire to eradicate death by creating life, the desire to be the puppeteer, to play God. After all, humans have tried throughout the history of literature, philosophy, and religion to transcend themselves, from Adam and Eve, to Prometheus, and Nietzsche's *Übermensch*. As David Koepsell states, 'the desire to surpass one's natural state *is* the original sin'.[19] It also portrays a deeper fear of understanding the human body and its mechanisms and, as Barbara Johnson suggests, the fear that the reverse might happen, i.e. the animate turning into the inanimate, life into stillness and death. Johnson supports this by pointing out

> the confusion between the vocabulary of death and the vocabulary of sex (both a corpse and a penis are 'stiff'; testicles are referred to as 'stones' and erections as 'bones'; orgasm is known as 'the little death'; the ecstasy of 'going outside oneself' suggests that the most intense moments of life resemble non-life most closely).[20]

The eighteenth century resonates with the Enlightenment celebration of reason and science, yet a century later, literature expresses doubt about scientific and rational notions of progress. As mentioned earlier, the discovery of electricity and its gradual integration into everyday life raised many doubts and fears at its early stages. Some examples of the archetype that express this mistrust in scientific progress and the Industrial Revolution include automata, like Olympia in E. T. A. Hoffmann's 'The Sandman' and Frankenstein's creature.[21] The creature longs for acceptance and when it cannot achieve that, it desires a companion of the same species. The melancholy and loneliness of Romanticism are prominent in Shelley's work and the creature can only have a bad ending, in the same way that Nathaniel, the young protagonist of 'The Sandman', does. Yet it is the scientific desire of Dr Frankenstein who brought his creature to life, which shows (as in all previous examples) that desire is the driving force that transforms inanimate matter into a living being.

Even though Collodi's *The Adventures of Pinocchio* is not so far apart in time from *Frankenstein*, it is nonetheless significantly different. Collodi's Italy does not have the bourgeois context of Shelley's protagonists. There is no space for melancholy, as the first priority is survival; Pinocchio must satisfy his hunger first before he can think of loneliness, as Charles Klopp suggests.[22] Another significant difference is Pinocchio's desire to become human, a 'real boy', in contrast to Frankenstein's creature who wants only acceptance and companionship. Collodi's text is the first instance in which the archetype manifests the desire of the simulacrum to become human, rather than the creator's wish for it to become human, as in all previous examples.

There are multiple layers in the turn the archetype takes with Pinocchio. The little puppet can be a metaphor for humanity and the way one feels one's destiny is controlled by the strings of a greater power or God. In other words, the insecurity of humans over defining their identity and their body boundaries is reflected in Pinocchio's desire to become something else, something better, that is, human. Being human may not necessarily mean being better, however. Pinocchio leads a careless life and he would not need to change it. Yet Collodi deliberately idealises humanity. By making his hero desire it so much, he raises humanity's value in his audience's eyes, perhaps necessary in a time when living conditions devalued human existence. In order to become a real boy Pinocchio has to stop lying, which is very normal among humans, and sacrifice himself for his father, an act very rare and highly valuable: 'In the end Pinocchio has become what we "real people" wish to be'.[23] Pinocchio's desire to become real also symbolises the desire to pass from childhood to adulthood and manhood.

Moreover, Pinocchio stands for the newly-formed state of Italy which wants to become a real and unified country and, as Collodi's story suggests, the way to do so is through the ethics of work and education. Asor Rosa emphasises how vagabondism was a real problem in Italy and, in particular, in the Tuscany of Collodi's time, and how the warnings of the cricket in Chapter IV that those who desire a vagabond life will 'end up in the poorhouse or in prison' reflected the reality of the time.[24] He goes on to explain how Pinocchio's transformation additionally signifies his class ascension, a topic that Nicolas Perella also touches upon in his Introduction to *The Adventures of Pinocchio*. Pinocchio's desire to become human is, therefore, not only ontological but also socio-political. This dual dimension of the main element of the Pinocchio myth is present in all the retellings I examine. As is made explicit in the following case studies, the protagonists' desire for change is not only of an ontological nature, but it also often reflects the desire for, or fear of, change in societal structure.

A very popular literary manifestation of the animate/ inanimate archetype is that of the robot that becomes (or desires to become) human. My research suggests that the first time such a robot becomes synonymous with Pinocchio is in Spielberg's *A.I.* The film is based on Brian Aldiss's short story 'Supertoys Last All Summer Long'.[25] It is important to stress that the idea of blending the robot and Pinocchio originally belonged to Stanley Kubrick, who had been planning to make the film since the early 1970s. As scriptwriter Ian Watson mentions, Kubrick gave him a copy of Collodi's book together with Aldiss's story when he asked him to write a script for the *A.I.* film: 'The movie was to be a picaresque robot version of *Pinocchio*, spinning off from the Aldiss story'.[26] It would have been Kubrick's next film, but he died before he could complete it. According to John Tibbetts, Kubrick had already suggested a possible cooperation, in which Kubrick would be the producer and Spielberg the director, so when Kubrick died, Spielberg took over the task of realising Kubrick's idea.[27]

In literary manifestations of the animate/ inanimate archetype prior to Pinocchio, the inanimate object or simulacrum is given life because of the wish or desire of its maker. As I mentioned before, Pinocchio is the first simulacrum to have his own wish to become human. It is not therefore a coincidence that Kubrick connected the story of Pinocchio to the motif of a robot seeking humanity. This motif has been very popular in film and literature over the last decades, for reasons that will be discussed later on. The similarity of the Pinocchio myth to the sentient robot/cyborg motif is striking. Considering that both puppets and cyborgs are human simulacra with artificial bodies, it is easy to understand why the myth of the puppet that wants to become human is so easily applied to all examples of sentient robots, cyborgs, or clones that desire humanity. In fact, even when a cyborg-desiring-humanity story is not a direct retelling of Pinocchio, the Pinocchio myth resonates in the story anyway, as will be shown in different examples further on.

Posthumanism

The case studies in this part all belong to the genre of posthuman science fiction, as explained earlier. 'Posthumanism' is a term used in many different contexts, as I mentioned in the Introduction, and it has become increasingly popular. Posthumanist scholars often define the direction of their analysis by going back and redefining or referring to the concept of humanism, humanity, and what it means to be human (Rosi Braidotti, Cary Wolfe, and Elaine L. Graham).[28] This is understandable, since the word itself implies a reference to something after humanism. However, as Ivan Callus, Stefan Herbrechter, and Manuela Rossini point out:

> The posthuman is arguably so unprecedented and so much a product of its time that it has to be viewed as distinct from its supposed affinities with earlier thought and representations. There is, then, much to unlearn before the posthuman as well as much to reaffirm.[29]

They add further on that 'posthumanism has now become so sufficiently established as an academic discourse that it warrants analysis of its diverse strands and configurations'.[30] The examples examined in this book relate to 'transhumanism' or, as Wolfe calls it, the 'cyborg' strand of posthumanism.[31]

According to Max More, on the Humanity+ (World Transhumanist Association) webpage, transhumanism is:

> (1) The intellectual and cultural movement that affirms the possibility and desirability of fundamentally improving the human condition through applied reason, especially by developing and making widely available technologies to eliminate aging and to greatly enhance human intellectual, physical, and psychological capacities.

> (2) The study of the ramifications, promises, and potential dangers of technologies that will enable us to overcome fundamental human limitations, and the related study of the ethical matters involved in developing and using such technologies.[32]

Transhumanism has been criticised by Hayles for 'performing decontextualizing moves that oversimplify the situation and carry into the new millennium some of the most questionable aspects of capitalist ideology'. More specifically, she claims that 'there is a conspicuous absence of considering socioeconomic dynamics beyond the individual'.[33]

Posthumanism is closer to a critical theory and approach that aims to explore, and possibly answer, socio-political, psychological and philosophical issues and thus answer Hayles's concerns regarding transhumanism. Yet it is very telling how within the definition of transhumanism lies a desire to 'overcome fundamental human limitations'; this is very relevant to the animate/ inanimate archetype and the analysis of the case studies that will follow.

In *Posthuman Life*, David Roden points out how 'the terms "humanism", "transhumanism" and "posthumanism" are widely used among philosophers, critical theorists and professional futurists, but often in ways that are insufficiently nuanced'.[34] He goes on to introduce a new term in order to clarify these terms, that of 'speculative posthumanism'. While for Roden 'transhumanism is an ethical claim to the effect that technological *enhancement* of human capacities is a desirable aim (all other things being equal)', speculative posthumanism

> is not a normative claim about how the world *ought to be* but a metaphysical claim about *what it would contain*. For speculative posthumanists, posthumans are technologically engendered beings that are no longer human. SP makes no commitments regarding ethical value of posthuman lives. It does not, for example, define the posthuman as an improvement or apotheosis of the human as transhumanist philosopher Nick Bostrom does in 'Why I Want to be a Posthuman When I Grow Up' (2008).[35]

The posthuman may refer to an actual being that has crossed the threshold of humanity, either with the help of humans or without, and is to be found within the spheres of science and speculative fiction as well as those of philosophy and ethics. These beings include robots or androids with sentient features, cyborgs, cylons, and clones, but they could also be humans with enhancements or modifications of a bio-robotic nature. Posthumanism may also refer to a society that has incorporated posthuman beings and, as a result, has an entirely different structure from modern society. As a theory, posthumanism raises issues of defining or redefining humanity. On a speculative plane, questions are raised regarding the posthuman beings' sentience and ability to have emotions and therefore their potential (legal and ethical) equality to humans. Consequently, a whole new sphere is explored regarding how humans respond to posthumanism, ranging from the desire for self-enhancement and even cloning, to fear and negation, and to a possible biological and societal change. More often than not, a posthumanist society implies one that has challenged hetero-normative values and is more liberal and inclusive, as in the recent example of the Netflix series *Sense8*.[36]

Very often, the posthuman is also mixed with the superhuman. In his article 'The Silver Age Superhero as Psychedelic Shaman', Scott Jeffery divides post-humanism into three subcategories: a) Transhumanism, b) Post/ Humanism, and c) Superhumanism.[37] The 2012 'Superhuman' exhibition at the Wellcome Collection in London, on the other hand, presented posthumanism as part of the larger topic of superhumanism.[38] This is one more indication of the fact that posthumanism is a very recent and therefore not yet very clearly defined field.

For the purpose of this study, my focus is on the socio-political and psychological questions that posthumanism invokes in contemporary literature. More specifically, and in relation to the Pinocchio myth, I explore the relationship between the posthuman being and humanity from the point of view of the posthuman: does it desire humanity or does it abhor it, and why? What does this desire or lack thereof signify or stand for? Another issue I will address is why this theme is so popular and often revisited in literature.

Moreover, through the analysis of the specific examples I use, I explore the development of the concept of humanity in relation to social structures in the last four decades. Even though *A.I.* is the first example in which Pinocchio is clearly related to the main protagonist and, as mentioned before, the first example where the connection between a robot and Pinocchio is so explicit, I start my analysis with a much earlier example. *Blade Runner* is a landmark in the genre of cyborg literature in relation to humanity and it resonates with all the film material that deals with the same topic thereafter. In many cases there are straightforward references to it, as for example in the television series *BSG*, which will be my third example.

The Confrontation Scene

In relation to the myth of Pinocchio, the most important scene in Collodi's story is the one that directly connects the three case studies to Pinocchio, and at the same time helps to answer the questions I posed earlier: 'the confrontation scene', in which Pinocchio is directly confronted with his corporeality.

The scene that gives birth to the Pinocchio myth, which has inspired most retellings and adaptations, is located in Chapter xxv. It is remarkable that up to that point Pinocchio had gone through so many adventures: he had been tortured, cheated, hung from a tree; he had been put in prison; and then he had willingly sacrificed himself by jumping into the sea to save his father. And throughout all these adventures there was not a single instance where Pinocchio desired to be human or anything other than he was. In Chapter xxv he is on the island of the Busy Bees and has just found out that the girl with the blue hair (the first manifestation of the Fairy) has not died, as was written on a gravestone near her house. Instead, she has been transformed into a woman, the lady he helped with carrying water.

Pinocchio is bewildered by her change:

> 'But how did you manage to grow up so fast?'
> 'It's a secret.'
> 'Teach it to me; I'd like to grow a little too. [...]'
> 'But you can't grow,' replied the Fairy.
> 'Why not?'
> 'Because puppets never grow. They are born as puppets, they live as puppets, and they die as puppets.' (*AP*, p. 283)

At this moment, Pinocchio realises how different he is. Even though he looks like a puppet, he has always behaved like any other child and this is how everyone has treated him so far, as just another disobedient child. This is the first time he hears from someone he trusts that he is not like everyone else. His immediate reaction is to reject his condition and desire change: 'Oh, I'm sick and tired of always being a puppet! [...] It's about time that I too became a man' (*AP*, p. 283). This is childish behaviour as well, in the manner of a child who is too eager to grow up. It also shows the desire of Pinocchio to match the grown-up Fairy, to be an adult.

What is particularly interesting is how she proceeds to manipulate him:

> 'And you will become one, when you learn to deserve it.'
> 'Really? And what can I do to deserve it?'
> 'Something quite simple: learn how to be a proper boy.'
> 'But isn't that what I already am?' (*AP*, p. 285)

Pinocchio has still not understood in what way he is not a boy. Besides, the Fairy, as well as others in the novel, keep calling him 'boy'. The difference lies in the adjective, 'proper'. This is a crucial point, as in the original Italian text what the Fairy says that he should be is 'un ragazzo per bene'. This could be interpreted as 'a real boy' or 'a proper boy'. In a sense, she means both, as Pinocchio in the end transforms into a human child and this happens after he has become 'proper', according to the Fairy's criteria. And these mainly involve obedience and hard work.

As Manganelli suggests (and as mentioned earlier, in the Introduction), if we consider Pinocchio a primal force that has animated a piece of wood, then his power must be much stronger than that of the Fairy since he manages to revive her. Following this reading, the Fairy will do anything she can to keep this power close to her. This is in relation to the realm of magic where animals talk and time is unimportant. For the readers of Collodi, though, the Fairy represents a work ethic that was believed to be able to help Italy become a strong, united country. More specifically:

> Whether one is born rich or poor, one has the duty to do something in this world, to keep busy, to work. Woe to those who yield to idleness! Idleness is a horrible disease, and it has to be cured early, in childhood; otherwise, when we are grown-up, we never get over it. (*AP*, p. 287)

Thus the Fairy aims to lead Pinocchio from his prelapsarian, careless state to that of a human — the fallen Adam, expelled from Paradise and condemned to work for the rest of his life. Ironically, Collodi reverses the punishment of man for disobeying God, a life of hard work, to the pre-requisite to deserve and earn humanity. Irony is a common element in Collodi's work and it is possible that he does not agree with the Fairy's doctrine. It is important to note, however, that the Fairy represents the society around Pinocchio, so what she says becomes a rule that the world she represents adheres to. She is this representative not so much because of her magical powers as because of her respected social position on the island of the Busy Bees.

The examples of the posthuman retellings of *Pinocchio* which I analyse have certain things in common with this crucial scene in Collodi's text — in particular the realisation of one's corporeality and true identity together with the reaction this confrontation inspires — thus making them semantic relatives and thematic cognates to *Pinocchio* and retellings of the Pinocchio myth. Furthermore, they not only are examples of androids desiring humanity but also share the confrontation scene, of the greatest importance in the formation of the Pinocchio myth.

Before I analyse the similarities between Pinocchio's posthuman retellings and Pinocchio's confrontation scene, it is important to show the strong similarities between the examples of humanoids I will examine:

1) All the humanoids are capable of emotions.
2) They look exactly like humans: they are exact replicas of the human body and nothing in their physical appearance or even behaviour betrays that they are not human.
3) The specific examples I use have something different from the rest of their kind; they are in some way one step ahead.
4) At some point in the narrative (even just briefly, as in *A.I.*), they are mistakenly perceived as humans.
5) In all three cases, the humanoids are not aware that they are not human.
6) They find out about themselves through a confrontation with the 'other', whether it be a human or an exact replica of themselves (for example, Sharon in *BSG*).
7) The 'other' that confronts them with their true identity represents the values of society and the establishment.
8) The humanoids are not at peace with their identity, desiring (to a greater or lesser extent) humanity.

In 'Picturing the Human (Body and Soul): A Reading of *Blade Runner*', Stephen Mulhall considers that

> the humanity of the replicants — or indeed of all human beings — is in the hands of their fellows; their accession to human status involves their being acknowledged as human by others. They can fulfil all the criteria, but they cannot force an acknowledgement from those around them; and if their humanity is denied, it withers.[39]

Taking as a reference-point the supposition that one is human (or not) because one is acknowledged and accepted as such by a human or a group of them, I examine the three scenes of confrontation: Rachael in *Blade Runner*, David in *A.I.*, and Sharon in *BSG*. My analysis also considers Stephen Mulhall's view of the humanity of the replicants and that of all human beings under the same lens.

Notes to Part I

1. Homer, *Iliad*, XVIII, ll. 416–21, translated by A. T. Murray <http://www.theoi.com/Text/HomerIliad18.html> [accessed 15 October 2021].
2. See Apollonius of Rhodes, *Argonautica, Book IV*, ed. by Richard Hunter, Cambridge Greek and Latin Classics (Cambridge: Cambridge University Press, 2015).
3. Roger Luckhurst, *Science Fiction* (Cambridge: Polity Press, 2005), p. 15.
4. Darko Suvin, 'On the Poetics of the Science Fiction Genre', *College English*, 34.3 (1972), 372–82 (pp. 372, 374).
5. Luckhurst, *Science Fiction*, p. 26.
6. Vivian Carol Sobchack, *Screening Space: The American Science Fiction Film*, 2nd enl. edn (New Brunswick, NJ, & London: Rutgers University Press, 1997), p. 87.
7. N. Katherine Hayles, 'Wrestling with Transhumanism', in *H+/-: Transhumanism and its Critics*,

ed. by Gregory R. Hansell and William Grassie (Philadelphia: Metanexus, 2011), pp. 215–26 (p. 216).

8. Barry Keith Grant, ' "Sensuous Elaboration": Reason and the Visible in the Science Fiction Film', in *Liquid Metal: The Science Fiction Film Reader*, ed. by Sean Redmond (London: Wallflower, 2004), pp. 17–23 (p. 19).

9. M. Keith Booker and Anne-Marie Thomas, *The Science Fiction Handbook* (Chichester & Malden, MA: Wiley-Blackwell, 2009), p. 11.

10. See Mark Bould, and Sherryl Vint, *The Routledge Concise History of Science Fiction* (New York: Routledge, 2011).

11. Stephan A. Hoeller, 'C. G. Jung and the Alchemical Renewal', *Gnosis: A Journal of Western Inner Traditions*, 8 (1988) <http://gnosis.org/jung_alchemy.htm> [accessed 15 October 2021]. See Carl Gustav Jung, *The Archetypes and the Collective Unconscious* (London: Routledge, 1968)

12. I will explain the relationship of Pinocchio to the archetype of the trickster in Part II when this aspect of Pinocchio will be more relevant to the retellings examined.

13. Ovid, *Metamorphoses*, ed. by Henry T. Riley (London: G. Bell & Sons, 1884), p. 358 (Book x).

14. Victoria Nelson, *The Secret Life of Puppets* (Cambridge, MA, & London: Harvard University Press, 2001), p. 37.

15. Lois Rostow Kuznets, *When Toys Come Alive: Narratives of Animation, Metamorphosis, and Development* (New Haven, CT: Yale University Press, 1994), p. 189.

16. Giambattista Basile, 'Pinto Smalto', in *Lo cunto de li cunti* [1674] (Turin: Einaudi, 2002), pp. 838–51.

17. Anon. 'The Gingerbread Boy', *St. Nicholas Magazine*, 2.7 (1875), 448–49.

18. See Barbara Creed, *The Monstrous-feminine: Film, Feminism, Psychoanalysis* (London: Routledge, 1993).

19. David Koepsell, 'Gaius Baltar and the Transhuman Temptation', in *Battlestar Galactica and Philosophy: Knowledge Here Begins Out There*, ed. by Jason T. Eberl (Malden, MA: Blackwell, 2008), pp. 241–52 (p. 241, my emphasis).

20. Barbara Johnson, *Persons and Things* (Cambridge, MA, & London: Harvard University Press, 2008), p. 20.

21. E. T. A. Hoffmann, 'The Sandman', in *The Golden Pot and Other Tales* [1817] (Oxford: Oxford University Press, 1992), pp. 85–118; Mary Shelley, *Frankenstein: or, The Modern Prometheus* [1818] (Oxford & New York: Oxford University Press, 1994).

22. Charles Klopp, 'Workshops of Creation, Filthy and Not: Collodi's Pinocchio and Shelley's Frankenstein', in *Pinocchio, Puppets and Modernity: The Mechanical Body*, ed. by Katia Pizzi (London & New York: Routledge, 2012), pp. 63–74.

23. Johnson, *Persons and Things*, p. 91.

24. Perella, 'An Essay on *Pinocchio*', p. 109. See Asor Rosa, '*Le avventure di Pinocchio*', pp. 922–27.

25. Brian Aldiss, 'Supertoys Last All Summer Long', in *Supertoys Last All Summer Long and Other Stories of Future Time* (New York: St. Martin's Griffin, 2001), pp. 1–11.

26. Ian Watson, 'Plumbing Stanley Kubrick', *The New York Review of Science Fiction* (2000) <http://www.ianwatson.info/plumbing-stanley-kubrick/> [accessed 21 March 2019].

27. John C. Tibbetts, 'Robots Redux: *A.I. Artificial Intelligence* (2001)', *Literature & Film Quarterly*, 29.4 (2001), 256–61.

28. Rosi Braidotti, *The Posthuman* (Cambridge: Polity Press, 2013); Cary Wolfe, *What Is Posthumanism?* (Minneapolis: University of Minnesota Press, 2010); and Elaine L. Graham, *Representations of the Post/human: Monsters, Aliens and Others in Popular Culture* (Manchester: Manchester University Press, 2002).

29. Ivan Callus, Stefan Herbrechter, and Manuela Rossini, 'Introduction: Dis/ Locating Posthumanism in European Literary and Critical Traditions', *European Journal of English Studies*, 18.2 (2014), 103–20 (p. 105).

30. Ibid., p. 106.

31. Wolfe, *What Is Posthumanism?*, p. xiii.

32. Max More, 'Transhumanist FAQ', *Humanity+* <http://humanityplus.org/philosophy/transhumanist-faq/#answer_19> [accessed 21 March 2019].

33. Hayles, 'Wrestling with Transhumanism', pp. 215, 217.

34. David Roden, *Posthuman Life* (London: Routledge, 2015), p. 9.

35. Ibid.

36. *Sense8*, dir. by The Wachowskis (USA: Netflix, 2015).

37. Scott Jeffery, 'The Silver Age Superhero as Psychedelic Shaman' (2011) <http://stir.academia.edu/ScottJeffery/Papers/1334997/The_Silver_Age_Superhero_as_Psychedelic_Shaman> [accessed 21 March 2019].

38. 'Superhuman' exhibition, Wellcome Collection, 19 July-16 October 2012.

39. Stephen Mulhall, 'Picturing the Human (Body and Soul): A Reading of *Blade Runner*', *Film and Philosophy*, 1 (1994), 87–104 (p. 90).

CHAPTER 1

❖

Blade Runner

In *Blade Runner*, the replicant Rachael thinks she is human because she has been manufactured with implanted memories of a supposed childhood. This is what makes it so difficult for blade runner Deckard to discover that she is a replicant after she has been given the Voight-Kampff test, an assessment that is designed to reveal the true identity of a humanoid robot or replicant. In Ridley Scott's futuristic world, replicants are created to be used as a labour force in Earth's stellar colonies. They are made with a lifespan of four years so that they can be kept under control. Those who escape to Earth are 'retired' or killed by a special police force, the blade runners.

It is important to note that I will refer to Ridley Scott as the authorial voice, since he differentiated his film from Philip K. Dick's *Do Androids Dream of Electric Sheep?*, the book on which the film was based. As Vernon Shetley and Alissa Ferguson highlight, 'the treatment of the theme of empathy marks perhaps the greatest divergence between book and film'.[1] In an interview with Paul Sammon, Dick explains how he meant the replicants to be:

> To me, the replicants are deplorable. They are cruel, they are cold, they are heartless. They have no empathy, which is how the Voight-Kampff test catches them out, and don't care about what happens to other creatures. They are essentially less-than-human entities.[2]

Scott had a more transhumanist, so less hostile, view of how he would depict the replicants. He might have depicted some of them as cruel and heartless, but he questioned Dick's notion of 'less-than-human'. This is a very important difference, as Rachael's feelings make the humanoid replicants less alienating and more accessible to the viewer. The Director's Cut is even more important, as it leaves doubts as to whether blade runner Deckard is a replicant himself.

Rachael thinks she is human and does not object to taking the Voight-Kampff test. Tyrell, head of the corporation that manufactures the replicants, sends her away and reveals to Deckard that Rachael is an experiment. By giving emotions to the replicants, people can manipulate them better and they do that by implanting them with fake memories. Without anyone telling her the truth, Rachael starts having doubts about her identity, quite as any human would. She visits Deckard in his apartment to learn the truth. 'You think I'm a replicant, don't you?' she asks him and takes an old photograph out of her bag. She points it out to him. 'Look. It's me with my mother'. Deckard does not even look at the photograph and continues to tidy up in an indifferent way:

> Yeah? Remember when you were six, you and your brother snuck into an empty building through a basement window, you were going to play doctor? He showed you his and when it got to be your turn you chickened and ran, remember that? Have you ever told anybody that? Your mother, Tyrell, anybody?

Deckard goes on to narrate another of Rachael's implanted memories, as she slowly realises the bitter truth. Then he quite simply goes on to explain: 'Implants. Those aren't your memories, they're somebody else's, they're Tyrell's niece's'. Rachael stares at him and tears start running from her eyes. Only then does Deckard realise how much she is hurt. 'Ok, bad joke,' he says, 'I made a bad joke, you're not a replicant. Go home, ok?', and the camera lens focuses on Rachael's crying eyes. Deckard is not used to dealing with such emotions. He cannot convince Rachael that he was joking and he offers her a drink. As he goes into the kitchen to fetch a glass, Rachael throws the photograph on the floor and leaves.

This is a highly emotional scene and Rachael, unlike all the other replicants in the film, looks nothing less than a hurt human being. As R. M. P. and Peter Fitting suggest, 'the robot and its ancestors and relatives have been used — at least since Mary Shelley's Frankenstein — as a figure for collective anxieties about the dangers of science and technology'.[3] However, Scott's camera sympathises with Rachael and opens up the possibility of welcoming the advances of technology, no matter how estranging they initially look. This is also suggested by the film's ending, which will be analysed in detail further on.

Unlike Pinocchio, who instantly decides he wants to become a man when he realises that he is a puppet, Rachael succumbs to her sadness and leaves in tears after being confronted with the fact that she is a replicant. While Pinocchio's wooden body shows from the start that he is a puppet, Rachael looks and behaves exactly like any other human. What might seem uncanny for the viewer is the supposition that her memories were implanted, since these are what give Rachael human feelings and emotions. Empathy, which is what the Voight-Kampff test aims to detect, comes as a result of having memories and is what distinguishes humans from replicants. This is quite the opposite of the world of Pinocchio, where it is not empathy that makes one human, but hard work. Besides, Pinocchio has empathy from the start, as he cares for his father, the Fairy, his friend Lampwick, and other characters around him. The realisation that her memories are not her own leads Rachael to resemble a tragic character. She is suddenly deprived of her identity and estranged from her newly-discovered body, as if left with an empty shell.[4] Recent research has proved that not only androids but also humans can have false memories, as was presented on the BBC radio show 'Past Imperfect'.[5] In it, Giuliana Mazzoni revealed how implanted false memories can change people's behaviour. This further emphasises Rachael's proximity to a human being.

Empathy is what distinguished humans from non-humans in Dick's novel and Scott's film and it is still a concept that concerns modern science. In the New Scientist article 'Too Close for Comfort', Joe Cloc tries to explain the reasons why humans feel uncomfortable with human-looking robots, a phenomenon described as 'the uncanny valley'.[6] One of these reasons is that humans are unable to empathise with human-like robots. This revealing insight, based on research by Kurt Gray at the University of North Carolina at Chapel Hill, collapses the notion of empathy, which was hitherto attributed to humans as their most distinctive feature. Gray's research suggests that 'the particular brand of sympathy we reserve for other people requires us to believe the thing we are sympathising with has a self. And this concession of a mind to something not human makes us uncomfortable'.[7] In that research study, the results refer to the reaction of humans to humanlike robots that were unable to have emotions, so self-less creatures. An immediate question is what would one consider necessary for these robots to acquire a 'self'? This changes in different times and Gray's study does not provide any further answers regarding the pre-requisites of selfhood. In Rachael's case, this would consist of having feelings of empathy towards humans and animals, which are what humans value as precious in Scott's film.

Collodi wanted his young readers to appreciate the ethics of work or at least he wanted to convince their parents that this is what his purpose was. Scott's purpose is a very different one: he wants his viewers to reflect upon what it is to be human. This question might have occurred to the reader of Collodi as well, but not as the main focus, as it is in *Blade Runner*. However, even though it is articulated in different terms, it is essentially the same ontological question in both works, one which continues to reverberate in modern research. What is real in Collodi's 'real boy' ('ragazzo per bene') is similar to what is 'human' in Scott's film and what is referred to as 'self' in Gray's research.

In *Blade Runner* Rachael represents the humanoids that have escaped to Earth illegally and, by their presence, threaten the human race. Deckard represents humanity in the form of the lawful police officer who keeps order and protects society. Yet it is Deckard rather than Rachael who lacks empathy. He is completely indifferent to the devastating emotions that Rachael is going through because of his revelation to her. When he realises her distress, he does not empathise with her; rather, he appears unable to deal with the situation and therefore tells her it was all a bad joke. But even in that response, he does not make an effort to sound convincing: it is quite obvious that he does not know how to deal with human emotions — and Rachael's emotions are exactly that. He offers her a drink, a gesture that suggests that this has been his way of dealing with unpleasant thoughts and emotions, portraying in the film what Philip Dick originally wanted to show in his book, namely how Deckard is dehumanised by his work. As a result, the viewer sympathises with Rachael, the humanoid who is 'more human than human', as Tyrell's advertisement proclaims and as is ironically portrayed in this scene.

The next scene in which Deckard and Rachael appear together is when she saves his life by killing one of her own, another replicant who was about to kill him. The blade runner has just killed Zhora, one of the four replicants who escaped to Earth and whom he was originally supposed to 'retire'. Immediately after that, he is told by Bryant, his supervisor, that he is supposed to add Rachael to the list because she has been reported missing from Tyrell headquarters. To the authorities that Deckard serves and represents, finding out about her identity makes Rachael dangerous enough to be killed. Yet her reaction is very normal and to be expected, having grown up in a society where it is quite clear that replicants found on Earth will be 'retired'. Her newly discovered self was her enemy just hours before. Once again, the humans display inhuman behaviour by creating a replicant with emotions like their own and then discarding the 'experiment' without the slightest remorse when things get complicated.

Rachael is out in the street watching Deckard, who is being watched by another replicant named Leon. Deckard is attacked and disarmed by Leon, but as Leon is about to kill him, Rachael shoots Leon from behind, saving Deckard's life. The next scene finds them in his apartment again. Rachael is aware that Deckard's job involves 'retiring' her. Before being able to come to terms with her identity, she has to run and hide and find a way to protect herself. 'What if I go north? Disappear?' she asks him, 'Would you come after me, hunt me?' 'No. No, I wouldn't. I owe you one. But somebody would'.

Deckard might lack the ability to express or share emotions, but he is clearly not happy doing his job. And he is very reluctant to include Rachael among his targets even when his supervisor mentions it. Even though his job is to kill replicants, Rachael feels safer with him, because he could have killed her if he had wanted to, during their first encounter in his apartment. The most important confrontation that entails the existential issues that the film raises is when Rachael starts asking Deckard questions. First she asks about the files on the length of her lifespan, but he tells her they were classified. And then, 'You know that Voight-Kampff test of yours, did you ever take that test yourself?', a question that he leaves unanswered.

At this central moment in the film, two major philosophical issues are touched upon: the time limitations of human existence and what makes one human. It is very interesting that both these questions are brought to the surface through a replicant; this is partly because it makes those issues more bearable to face than if they were articulated by a human. The way Rachael functions as a mirror — reflecting human anxieties back to Deckard and the viewer — is significant because the viewer can experience her anxiety from the safety of their own position, much like the relief (catharsis) that the viewers of tragedy experience according to the Aristotelian definition of tragedy.[8] This effect is doubled because normally an actor suffices to distance the viewer from the act he/she is representing, but in this case the actor herself represents a non-human. The questioning of one's own nature is an extremely delicate matter and can still cause anxiety in the viewer; therefore a second layer of estrangement and distancing is needed: a woman acting the role of a humanoid, one representation within another.

The main difference between Rachael and the four replicants that have escaped to Earth is that, unlike them, she was not always aware of her non-human identity. They travelled all the way to Los Angeles in order to locate the Tyrell Corporation (their maker) and find a way to prolong their lives. They do not desire humanity as such, only a feature of it, the duration of a human life. They are stronger and more developed than humans, they experience everything at a much greater intensity than humans, but they only have a four-year lifespan. Rachael's reaction is not to join forces with them to try to obtain the information about how to prolong her lifespan; since she has lived with Tyrell and knows him, she can do so directly. Instead, she accepts her fate with a determinism that recalls the 1950s femmes fatales and the film noir atmosphere that *Blade Runner* so convincingly reproduces. All she desires is to stay alive for as long as she is able and to seek Deckard's protection. Since *Blade Runner* is stylistically a neo-noir film, we expect the heroes to be doomed no matter what, as all film noir protagonists are. Even though the ending of the film is ambiguous, the characters remain outcasts from society, each of them for a different reason.

What Pinocchio and Rachael have in common is that they both suddenly discover something about their nature they did not know before: that he cannot become a man and that she is not human. What they also have in common is that they seek advice and protection from a person they trust. Ironically, the Fairy in Pinocchio is not really human; rather she is closer to Pinocchio's magical nature than to the human Geppetto, yet she represents the society of Pinocchio's world. The same irony occurs in *Blade Runner*: according to the book and the original script, Deckard has been dehumanised by the brutal nature of his work. In order to be able to perform the killings, or 'retirings', of the replicants, he has to follow his purpose very rigidly and ignore any feelings that might interfere with doing his job. His name — Deckard — sounding so similar to 'Descartes', works as a constant reminder of and reference to Cartesian rationalism and thought. Moreover, in the Director's Cut, the irony is even stronger, as Deckard is himself a replicant, which he does not know but possibly suspects.

Yet Rachael is different from Pinocchio in her lack of desire to change her nature. She takes action, but only in order to preserve her current state. She also has trouble accepting that she could be happy in her new identity. Still, in the same scene in Deckard's apartment, the two come closer and he tries to kiss her. She avoids him, but not because she does not want him; she is not sure how to act according to the new facts that define her life and identity:

DECKARD   Say 'Kiss me'.
RACHAEL   I can't rely on...
DECKARD   Say 'Kiss me'.
RACHAEL   Kiss me.
DECKARD   I want you.
RACHAEL   I want you.
DECKARD   Again.
RACHAEL   I want you. Put your hands on me.

Deckard pushes her to acknowledge her feelings and accept them and, after repeating his words, she finally finds her own voice and allows herself both to desire and to express that desire. This scene might initially reflect Rachael's identity as a replicant since she replicates Deckard's speech, yet she is more similar to a child who learns by repetition until it finds its own voice. In that sense, she is closer to the childlike state of Pinocchio or David, the protagonist of *A.I.*, which will be examined next. In the same way that childhood is a learning process that allows humans to reach their full potential, so is this a phase for Rachael in order to learn to express herself in her new identity.

Rachael's desire to be loved indirectly reflects her wish for humanity. She stays in Deckard's apartment, waiting for him; after he has killed the other two replicants, he returns. His door is open and he enters, calling Rachael and pointing his gun in all directions. Rachael is lying on the bed, covered by a sheet. A very anxious Deckard approaches and lifts the sheet slowly, afraid that someone might have harmed her. Rachael is sleeping and so he bends over to hear if she is breathing. Noticeably relieved, he wakes her with a kiss. He asks her if she loves him and if she trusts him. Rachael says yes and shortly after they escape together. This is the extent of Rachael's becoming human: her being loved and accepted by a human and sharing her future with him. It is not so important if Deckard is human or not, because she does not know one way or the other. In the final scene, they are driving in the countryside, a marked contrast to the bleak and dark cityscape of the rest of the film. Rachael is looking happy and Deckard says in a voiceover, 'Tyrell had told me Rachael was special: no termination date. I didn't know how long we had together. Who does?' Thus Rachael will live a human life in the sense that no human knows how long they have to live.

It is remarkable that those who tried to change their nature in a more direct and radical way (i.e. the other four replicants) all found death. Even though in the first instance they seem to be more eager to change their future and prolong their lives to be like humans, essentially they do not appreciate or respect human life. The only one who does is Rachael, but she has 'grown up' as a human; she has all the memories of one. This contradistinction between Rachael and the other replicants emphasises the importance of memory and personal history to the essence of humanity.

Ridley Scott's tolerant and positive attitude towards humanoids is noticeable in the context of the 1980s, when there was widespread anxiety regarding the introduction of PCs into everyday life. Machines and robots were still seen as foreign to daily life: there was a fascination with them, but not yet a familiarity. This is also evident in many episodes of *The Twilight Zone* series, first revival (1985–89), among many films and series of the time. As mentioned before, the original book by Philip K. Dick, *Do Androids Dream of Electric Sheep?*, did not include any empathetic replicants. In fact, Dick chose the replicants to stand as a metaphor for Nazis. Stephen Dalton mentions that Dick's 'key inspiration was not the dawning age of robotics but the real-life Nazi mass murderers whose diaries he had studied for his previous novel, *The Man in the High Castle*'.[9] The fact that he chose androids to represent Nazis reveals that he had no friendly attitude towards human-like robots. Scott's contribution, therefore, in predisposing the viewer towards an acceptance of the humanoid has to happen in an environment where a risk to them is also acknowledged. By providing two different types of replicant, he opens up the possibility of including them in human society. The four rebel replicants may embody a human fear of the machine but they are earlier models, before an improved version like Rachael was made. They are a step along the technological path towards making human replicants that cannot be distinguished from humans, not only because of their perfect physical likeness, but also because of their inner, emotional similarity. The rebel replicants have a four-year lifespan; Rachael's is unknown. Had she not found out from Deckard that she was a replicant, she would always have thought that she was a human. This has several disturbing implications for the viewer: she finds out about her nature at the same time as the viewer does. In this manner, she can be included by exclusion; having been identified as a different 'species' and then controlled so that she does not pose any danger, she can then be accepted as long as the boundaries of her identity and her rights are clearly stated. This does not sound very progressive by contemporary standards, but it was a very big step forward in the technophobic atmosphere of the 1980s.

Notes to Chapter 1

1. Vernon Shetley, and Alissa Ferguson, 'Reflections in a Silver Eye: Lens and Mirror in *Blade Runner*', *Science Fiction Studies*, 28.1 (2001), 66–76 (pp. 72–73).
2. Paul M. Sammon, *Future Noir: The Making of 'Blade Runner'* (London: Harper Collins, 1996), p. 285.
3. R. M. P., and Peter Fitting, 'Futurecop: The Neutralization of Revolt in *Blade Runner*', *Science Fiction Studies*, 14.3 (1987), 340–54 (p. 341).
4. Another sentient cyborg exploring her fragmented identity worth comparing with Rachael is Motoko Kusanagi in the animation film *Ghost in the Shell*, dir. by Mamoru Oshii (Japan & USA: Bandai Visual Company, 1995).
5. 'Past Imperfect', BBC Radio 4, 22 July 2015 <http://www.bbc.co.uk/programmes/b062kx4x> [accessed 21 March 2019].
6. Joe Cloc, 'Too Close for Comfort', *New Scientist*, 2899 (12 January 2013).
7. Ibid., p. 37.
8. 'Tragedy, then, is an imitation of an action that is serious, complete, and of a certain magnitude; in language embellished with each kind of artistic ornament, the several kinds being found in separate parts of the play; in the form of action, not of narrative; through pity and fear effecting the proper purgation of these emotions'. Aristotle, *Poetics*, trans. by S. H. Butcher <http://classics.mit.edu/Aristotle/poetics.1.1.html#200> [accessed 21 March 2019].
9. Stephen Dalton, 'Blade Runner: Anatomy of a Classic', BFI homepage, 29 June 2015 <http://www.bfi.org.uk/news-opinion/news-bfi/features/blade-runner> [accessed 21 March 2019].

CHAPTER 2

❖

A.I. Artificial Intelligence

Blade Runner is not the only example of a 1980s film that portrays the fear of machines. Many films with this topic were produced around that time, ranging from children's animation such as *Andromeda Stories* to popular films such as *The Terminator.*[1] As mentioned earlier, the original idea for *A.I.* was born in the late 1970s; the 2001 film, though, has a different, more robot-friendly approach than the predecessors of its genre. To a large extent, the film follows the storyline of *Pinocchio* and the robot boy David desires humanity, as Pinocchio did. All David desires is to be loved and accepted and the way to achieve this is by becoming human. Pinocchio had to fulfil certain tasks in order for the Blue Fairy to grant him his wish to become human. David's self-imposed task is to become human in order to achieve his goal, which is to be loved.

A.I. is the story of David, the first mecha boy (the name is short for mechanic) in an imagined twenty-second century. He is the first robot child to be designed and the first robot to have emotions, and in particular, emotions of love. When his love becomes too dangerous for the members of his foster family, they decide to abandon him in the forest. Having listened to the story of Pinocchio when his mother Monica was reading it to him and her real son, he firmly believes that if he becomes a real boy, then Monica will accept him back and love him. So he starts on a quest to find the Blue Fairy, who he believes will turn him into a real boy.

David identifies with Pinocchio after he is confronted with his artificiality, which happens after Monica's biological son recovers from a rare disease and returns home. It is the human boy and his friends who constantly point out to David that he is not real, and in this *A.I.* is very similar to the story of Pinocchio.

However, there are many fundamental differences between the two narratives. To start with, the Fairy has promised Pinocchio that she will make him real if he behaves well, while David never meets the Fairy he is looking for. Pinocchio's journey begins because of his appetite for adventure and his desire to explore the world, and part of this involves exploring himself and becoming a real boy. For David, by contrast, there is no self-exploration: his quest is to return home after being abandoned. It is for this reason only that he wants to become real: to be accepted and loved by his mother. This is his obsession throughout the film. As Tim Kreider points out, 'it looks more like a scary parody of love, a monomaniacal obsession that renders him oblivious to the ugly realities around him'.[2] There is no self-discovery in David's journey; even when he is given the chance to understand why he was abandoned and how humans see him — when Gigolo Joe, the mecha love robot that David meets on the way, and who has been helping him all along, tries to tell him the truth — David is in complete denial and remains so until the end.

Pinocchio also had a quest (that of finding his father), being led by his feelings of guilt and love towards Geppetto. Becoming a real boy became a parallel quest on the way to finding Geppetto, as the schematic representation of the structure of *Pinocchio* shows in my Introduction. However, Pinocchio, like any normal child, gets distracted on the way to fulfilling his quests and repeatedly deviates from his original intention. This is not the case with David. Like a psychotic person, David ignores everyone and everything on his way until he finds the Blue Fairy. It is a linear and agonising journey that never stops until David reaches his goal.

Another difference between the two heroes is that Pinocchio manages to become a real boy in the end. David, on the other hand, does not. He finds a statue of the Blue Fairy in the sea surrounding sunken Manhattan, a simulacrum that used to be part of the 'Pinocchio World' in a fairy-tale fair on Coney Island. Even then, David is unable to face reality and begs the Fairy to make him real. Two thousand years later, the sea has frozen, humanity is extinct and robots of advanced intelligence live in what remains of the world. They discover David, who awakens from a long sleep and turns towards the Blue Fairy again, full of hope. In order to make him happy, the robots simulate the Blue Fairy, who then explains to David that she cannot make him real. What she can do, however, is recreate his mother, Monica, from the DNA of her hair that Teddy, David's supertoy, has been carrying with him all along. The robots explain to David that the clone can live only for one day, but he is still unable to accept reality. He hopes that this clone of his mother will be able to stay longer. In the end, he spends the best day of his life with Monica. She tells him that she loves him, which is what he has been waiting to hear all his life. Then Monica goes to sleep for ever and David decides to sleep (and possibly die) there with her.

As mentioned earlier, theorists of posthumanism often refer to humanism and humanity in order to explain their approach. In *A.I.,* through David's character, questions about the nature of humanity are raised as well. It is not so much his robot nature that arouses some unease in the viewer, as his human emotions. The idea of giving human emotions to a machine is uncanny, mostly because we have not entirely deciphered the complexity of human nature, especially with regard to emotional intelligence. David manifests the psychopathology of a disturbed human but with the resilience and veracity of a robotic machine, magnifying these human elements, which creates uneasiness. He is a reminder that through technologies of artificial intelligence, we are trying to reproduce something we have not entirely understood and that sentient robots can create uneasiness because they function as a magnifying glass on a flawed humanity.

David's journey of self-discovery is very different from Pinocchio's and yet for the entire second half of the film, all the themes resonate with Pinocchio and the Blue Fairy. It is very characteristic that from all the elements of Collodi's novel,

Spielberg decided to keep only one and then emphasise it to the extreme: the desire to become real, the core of the Pinocchio myth. What in Collodi's original story is one theme among others becomes exaggerated and overstretched in *A.I.* This is very interesting if we consider that the story the film was originally inspired by, Brian Aldiss's 'Supertoys Last All Summer Long', was not a story of hope, but one of loneliness. In that story, robot children replace human children because of governmental fertility control. When David's foster parents get permission from the government to procreate, his future is uncertain. In a way, it seems as if Spielberg needed the myth of Pinocchio in order to smooth out the bleakness of Aldiss's story. Spielberg's view of the future in 2001 could not be the same as Aldiss's in 1969, when he wrote the story.

Spielberg has a non-threatening approach to the topic of a robot desiring humanity. There is no implied fear of machines taking over or of an artificial intelligence desiring humanity in order to evolve. The storyline of David takes the viewer gradually on an emotional roller coaster of utter sympathy and identification with the little robot boy who seeks love. The *A.I.* version of *Pinocchio* is very different from that of *Blade Runner*. David is a robot rather than a cyborg/replicant. The viewer gets to see the interior of his body, which mainly consists of metal parts and wires. He has organic parts as well, but not as many as Rachael. He is closer to Pinocchio as far as his mechanical body is concerned. He is not as developed or intelligent as Rachael, but this is because he was designed to have the intelligence and emotions of a child. Throughout the film, his identity is clear to most characters; he is recognised as a robot — a mecha, as they are called here. In this film humans are used to having mechas among them. However, a mecha child is something entirely new. This is why, during a 'flesh fair', an entertainment event for humans during which robots are tortured and destroyed, the fact that he is mistaken for a boy is what eventually saves his life.

In David's case there is not only one confrontation scene, as was the case with Rachael, but a series of scenes that climactically lead to the most important one near the end of the film, in which David fully realises his true identity. The first time he is confronted with his nature directly is when Monica's real son, Martin, returns home. The first time we see them together, Martin is trying to understand David or perhaps make him understand who is in charge. 'So, I guess now you're the new Super-toy, so what good stuff can you do? Oh, can you do "power" stuff, like, uhhh, walk on the ceiling or the walls? Anti-gravity? Like, float or fly?' 'Can you?' asks David, quite confused. 'No, because I'm real'. The conversation goes on and David finds out that he has no birthday or memory of it. This is the first time David is confronted with the fact that he is not real; he does not want to accept this as the truth, yet doubt has entered his mind. This is why when he listens to the Pinocchio story that Monica is reading to him and Martin, he is entirely absorbed, a smile drawn on his face, a smile full of hope.

Another instance of David being confronted with his nature is at Martin's birthday party. When he brings a present to his foster brother, one of Martin's friends asks: 'This him? This your little brother?' 'Technically... no,' says Martin.

Then Tod, Martin's friend exclaims, 'He's mecha!' David is perplexed: 'What's mecha?' he asks. 'We're or-ga-nic, you're mecha-nical. Orga, mecha, orga', and he points his finger once to himself, and once to David, as he distinguishes between the two. This scene ends badly as the children hurt David and he grasps Martin in a tight embrace, asking for protection; they both fall into the swimming pool and Martin is saved at the last minute by panicked adults. David's foster parents decide to return him to the factory as he is posing a danger to them, but Monica knows that if they return him, he will be terminated so she decides to abandon him in the forest instead, to save his life. During that very intense and dramatic scene, David tries to understand what he has done wrong and then begs her to accept him back once the Blue Fairy has made him a real boy. Monica warns him that this is just a story, but David is determined to get his mother back and earn her love.

The ultimate confrontation scene is when David arrives at the place where he thinks the Blue Fairy is, but in reality it is the headquarters of the company that made him. This is an indirect link connecting the idea of the Blue Fairy with that of the God the Maker. This is of significance regarding Professor Hobby's part, and also regarding the crucial role that the Blue Fairy plays in Coover's retelling of *Pinocchio*, which will be analysed in Part II. David opens the door and comes face to face with a boy who looks exactly like him. He finds out he is called David too, and then, full of jealousy, he destroys the other robot, yelling 'I'm David! I'm David! I'm special, I'm unique, you can't have her! I'm David!' Professor Hobby, his maker, finds him and calms him down.

> PROFESSOR HOBBY   Yes, you are David.
> DAVID   Professor Hobby?
> PROFESSOR HOBBY   Yes, David, I've been waiting for you.
> DAVID   Dr Know told me you'd be here. Is Blue Fairy here, too?
> PROFESSOR HOBBY   I first heard of your Blue Fairy from Monica. What did you believe the Blue Fairy could do for you?
> DAVID   She would make me a real boy.
> PROFESSOR HOBBY   But you are a real boy. At least as real as I've ever made one which by all reasonable accounts would make me your Blue Fairy.

At this point, just before the revelation of the last details of David's identity, Professor Hobby's attitude starts to reveal an uncannily emotionless human side: he does not seem to care if he hurts the feelings of the robot-boy he created, reminding us of Deckard's indifference towards Rachael's feelings. He is so absorbed in his self-admiration for having created the life that stands before him that his speech sounds almost self-deluding. This reflects perfectly one of the desires that the animate/ inanimate archetype expresses — the primal human wish to play God.

The primal desire to create life and play God becomes even more evident through a cyborg-friendly approach in different literary and film versions. This happens because if we accept the cyborg's human attributes or even the hypothesis that it can be equal to a human, then man is able to create humans and this makes him equal to God. In short, if man is able to clone himself or create an android and then upload his consciousness to it, rendering it into a being with a human consciousness, a human being, then he has become the Creator. Therefore, the more examples appear in literature portraying cyborgs as sentient beings with human attributes, the more the forbidden wish of becoming God resonates in the human psyche. This is a particularly male fantasy, to become the Creator, according to the Judaeo–Christian image of God, who first creates Adam and breathes life into him.

In Genesis 1:26, God says 'Let us make man in our image, after our likeness', and therefore it is implied that the human race has the face of God. According to the biblical texts, the most significant manifestation of God's power is the creation of the universe, including the human species. By building androids in his likeness, man imitates God and like him gives his face to his creations. And if his creations manage to become human, then he will have been able to match the power of God to create humans and so become exactly like him.

David reacts to Professor Hobby's claim that he is the Blue Fairy, feeling his world collapse:

> DAVID   You are not her. Dr Know told me that she would be here at the lost city in the sea at the end of the world where the lions weep.
>
> PROFESSOR HOBBY   And that's what Dr Know needed to know to get you to come home to us. And it's the only time we intervened, the only help that we gave him to give to you, so you could find your way home to us. Until you were born, robots didn't dream, robots didn't desire, unless we told them what to want. David! Do you have any idea what a success story you've become? You found a fairy tale and inspired by love, fuelled by desire, you set out on a journey to make her real and, most remarkable of all, no one taught you how. We actually lost you for a while. But when you were found again we didn't make our presence known because our test was a simple one: Where would your self-motivated reasoning take you? To the logical conclusion? The Blue Fairy is part of the great human flaw to wish for things that don't exist. Or to the greatest single human gift — the ability to chase down our dreams. And that is something no machine has ever done until you'.
>
> DAVID   I thought I was one of a kind.
>
> PROFESSOR HOBBY   My son was one of a kind. You are the first of a kind. David?
>
> DAVID   My brain is falling out.

This is the moment at which David fully realises the truth and is shocked by it. Unlike resourceful Pinocchio, who tried immediately to change his fate after he realised his difference from other boys, David is emotionally broken. As Professor Hobby goes to bring in the creative team — David's 'real mothers and fathers', as he calls them — David enters the room where he was born. He sees the numerous copies of himself, looking at them in horror. Then he sees the big bird he had as a first memory, realising that it is the company's logo. In the next scene, he is sitting on the outside ledge of the Cybertronics building; he looks psychologically shattered. Like any traumatised child, he seeks his mother's soothing presence. He whispers 'mommy' and falls into the abyss.

David sinks into the water below, which used to be the ground level of New York City, and a school of fish carries him around, in a scene strongly reminiscent of the fish that eat Pinocchio's donkey skin and liberate him. These fish, though, do not quite liberate David. Instead, they bring him closer to his obsession, the Blue Fairy. And this is exactly what he needs — motivation in order to go on. In that sense, then, the fish save David's life just as they saved Pinocchio's life. Whether this reference is deliberate or not, it is one of the few instances where *A.I.* is closely connected to Collodi's text. It is likely that Spielberg based his *Pinocchio* references largely on the Disney version, as he was mainly addressing an audience that would be familiar with Disney rather than Collodi. However, this scene allows for the assumption that Spielberg is paying tribute to the original *Pinocchio*, since this scene in the original text is missing from the Disney version. The fish leave David in front of a statue of the Blue Fairy, in what used to be an attraction at the Coney Island amusement park. His desperate face fills with hope again. When Joe is arrested, he leaves David the amphibicopter and David uses it to go underwater to the Blue Fairy.

As I described earlier, the ending of *A.I.* is very ambiguous as David's dream comes true and he is finally loved by his mother. He does not become a real boy — the robot-Blue Fairy explains that. But it does not matter anymore for David as long as he can be loved by his mother; his life's purpose and obsession from the day Monica decided to make him 'her son' and activated his emotions. Even though David was obsessed with becoming real, he wanted this transformation only in order to be loved. Once he is loved by Monica, it does not matter if he stays as he is. His need for humanity is not, therefore, an existential one, as it was with Rachael and the other replicants in *Blade Runner*, but a need for love and acceptance. Pinocchio is similar in the way that he needs to be a real boy in order to grow up and be a man. He desires to be like everyone else, so too wants acceptance, but without David's obsession. Kreider describes *A.I.* as:

> A story about hopeless human attachments and our bottomless capacity for self-delusion. David's Oedipal fixation remains utterly static throughout two thousand years, in spite of the fact that no human being — including his mother — ever shows him any reciprocal affection. The fact that his devotion is fixed, helpless, and arbitrary ultimately makes his heroism empty and the happy ending hollow. David searches and suffers and waits all those eons for a goal that's not of his own choosing; it's irrational, unconscious — what we might call hard-wired. This is what makes him a tragic figure, and, in a way his manufacturers never intended, also what makes him human. This is a bleakly deterministic, distinctly Freudian view of the human condition, a vision of human beings wasting their lives blindly chasing after unconscious goals just as hopelessly fixed and childish as David's — most often the idealized image of a parent.[3]

Kreider's observation about the deterministic view of the human condition chimes with the film noir determinism seen in the stylistics of *Blade Runner*, as does his view of David as a tragic figure, a parallel to Rachael. *A.I.* may be a film that does not perpetuate the fear of the machine; it is not, however, ready to defend a pluralistic posthuman society either, as the bleak ending suggests. Moreover, I disagree with Kreider that David's goal is not of his own choosing. David is programmed to have human emotions, but what these will be depends solely on him. As seen earlier, Professor Hobby confirms this when he meets David and is astonished by his determination, which was 'fuelled by [David's own] desire'.

A point of commonality between David and Pinocchio is that they both possess characteristics of human children from the start. Pinocchio is a normal child in a wooden body; and because of this body he cannot achieve his desire to grow up. David has all the feelings of a human child and, as is clearly shown, behaves better than human children or adults who are cruel towards him and hurt his feelings. As J. Hoberman emphasises, 'he's been designed as a perfect reproach to humanity, hard-wired for innocence. (Thus Spielberg circumvents the moral of the Aldiss story — which is also the pathos of *Blade Runner*, namely that the robots are more human than their creators)'.[4] Spielberg plays a lot with the viewers' reactions and expectations as to what is real, or human, and what is artificial. David has one more human characteristic, what Timothy Dunn describes as 'a pervasive human desire, the desire for uniqueness'.[5] He goes on to explain that all humans desire to be one of a kind, unique, 'or perhaps more accurately, we fear the loss of our identity, our uniqueness, or whatever makes us irreplaceable'. *A.I.* addresses the issue of replaceability by the constant presentation of simulacra:

> Every character in the film seems as preprogrammed as David, obsessed with the image of a lost loved one, and tries to replace that person with a technological simulacrum. Dr Hobby designed David as an exact duplicate of his own dead child, the original David; Monica used him as a substitute for her comatose son; and, completing the sad cycle two thousand years later, David comforts himself with a cloned copy of Monica.[6]

As Nigel Morris suggests, 'implied narcissism raises awkward issues in relation to Hobby replicating his dead son and Monica adopting, then abandoning, David'.[7]

Another common element between *A.I.* and *Pinocchio* is that both texts are addressed to a double audience: they are both for children and for adults. Collodi's text is didactic and ironic, entertaining and symbolic at the same time. Similarly, Kreider highlights the double message of *A.I.*: 'However brightly the children's story may end for David, the grown-ups can't help but notice, in the background, the death of the human race'.[8] What additionally connects *A.I.* to Collodi's text are the numerous references to fairy tales, whose language and motifs are already present in *Pinocchio*. *A.I.* contains references to the fairy tale of 'Hansel and Gretel', as David is abandoned in the forest, but also to *The Wizard of Oz*, with David's visit to Dr Know.[9]

Collodi's text pointed towards an understanding of the work ethic as an indispensable part of human values. Ridley Scott's *Blade Runner* raised uncomfortable questions about human nature. Spielberg, however, very much like the Disney interpretation of Pinocchio — and despite the uncanny scenes of David's exaggerated behaviour — suggests that humanity's essence lies in the ability to chase one's dreams, a notion that is directly linked to the rhetoric of the American dream: the right and ability to chase one's happiness. This ties in very well with the core of the Pinocchio myth: Pinocchio's desire (and its fulfilment) to become a real boy.

Notes to Chapter 2

1. *Andromeda Stories* (released in the USA as *Gemini Prophecies*), dir. by Masamitsu Sasaki (Japan: TOEI Company Ltd., 1982); *The Terminator*, dir. by James Cameron (UK & USA: Helmdale Film & others, 1984).
2. Tim Kreider, 'A.I. *Artificial Intelligence*', *Film Quarterly*, 56.2 (2002), 32–39.
3. Ibid., p. 33.
4. J. Hoberman, 'The Dreamlife of Androids', *Sight & Sound*, 11.9 (2001), 16–18.
5. Timothy Dunn, '*A.I.: Artificial Intelligence* and the Tragic Sense of Life', in *Steven Spielberg and Philosophy: We're Gonna Need a Bigger Book*, ed. by Dean A. Kowalski (Lexington: University Press of Kentucky, 2008), pp. 82–94 (p. 86).
6. Kreider, 'A.I. *Artificial Intelligence*', pp. 33–34.
7. Nigel Morris, *The Cinema of Steven Spielberg: Empire of Light* (London: Wallflower Press, 2007), p. 302.
8. Kreider, 'A.I. *Artificial Intelligence*', pp. 33–34.
9. Frank L. Baum, *The Wonderful Wizard of Oz* (New York: Bobbs-Merrill, 1900).

CHAPTER 3

❖

Battlestar Galactica

In the universe of the reimagined 2004 television series *BSG*, issues similar to those related to Rachael and David concern a type of further evolved cyborg, the cylons. 'Cylon' stands for 'Cybernetic Lifeform Node'; they were originally robots, used by humans as workers or soldiers. They developed their own consciousness after the accidental transfer of a human's avatar into one of these robots, as is shown in the prequel to the series, *Caprica.*[1] This happens when Zoe Graystone, the daughter of the technology CEO, creates a double of herself in a virtual reality game. When she dies in an accident, her avatar is mistakenly downloaded from the virtual world into a robot, the model of a robot series that was originally created as a war robot. Zoe is the predecessor of the cylons who have different models and forms, ranging from chrome robots to humanoids, as they are highly developed in bioengineering. The humanoid cylons are composed of many copies of eight different models. They do not die, as their consciousness is immediately downloaded into an identical body after their death; this way they carry their memories and experiences into the new body, and so live on. For this to happen they need to be close enough to their Resurrection Ships, which carry the new bodies, into which the cylons can download their consciousness.

The series starts following the second Cylon War, after the cylons had rebelled against their creators who had exploited and mistreated them. In the first Cylon War, the cylons infiltrated technology to attack humans, and in the second, they attacked all the twelve colonial planets inhabited by humans, with nuclear weapons. In the *BSG* world, there were twelve tribes of humans who had escaped from their original planet, Kobol, to escape war, and had colonised twelve planets. The Cylon War happened as a result of their advances in technology and the misuse of their robots. At the time that the series starts, only two battleships carrying humans have escaped. They are trying to find a planet to inhabit, searching for the legendary Earth, which a thirteenth tribe of the original humans allegedly inhabit.

Even though the series starts from the point of view of the humans, it gradually shows the cylon and human views equally and does not always take clear sides. It is also gradually explained that the reason why the cylons declared war against humanity was because of the humans who enslaved them. As the series progresses, the cylons disagree amongst themselves as well, as some of them desire peaceful co-existence with humans and others do not. It is also significant that some of those who are more religious feel the urge to spread the word of their God among sinful

— as they consider them — humans and save them. The fact that cylon behaviour is often indistinguishable from human behaviour makes it more difficult for the viewer to decide which side they should support. The series starts with a very technophobic approach and portrays the cylons as the enemy, a familiar topic in science-fiction films whose visual reference invokes in the viewer all previous debate on the subject. In this case, it refers to all films that revolve around the scenario of man-made robots reaching what Ray Kurzweil has named 'the singularity', the point at which they become more intelligent than their makers and wage war against them.[2] With this as a starting point, there are many twists and turns before the series ends on an optimistic note. The advantage of starting with such negative visual references is that it gains the trust of even the most technophobic viewers, and then it is easier to convince them gradually of the transhumanist ending that I will discuss further on.

In the first episode of *BSG*, the crew of the battleship Galactica have just found out that cylons have advanced their technology and now look exactly like humans, so making each one a possible spy on the humans amongst whom they reside. The cylons have also managed to plant sleeper agents among the humans. These sleeper agents are cylons who think they are human and can be activated and manipulated only when needed. One such agent is Lieutenant Sharon Valerii, otherwise known as 'Boomer'. The viewer realises that she is a cylon before she or anyone else around her does. This is because she is on board the Battlestar Galactica, while another identical Sharon appears on the cylon-occupied planet Caprica. When cylons seem to have no other choice but to infiltrate Galactica, they remotely activate Sharon after one of their spying ships is destroyed. Episode 2 starts with her sweating excessively and having no memory of how she found herself in the room. Then she finds a detonator in her bag and, when she returns it to its place, she realises that more detonators are missing. It is clear to the viewer that she has been activated by the cylons, yet it is dramatic to watch, as she does not realise it. Her tortuous self-conflict is at its most intense when she is flying on her raptor (a fighter aircraft) in search of water, which is vital, at this point of the story, for the survival of the human race. On her screen it says that water has been found, but when they ask her to report, she says it is negative. Then she asks to search again and in looking at the screen, she tries to say that water has been found, but it seems as if she is fighting against herself. She complains that she cannot see well and then after another struggle, she finally manages to go against her cylon programming and follow her feelings, saving them all.

Later on, there are more instances where Sharon is torn between her two identities, not really realising that she is a cylon, but suspecting it, in the same way Rachael suspected that she was a replicant. Sharon's doubts escalate and in Episode 8 of the first season, she approaches Dr Gaius Baltar, who is setting up a test for cylon detection, and asks to be tested first. He tests her and finds out that she is a cylon but he does not tell her; instead he lies, reassuring her that she is human. And he lies in a convincing way, quite unlike blade runner Deckard. His motives are very different, however, from those of Deckard. Baltar is not interested in protecting

Sharon from being hurt. He is instead protecting himself, fearing that if she finds out from him that she is a cylon, she might try to kill him to protect her secret. Baltar is the renowned and respected scientist who represents human values in *BSG*'s universe; and he lets her down. This could have been Sharon's confrontation scene, in which she learnt the truth from a reliable human (as in the previous case studies); however, this revelation has only occurred for the viewers and not for her.

In the penultimate episode of the first season, Sharon puts her gun into her mouth and then changes her mind. Throughout the series, doubt has been torturing her, despite Dr Baltar's fake reassurance. And it is he again who finds her holding her gun and looking thoughtful. She confesses to him that she has dark thoughts and that she is afraid that she might hurt someone. Knowing who she really is, Baltar encourages her to 'embrace what she knows to be the right decision', leading her, in a way, to suicide. Sharon shoots herself, but she is not killed. In the hospital bed, she confesses to Chief Tyrol — the closest person to her, as they used to be a couple — how she feels: 'I wake up in the morning and I wonder who I am. I wake up and wonder if I'm going to hurt someone' (S01E14, 26.43).

In the last episode, after Sharon has recovered, Commander William Adama, the leader of Battlestar Galactica, assigns her to a highly confidential and dangerous mission. She is to fly to one of the cylon base stars and release a nuclear bomb. The way to do that is by pretending she is a cylon, with a cylon transponder in her raptor. This mission will also lead to Sharon's confrontation scene, which has been building up throughout the season. Once on the cylon base star, Sharon gets off her raptor to release the bomb manually. She is then approached by a whole group of models identical to her. This is the most shocking moment for Sharon, to see multiple copies of herself, confirming her darkest fear that she may be cylon. 'This is not happening' is all she can say in response to the truth she is facing up to. As seen earlier, this is very similar to David's shocking confrontation with a copy of himself, and then many more copies, and reflects the human fear of being replaceable.

One of her identical sisters approaches her and takes off Sharon's helmet. 'You're confused and scared, but it's ok,' she says, trying to calm Sharon. Theoretically, if Sharon were a human, she would not be able to breathe for lack of oxygen, but as a cylon she has no problem. Yet, she is still unable to accept the truth. She denies what is so obvious to her, just as David in *A.I.* denied the bitter truth in front of him and kept repeating that he was unique. This is very similar to Sharon's next words: 'I am not a cylon. I am Sharon Valerii. I was born on Troy, my parents were Catherine and Abraham Valerii' (S01E15, 31.30). She is trying to convince herself, rather than her cylon sisters around her. Her confrontation moment is a traumatic one, as was that of David. Their similarity is striking, as they both react by speaking aloud about who they are. And, similarly to Rachael, Sharon refers to memories of her parents to confirm her identity — memories which seem to be implanted, as were those of Rachael.

In all previous examples of the confrontation scene (*Pinocchio*, *Blade Runner*, and *A.I.*), the character is told of their different nature by someone who has power over them. In all three cases, the bearer of news represents what the main character desires to be. This could have been the case for Sharon too, if Dr Baltar had revealed the truth to her. However, for reasons that will be explored later, *BSG* offers an alternative to the tradition of the cyborg confrontation scene. Sharon finds out about her identity through one of her own, someone who has no power over her, but only love. This is what all the cylon copies tell her, each one completing the words of another: 'You can't fight destiny, Sharon. It catches up with you, no matter what you do. Don't worry about us. We'll see you again. We love you, Sharon, and we always will' (So1E15, 31.46).

Sharon runs back to the raptor and takes off, watching the cylon base star explode. She reports back to Galactica that her mission has been accomplished. When she returns and is about to receive congratulations for her bravery, she points her gun at Commander Adama and shoots him twice, surrendering to her cylon nature and to the destiny she had to fulfil, as her cylon sisters told her. It is not revealed at this point whether her choice to embrace her cylon nature was a conscious one, or if her human resistance was lower once she had found out the truth and cylon programming took over. At the beginning of Season 2, though, Sharon does not remember shooting Commander Adama.

While Sharon 'Boomer' Valerii is moving towards her cylon side throughout the first series, in a parallel storyline, another copy of her model, fully aware of her cylon nature, is discovering her human side. She has found Karl 'Helo' Agathon, Boomer's co-pilot on planet Caprica, where Boomer had to leave him in order to rescue civilians. Pretending to be Boomer, who has come to bring him back to Galactica, she is in fact on a major cylon mission. Cylons have been trying to reproduce with humans in order to come closer to their god, as they believe. They are monotheistic, in contrast to humans, who are polytheists. They have concluded that the only way for a cylon to conceive with a human is if the human feels love for them. This is why Sharon 'Athena' Agathon is posing as Boomer and trying to make Helo fall in love with her. As the series progresses, she realises that she loves him in return. Even the other humanoid cylons have noticed that she has changed because of her love for him. Number 5 and Number 6 are waiting for her at their secret meeting place.

> NUMBER 6   Sharon's late.
> NUMBER 5   Half an hour. I notice you're calling her Sharon now.
> NUMBER 6   Yeah, well, I choose to think of her as one of them.
> NUMBER 5   Because you dislike her?
> NUMBER 6   Because, in the scheme of things, we are as we do. She acts like one of them, thinks like them — she is one of them. (So1E10, 19.15)

Number 6's phrase, 'we are as we do', is a statement that stirs the debate on ontological questions touched upon in the previous examples. Being and identity are defined by one's actions, according to Number 6. Contrary to the Aristotelian understanding of essence, she claims that one's being is subject to change and one becomes something else according to one's deeds. In that sense, as a result of his conscious actions, Pinocchio's essence changed and he became human. David's monomaniacal psychosis did not let him change and become something else; he remained a robot with the feelings of a child. Even though he was given the chance to mature and to grow, he did not respond to any of that, so his actions condemned him to his perpetually unchanging state. Rachael's decision to save Deckard's life, even though she knew he could go after her, was what made her ultimately human: she gave herself the choice to become human by not letting her nature define her feelings or actions.

Similarly in *BSG*, Number 6 is proved right because, when Sharon 'Athena' finally gets pregnant with Helo's child, she is not willing to co-operate with the cylons any more and helps him escape — following him, too — even though he rejects her after he discovers the truth about her nature. It is very interesting to observe the storylines of these two identical cylon models (Boomer and Athena) moving in opposite directions, since they are played by the same actress and therefore emphasise even more the questions about humanity and identity.

A very significant concept in the *BSG* universe is that of the cylons 'downloading' their consciousness to an identical body. This reflects recent research and theories that explore the possibilities of uploading one's brain into a machine or one's memories into an online avatar. However, another important link to Collodi's work is evoked through this visual representation. *Pinocchio* finishes with Pinocchio waking up in the body of a real boy, while his old wooden body hangs awkwardly on a chair. This is a very early version of uploading one's consciousness into another body: Pinocchio is not 'transformed' into a real boy; no metamorphosis has taken place in the end. The transformation happened inside him when he became obedient. The physical transformation, though, never happened: he abandoned his old body for a new one. Even though myths and fairy tales are rich in examples of transformation, Collodi very consciously chose not to follow that path. Pinocchio had already been transformed into a donkey and back to a puppet, so it would not be impossible, according to the laws of the fictional universe, to transform into a boy, but despite that Collodi deliberately chose for Pinocchio to observe his old wooden body with his brand-new human eyes, making him the precursor of the cylons and their resurrection technology.

This is emphasised by Gianfranco Marrone who claims that Pinocchio's apparent transformation at the end is essentially not a transformation, but his death — Pinocchio's suicide:

> Alla fine, Pinocchio si suicida decidendo di fare tutte quelle cose che aveva sempre odiato, innanzitutto lavorare, e che gli consentono di diventare finalmente un ragazzino come tutti gli altri, rinnegando la sua natura fantastico-vegetale, e soprattutto il suo celebre, fanciullesco programma narrativo: 'mangiare, bere, dormire, e fare dalla mattina alla sera la vita del vagabondo'.[3]

> [In the end, Pinocchio commits suicide by deciding to do all those things he had always hated, above all work, and which enable him finally to become a boy like any other, denying his fantastical-vegetal nature, and especially his famous boyish life plan: 'to eat, drink, sleep, and live the life of a vagabond from morning until night'.]

This death becomes a learning experience for Pinocchio, changing him into his new human self, exactly as death is a learning experience for every newly-downloaded cylon.

Notes to Chapter 3

1. *Caprica*, dir. by Michael Nankin & others (Canada & USA: David Eick Productions, 2009–10).
2. Ray Kurzweil, *The Singularity is Near: When Humans Transcend Biology* (London: Gerald Duckworth, 2005).
3. Gianfranco Marrone, 'Parallelismi e traduzione: il caso Manganelli', in *Le avventure di Pinocchio: tra un linguaggio e l'altro*, ed. by Isabella Pezzini and Paolo Fabbri (Rome: Meltemi, 2002), pp. 257–76 (p. 261).

❖

CHAPTER 4

Possible Futures

The various examples of confrontation scenes that were examined in my previous chapters emphasise the importance of the notion of identity in relation to the existential aspect of becoming, which is so central in the myth of Pinocchio. Each example differs with regard to acceptance of technological progress, and the myth of Pinocchio is used to express this debate. In order to highlight this, in the next section I examine the contrast between the fictional present and the possible future that is suggested by the ending of each of my case studies. I begin by explaining the context of the three examples and then analyse what the different endings suggest.

In *Blade Runner* 'the postindustrial city is a city in ruins', as Giuliana Bruno suggests:

> The psychopathology of J. F. Sebastian, the replicants, and the city is the psychopathology of the everyday postindustrial condition. The increased speed of development and process produces the diminishing of distances, of the space in between, of distinction. Time and tempo are reduced to climax, after which there is retirement. Things cease to function and life is over even if it has not ended.[1]

As Bruno points out, time does not function in favour of humanity: speed is not beneficial. Instead, it creates alienation, as most of the characters in the film suggest. Even the aesthetics of the futuristic city that Scott imagines is one of gloom and estrangement. Douglas Kellner, Flo Leibowitz, and Michael Ryan highlight this point as follows: 'The colored neon billboards and corporate ads dominating the skyline signify commercialization and are the dominant source of light in an otherwise obscure environment'.[2] In fact, not a single scene of the film is shot during daylight, apart from the ending, but this only occurs in the original version, also known as the Domestic Cut.

> The gaudy neon pink and red evoke a reference to Hell. In their sharp contrast to the dark streets below, the neon colors suggest the incongruity in late capitalism between the dazzling promises of consumption and the harsh realities of production and everyday life. The mixture of signs from Japanese, European, and U.S. capitalism points to a future society where trilateral capitalism has achieved its dream of a world economic system.[3]

That sort of capitalism is portrayed as a devastating wasteland, both in the original book and in Scott's film: 'The cinematic play of bright, artificial images against a hazy background creates unsettling effects through which the urban scenes express social fears about urban decay and anxieties about total domination by corporations'.[4]

The final scene of the film is the only one shot during the day, with brighter colours, without rain or smoke like most of the film's scenes. It is the scene where Deckard and Rachael escape out of the city towards a common future somewhere safer. Despite the bleak, dystopian vision of the whole film, the ending offers a ray of hope. It allows for a wider definition of humanity and suggests the possibility of human-machine co-existence. Even in the less optimistic ending of the Director's Cut (as well as the Final Cut), in which Deckard and Rachael escape into a fragile future — not in the bright surroundings of the original version — the acceptance of Rachael as a person is significant. The Director's Cut ends with the possibility that Deckard might also be a replicant; since he is the protagonist and the representative of order, this suggests even more strongly that it is not what one is made of that matters, but one's personality. In the end it does not matter if Rachael's memories were implanted; she is a person nonetheless.

Despite a hint of optimism at the end, the overall atmosphere remains pessimistic. Even though the viewer is invited to sympathise with Rachael, it is made very clear that she does not have a place in human society. Her humanity is acknowledged at an existential level, but not at a societal one. The only way for her to survive is on the margins of society, as a fugitive. Even though the final scene uses different colours and breaks away from the film noir aesthetic of the rest of the film, it is still a scene outside the film's universe so far. Even more, the final scene of the Director's Cut does not even allow the viewer the hope of some brighter colours: the future for Rachael is one of exile and hiding. Moreover, the film's pessimism lies in the portrayal of the dark future of a dehumanising society run by corporations. As mentioned earlier, with its dark vision of the future, alienating cities and alienated individuals, *Blade Runner* set an example for many to follow. The most characteristic films to follow *Blade Runner*'s cyberpunk aesthetics of social pessimism were the *Ghost in the Shell* and *The Matrix* trilogies. In Scott's film, humans have managed to inhabit other planets, yet life on earth has deteriorated and the progress of technology has spun out of control and turned against humanity. This is in part a reflection of the anxieties about emerging technologies in the 1980s, but it also reflects the alarming consequences of the politics of the Reagan administration in the US. Reagan's disregard of the jobless and homeless, and his failure to provide for the weaker layers of society are reflected in several scenes in the film. Cyberpunk literature and film have consistently used the theme of technological progress contrasted with socioeconomic degradation to convey social criticism.

★   ★   ★   ★   ★

A.I. begins on a somewhat more positive note than *Blade Runner* since no rebellion of the machines has occurred. Technological progress is similar to that in the *Blade Runner* universe, as far as humanoids are concerned: they are created to serve humans. As is revealed in several ways in the film, humans do not treat their humanoid servants well, even if they know that the latter have real feelings. David's happy-ending resolution happens in an extremely devastating context. In Spielberg's film, humanity is wiped off the face of the Earth and advanced-intelligence robots treat any remainders of the human past with the same respect and curiosity with which we approach museum exhibits. As Erik Blankinship remarks:

> At the end of the film, the role of god-like creator is taken from Geppetto, and assumed by the machines, which now create human lives to love robots. It should be an eerie, unnerving future where only echoes of humanity reverberate. But Spielberg plays down the haunting sci-fi aspects, focusing on what the machines were programmed to acquire: the love of humans. We have to remind ourselves that this is a horrifying future, one where David completes his Oedipal quest to take his father's place in his mother's bed. But it is told lovingly, as a fairy tale, an ever-after ending.[5]

Yet the sweet note that is added to the very morbid ending is exactly what makes it even more disturbing. It is what is not said that matters most: David never laments the end of humanity or the death of his mother. If she can be recreated as a clone to utter those long-desired words of love for him, then this is enough for David, nothing else interests him. Even though Spielberg invites the viewer to sympathise with David all along by using archetypical scenes and symbols that invoke sympathy (for example, the child abandoned in the forest running after his mother and begging her to love him), the ending of the film reminds us very strongly that David is a robot after all. He may have human feelings but he lacks human empathy. He is very different from Rachael who has the full range of human thoughts and emotions. On the scale of humanoid affinity to human nature, David rates quite low.

A.I. is the only example among my three cases in which no danger from machine to human is directly expressed. It should be the film that eases the viewer towards a technology-friendly approach, yet it fails to do so dramatically because of its almost inexplicably uncanny ending. The machines might not be the danger, yet the future that is presented is one where they outlive humanity. Even in 2001, it was difficult for Spielberg to present a pluralistic, posthuman society, that is, one that embraces technological process and is tolerant to all differences within its strata. Spielberg remains conservative in his approach as, to paraphrase Fredric Jameson, it is easier for him to imagine the end of humanity than a transhumanist future.[6]

★   ★   ★   ★   ★

The universe of *BSG* shares with the two previous examples the vision of technological progress: technology has moved in the same direction of creating humanoids to be used as free labour. In *BSG*, as in *Blade Runner*, those humanoids have evolved and rebelled against humans, who had treated them badly. Both *Blade Runner* and *A.I.* start in the context of a devastated Earth. In *A.I.*, global warming has affected the planet, drowning cities like Venice, Amsterdam, and New York. As the narrator says at the beginning of the film:

> Hundreds of millions of people starved in poorer countries. Elsewhere, a high degree of prosperity survived when most governments in the developed world

introduced legal sanctions to strictly license pregnancies, which was why robots, who were never hungry and who did not consume resources beyond those of their first manufacture, were so essential an economic link in the chain mail of society.

Despite all this, humanity comes to an end. In *Blade Runner*, we are left with some hope, even though quite limited. *BSG* starts with the hope that humanity will survive. In all three examples, the question is stated directly or indirectly whether humanity deserves to survive, which goes together with the other prevalent question: what constitutes human nature? These two questions are related and this is more clearly stated in *BSG*. The following examples emphasise that evil and darkness are part of human nature and it is suggested that this is one reason why humanity does not deserve to survive. When Commander Adama asks Sharon-Athena why cylons hate humans so much, her answer raises exactly this point:

> I'm not sure I know how to answer that. I mean 'hate' might not be the right word. [...] It's what you said at the ceremony, before the attack, when Galactica was being decommissioned. You gave a speech it sounded like it wasn't the one you prepared. You said that humanity was a flawed creation and that people still kill one another for petty jealousy and greed. You said that humanity never asked itself why it deserved to survive... Maybe you don't. (S02E12, 17.40)

Sharon's reply reflects ideas by Thomas Ligotti, who sees life and human existence as 'malignantly useless'.[7] The most recent of many pessimistic philosophers, he considers consciousness as a mutation that happened to human organisms, a mutation that led to our current state, but which is a tragedy: 'consciousness has forced us into the paradoxical position of striving to be unself-conscious of what we are — hunks of spoiling flesh on disintegrating bones'.[8] In *A.I.*, humanity disappears in the end, but the viewer is not given the exact details of how this occurred. In *BSG*, through dialogues like the above, it is suggested that humanity could end, mainly as a result of human arrogance, which caused the cylon war when humans treated their creations inhumanely. In several instances it is suggested that cylons are improved versions of humans and that humans may not deserve to live after all. Such views express the opposite philosophy to transhumanism and are closer to what I mentioned in the Introduction as speculative posthumanism

Gaius Baltar often discusses this with Caprica Six, who confronts him with the cylons' version of what humanity is: 'You, your...race invented murder, they did killing for sport, greed, envy. It's man's one true art form' (S02E03, 10.55). Later on, when at a very crucial moment Baltar shoots a man in order to protect the rest of the people in his group, Caprica Six whispers in his ear:

> CAPRICA SIX   I'm so proud of you, Gaius.
> BALTAR   Why? Cause I've taken a life?
> CAPRICA SIX   That's what makes you human.
> BALTAR   Is it? No conscious thought, poetry or art, music, literature? Murder? Murder is my heritage? (S02E03, 40.15)

Since these conversations between Baltar and Caprica Six are not witnessed by anyone else, it is suggested that this might be the conscience of Baltar speaking, personified in the form of the woman he loves. Besides, it would fit the persona of the megalomaniac genius scientist he is to have some crises of conscience and self-doubt. Baltar represents science and reason throughout the series: he is the scientist-researcher aboard Galactica and his knowledge is based on facts and scientific data. This is further emphasised when, during his campaign for the presidency, he is contrasted with the other candidate, President Laura Roslin, formerly a teacher, who is religious and spiritual. Baltar discards religion, both human and cylon. Since he represents science in the *BSG* universe, his doubts about humanity and its nature can be viewed through the lens of a wider, existential angst. Moreover, further issues that scrutinise the different manifestations of human nature are raised throughout the series, such as religious fundamentalism, political crises and extremism, democracy, and corruption, among others.

It is important to mention, however, that cylons are divided amongst themselves as to their feelings and beliefs about humans, in the same way that humans have conflicts, whether these are religious, political, or of any other nature. In 'Downloaded', Episode 18 of the second season, the viewer sees for the first time how the 'resurrection' function of the cylons is actually performed. The cylon soul is downloaded into a new body in a bathtub full of a liquid gel, directly reminiscent of the amniotic fluid in the womb. The process is painful for the cylons because they are re-experiencing their previous lives, including their deaths. Caprica Six and Sharon Valerii are the two cylons that are portrayed as being reborn in this episode. They are war heroes for other cylons, but their experience among humans has changed them both. They are convinced that the attack against humanity was a mistake. In the subsequent episodes, they manage to influence the other cylons who notify the humans in Galactica about their decision to end the war and leave them in peace. This message is delivered in a very significant, philosophical speech by a cylon model Number One who has been infiltrating Galactica as a priest:

> People should be true to who or what they are. We are machines; we should be true to that: be the best machines the universe has ever seen. But we got it into our heads that we were the children of humanity, so instead of pursuing our own destiny of trying to find our own path to enlightenment, we hijacked yours. (S02E20, 23.20)

At this point, in the last episode of the second season, the Pinocchio myth is being exposed and debunked. Symbolically delivered out of the mouth of a priest, the idea of 'becoming' is dismissed in favour of being true to one's own nature. Once again, the philosophical debate between one's nature (or being) and that of becoming (or changing) is addressed. Believing in the nature of oneself is supported here by Number One, or John Cavil, a cylon model that throughout the series is particularly negative towards humans and in constant conflict with other cylons and even with himself. Towards the end of the series, it is revealed that the eight cylon models were made by another five humanoid cylons who were their ancestors and John Cavil was the first one to be designed by his five cylon makers. Clearly reminiscent of the story of Cain and Abel, John Cavil destroyed the entire line of his brother Daniel, Number Seven, because he was jealous that Helen, one of the five makers, favoured Daniel over him. John's character seems to embody many human vices and faults and this does not make him a reliable advocate of his ideas regarding his machine nature. Yet he is the most passionate of all about cylon nature: in a dialogue with Helen, his maker, he reveals why. This dialogue is a direct reference to a very famous scene from *Blade Runner*, in which replicant Roy and Blade Runner Deckard are fighting on the roof. Just when Roy is about to die and as the rain is falling on him, he says to Deckard, 'I've seen things you people wouldn't believe. Attack ships on fire off the shoulder of Orion. I watched C-beams glitter in the darkness at Tannhäuser Gate. All those moments will be lost in time like tears in rain'.

John has similar feelings to Roy when he tries to explain to Helen his hatred for humanity:

> JOHN CAVIL (NUMBER ONE) In all your travels, have you ever seen a star supernova?
> HELEN No.
> JOHN CAVIL No? Well, I have. I saw a star explode and send out the building blocks of the universe: other stars, other planets and eventually other life. A supernova, creation itself. I was there, I wanted to see it and be part of the moment. And you know how I perceived one of the most glorious events in the universe? With these ridiculous gelatinous orbs in my skull; with eyes designed to perceive only a tiny fraction of the EM spectrum; with ears designed only to hear vibrations in the air.
> HELEN The five of us designed you to be as human as possible.
> JOHN CAVIL I don't want to be human! I want to see gamma rays, I want to hear X rays and I wanna, I wanna smell dark matter. Do you see the absurdity of what I am? I can't even express these things properly, because I have to, I have to conceptualise complex ideas in this stupid, limiting, spoken language. But I know I want to reach out with something other than these prehensile paws and feel the solar wind of a supernova flowing over me. I am a machine and I could know much more, I could experience so much more, but I'm trapped in this absurd body. Why? Because my five creators thought that God wanted it that way. (So4E15, 21.25)

Helen and the other four cylon models which originated from the thirteenth tribe that once inhabited Earth believe in the co-existence of humans and cylons, and this was their plan in creating the eight cylon models. As she explains to John, 'We didn't limit you. We gave you something wonderful: free will. The ability to think creatively, to reach out to others with compassion, to love'. It is this free will that determines in the end what each human or cylon wants to be and become. This is also what is represented by the element of desire in the animate/ inanimate archetype, which is reflected in *Pinocchio* and in all the examples of its retellings that have been discussed so far.

The two figures that are juxtaposed in the second season of *BSG* to emphasise the ongoing debate about human nature versus cylon nature — similar to the two versions of Sharon in the first season — are Gaius Baltar and Caprica Six. Throughout the series, Baltar has held conversations with Caprica Six in his mind. Nobody else could see her and therefore it was not made clear whether it was a cylon function that she can appear only to him and live inside his brain or whether he was paranoid. In 'Downloaded', it is the first time that Baltar takes a similar role in the mind of Caprica Six. She is the only one who can see him. Both were exposed to the other species with great intensity and love. It is implied, therefore, that it is this experience of close exposure and emotional intensity that has allowed this becoming the projected conscience in the mind of the other.

For the first two seasons, the narrative has been escalating towards an ever more favourable view of the cylons, inviting the viewer to understand and sympathise with them, particularly those cylons that show human emotions and devotion to humans, like Sharon Valerii, Sharon Athena, and a Number Six that was severely tortured on Battlestar Pegasus. After the cylons declare that they will go their own way, the fleet of Galactica settle on a new planet they have found, which they name New Caprica. After a year of peaceful existence, however, the cylons strike back and catch the humans unawares. The President at the time, Gaius Baltar, surrenders and the second season ends with a scene that portrays one of the worst fears that machine and human co-existence has inspired: giant war robots made of steel march through masses of enslaved humans, spreading fear. This scene, visually revisiting one of the most common scenes in the cyborg science-fiction genre (that of robots enslaving humans), allows for a regression to technophobic sentiments to emphasise the turn towards a positively transhumanist direction in the following seasons until the end of the series.

During the third season, the humans in New Caprica manage to liberate themselves from the cylons. Gaius Baltar is considered a traitor and is to be executed for his co-operation with the cylons, but Caprica Six saves him and takes him with her in the cylon base ship as the cylons leave. With Baltar living with the cylons, a lot of information is revealed about cylon nature, including their weaknesses and beliefs. Interestingly enough, both human and cylon religions instruct humans and cylons to find their home on planet Earth. This is what drives the narrative from that point on and meanwhile the issue of identity is emphasised repeatedly. This season focuses on all the common elements between humans and cylons and these seem to be more numerous than their differences. The main concept of the season is articulated by Baltar when talking to D'Anna, a Number Three: 'Cylons, humans, we're all just trying to discover... who we are' (S03E10, 24.25).

There are instances in the narrative when Baltar wonders if he is a cylon and others when he desires to be a cylon: this functions narratively as the reverse of the Pinocchio myth, as a human desires to become a machine. The main juxtaposition between the character of Baltar and that of Caprica Six continues in the third season. Caprica Six helps Sharon Athena to get her daughter back to Galactica. Caprica Six is held prisoner there and has more and more conversations with imaginary Baltar, possibly the voice of her conscience. When he asks her why she came to Galactica and helped Sharon, she does not know herself what her real motivations were. Then imaginary Baltar answers for her: 'You're here because you want to be human. But there's a trick to being human: you have to think only about yourself' (S03E14, 18.20). These imaginary conversations that both Baltar and Caprica Six have are vivid projections of their consciences and inner monologues. They occur with these two characters who have had similar experiences: they have been in the intimacy of someone from another species and they have feelings for that other person. Whether because of this particular relationship with the 'Other' or because of their feelings of guilt towards their own species, or both, they experience these dialogues as sharply as if they were with people physically next to them. It is important to clarify, though, that all these dialogues are created by themselves. At least this is what is implied throughout the series, even though the ending suggests otherwise. Therefore, when imaginary Baltar tells Caprica Six that she wants to be human, it is she who says that. This is the first instance in the series when a cylon expresses that desire. It is also quite significant that all this is left to the viewer to assume. In short, Caprica Six never uses the first person to express this desire; it is her imaginary Baltar who expresses it for her. As was shown in the previous season through the character of Gaius Baltar, his imaginary Caprica Six expresses the most hidden part of himself, his suppressed desires and forbidden thoughts. He is the rational, intelligent scientist and his imaginary Caprica Six talks to him about God. She (or that part of himself) wonders about human nature.

However, the desire of Caprica Six to be human cannot be compared to that of Pinocchio or David, as she knows from the start that she is a cylon and has no confrontation scene as Sharon. Her desire has been carefully built up throughout the series and features in the narrative after Baltar's desire to be a cylon. In that sense, it portrays more the desire to be the 'Other' and to question one's own nature, a distinctive human trait. As the narrative climaxes through the fourth season, the question of identity becomes more and more prominent. Cylons have serious conflicts with each other, stemming from disagreements regarding their nature and the purpose of their existence. On the Galactica, four more characters find out that they were sleeper agent cylons and struggle with accepting their new identity.

In the fourth season, the narrative starts with a cylon civil war, soon to be followed by a human civil war in the form of a mutiny on the Galactica. This emphasises once more the similarities between the two species. The rebel cylons, those who believe in pursuing their destiny, in opposition to those who perceive themselves as 'only machines', form an alliance with the humans in order to find Earth, which appears in the religious beliefs of both cylons and humans. This is supposed to be the original home of the thirteenth tribe. *BSG* refers to already known religions with allusions and symbols. The humans believe in polytheism, referring mainly to the ancient Greek and Roman gods. At the same time, their scriptures and history refer to the twelve tribes that escaped from a great catastrophe and made new homes on the twelve planets of the colonies, as they call them. This is a clear reference to the Jewish twelve tribes. The cylons' 'one true God' refers to Judaeo-Christianity. Robert Sharp considers that their belief that they have a soul is an element that links them with the Christian religion, spreading among the slaves of the Romans, whose polytheism did not include any reference to a soul. 'The notion of a soul — a non-material part of the person that survives the death of the body — allowed Christians to wage war with the Romans on a different metaphysical plane, one where worldly power didn't matter'.[9] Similarly, the cylon slaves differentiate themselves from their masters by embracing the faith of the 'one true God'. In the fourth season, Gaius Baltar, who has been familiar all along as the representation of science, rationalism, and scepticism openly converts to the 'one true God' of the cylons and preaches his word in the Galactica, dressed as a prophet and visually strongly reminiscent of common depictions of Jesus Christ.

Joining forces, rebel cylons and humans find what they call Earth, only to discover the fallout of a nuclear holocaust. They find human skeletons and robot parts; when they analyse the bones, they discover that all the residents of this planet were humanoid cylons. In short, the thirteenth human tribe was a cylon tribe, meaning that their very remote ancestors had already created robots that had evolved and rebelled against humanity, ending their conflict in a nuclear war that resulted in the destruction of the planet and the fleeing of the few survivors. This is why, at that point in the narrative, the opening credits are: 'This has all happened before and it will happen again', a phrase that strongly emphasises the inevitability of human nature and a reminder that history repeats itself.

The series ends with both rebel cylons and humans finding a planet that looks exactly like the real Earth, implying that what the viewer had been watching so far was the prehistory of humanity. The planet is very fertile and they find that it already has inhabitants, animal and human, in a primitive state. The fleet of the Galactica decide not to impose their technology upon the inhabitants of the planet and instead to live with them peacefully. They name this new planet Earth, after the real Earth which they had been longing for and which was devastated by their ancestors' nuclear war. Cylon and human will live peacefully together and procreate. Hera, the daughter of Karl 'Helo' Agathon and Sharon 'Athena', is the living proof of this. She has been important for both cylons and humans throughout the series and is to be understood in narrative terms as the message that *BSG* intended to convey: humans and machines can co-exist. All the fighting and wars between humans and machines throughout the series do not prove the opposite, because one more thing that has been emphasised throughout is that warcraft is a very distinctive human trait and not specific to the cylons. Caprica Six points this out during a dialogue with Baltar. When he confronts her with the fact that cylons have also provoked killings and genocide, she answers, 'Yes, well we're your children, you taught us well' (S02E03, 10.55). Cylons have seen themselves as children of humanity because humans created them. Yet by genetically procreating together, human and cylon are left on Earth to decide its future.

The final scene of *BSG* is telling. In the last episode, the imaginary Baltar and the imaginary Caprica Six are shown together with the real ones, and for the first time all of them can see each other. According to a symbolic interpretation, this might be happening because the human–cylon conflict is finally resolved and therefore Gaius Baltar and Caprica Six completely trust and understand each other and so have access to each other's unconscious voices. In the last scene, the imaginary couple are seen on the same planet, 150,000 years later than the narrative so far. Earth looks like the contemporary Earth with the same technological advances. A news bulletin is heard:

> At a scientific conference this week at the Smithsonian Institution in Washington, the startling announcement was made that archaeologists believe they have found fossilised remains of a young woman who might actually be mitochondrial Eve. Mitochondrial Eve is the name scientists have given to the most recent common ancestor for all human beings now living on Earth. She lived in what is now Tanzania. (S04E20, 1.33.00)

Imaginary Baltar and imaginary Caprica Six lean over someone reading the news in a magazine that looks like *National Geographic*. 'Over 150,000 years ago,' says Caprica Six, and Baltar continues, 'along with her cylon mother and human father' (S04E20, 1.33.15). It is therefore suggested that the series was a narration of true events and that Hera was the mother of all humanity as we know it. In short, it leads to the conclusion that humanity is a hybrid of what used to be a humanoid cylon and an original human. And once more it is implied that history repeats itself, as the camera focuses on robot toys and gadgets that contemporary humans are creating. Caprica Six goes on to remark:

> CAPRICA SIX Commercialism, decadence, technology run amok, remind you of anything?
> BALTAR Take your pick. Kobol, Earth, the real Earth before this one, Caprica before the Fall...
> CAPRICA SIX All of this has happened before...
> BALTAR ...but the question remains, does all of this have to happen again?
> CAPRICA SIX This time, I bet no.
> BALTAR You know, I've never known you to play the optimist. Why the change of heart?
> CAPRICA SIX Mathematics, law of averages. Let a complex system repeat itself long enough, eventually something surprising might occur. (S04E20, 1.33.50)

In short, *BSG* finishes on a very positive and optimistic tone. Even though history seems to repeat itself, at some point something changes. In this case, we have seen in the narrative that the original cylons of the thirteenth tribe, having learnt what went wrong between humans and cylons, tried to do things differently. They wanted to warn future humans to treat machines and cylons well so that a rebellion and war could be avoided. They failed in the first place, but this does not mean that a second or third effort would fail. One of the messages that the series conveys is to treat the other well and with respect, no matter who they are: all wars can be avoided as long as we treat each other with respect. Clearly, this is a message that does not refer only to human-machine relationships, but to all interpersonal relationships. The cylon here stands for the Other, whether that is a person of a different class, race, gender, religion, sexual orientation, or whichever minority is opposed to the dominant order. Therefore, the overall narrative of *BSG* can work as social criticism if one substitutes cylon with any minority or socially marginalised group. At the same time, this is one of the most machine-friendly audio-visual examples of the last decades, suggesting that twenty-first century Western society is not so technophobic anymore and that its focus has shifted towards the benefits of integrating technology into everyday human life.

The positive approach towards human-machine co-existence is highlighted through the example of a human-cylon child, as shown earlier. Reproduction is a major theme in many cyborg-related narratives and not entirely absent from Collodi's text. By following the Blue Fairy's hard work ethic, Pinocchio is rewarded in the end by being granted a human body. His work and production have awarded him the ability to reproduce. David, in *A.I.*, foreshadows a future where the human reproductive function has been nullified and the human race has become extinct. In the original Aldiss story, he replaces the child that his parents cannot have. In Philip Dick's novel that inspired *Blade Runner*, humans are only allowed by law to reproduce if they pass the required IQ test. Reproduction is the hope for future survival, whether for humans or for cylons, as shown in *BSG*. This focus towards the future is among the core principles of transhumanist philosophy, which advocates human lives that are enhanced, improved, and prolonged by technology. This hope for survival, which reproduction embodies, is emphasised by the contrast with another connotation this term has: that of the simulacrum that reproduces human features and emotions, whether it is a replicant, a cylon, or a robot. This contrast can sometimes emphasise the pessimistic approach of robots eradicating human reproductive capability and the simulacrum replacing its original, as in Spielberg's film, but it can also function in the reverse direction, as in *BSG*, where the copy was merged with the original, creating an improved version that combined the abilities and capabilities of both species. This is a positive message with regard to a posthuman society, one that merges all differences — not only those related to technology — and its multifacetedness proves to be its strength.

In her extensive analysis of the history of the robot and its reception, Rosi Braidotti mentions that 'the automaton is monstrous because it blurs the boundaries, it mixes the genres, it displaces the points of reference between the normal — in the double sense of normality and normativity — and its "others"'.[10] *BSG* reverses this rhetoric of monstrosity: by presenting the human race as the result of blurring the boundaries, the hybrid becomes normal and the 'other' becomes familiar. This change of approach towards human-machine blending did not happen overnight: it started with *Blade Runner* and since then the number of films with transhumanist views has been growing steadily and consistently.

The current cyborg-friendly approach in popular culture is confirmed by recent filmic examples, such as the fourth volume of the Terminator saga, *Terminator Salvation*.[11] Even though the Terminator universe is built on the main concept of war with the machines, and all the differentiation this universe could offer was between good and bad machines, the fourth instalment of the film took a different turn. For the first time a new type of character was introduced, one that blends human and machine. Marcus Wright plays a vital role in the film plot. He is a cyborg, a death row inmate who offered his body to science and woke up as a cyborg after 'Judgment Day' and the war with the machines. He looks exactly like all other humans, but he has mechanical skeletal parts and a partly-artificial cerebral cortex. He does not know that he is not human and he only finds out through John Connor, the head of the Resistance of humans against the machines. His confrontation scene is more dramatic than all the previous ones, as he finds out the truth about his new identity by finding himself in the position of the accused, in chains, as the Resistance considers him a spy working for the machines.

After Marcus escapes, John Connor finds him once again, but Marcus manages to convince John to let him live by promising to help him find Kyle Reese, John's father. In a very significant scene, where half of Marcus's face has been melted away, reminding spectators of previous Terminator films, Marcus tells John, 'I'm your only hope' — a scene that was also included in the film's trailer and therefore available to larger audiences. It is significant because it hints at the possibility that the only hope for a peaceful future is that of a blended society — a posthuman and hybrid one — as was suggested at the end of *BSG*. It is very important to see that the Terminator brand changed direction when it added this new element. Even though Marcus does not survive in the end, as he gives his life to save John, he dies as the 'good guy', in the simple language of big Hollywood blockbusters, changing the symbolism of the cyborg in a very (until then) machine-hostile series.

In the latest instalment of the Terminator franchise, *Terminator Genisys*, the idea of the hybrid that was introduced in the previous film is approached from the opposite angle to *Terminator Salvation*.[12] While in the previous film a human becomes hybridic by having machine elements introduced into his body, this time the hybrid is touched upon from the perspective of the machine. More specifically, the good machine seen in previous films (the Terminator who has been reprogrammed to be good) has his own human emotions for the first time. In several instances in the film, the Guardian Terminator, as he is called since he saved Sarah Connor when she was nine years old from the bad Terminator and has acted as her protector and father-figure ever since (she calls him Pops), manifests fatherly emotions towards her that are not part of his programming. He is a robot that has learnt to love, a machine capable of human emotions. What could be mistaken as a hybrid character in the film is the transformation of hero John Connor into a Terminator (T-3000), who owns John's memories and can therefore trick his mother. The reason why this does not qualify as the hybrid introduced in the previous film is because John Connor was attacked by a Terminator, who then infected and transformed John into a similar unit. In *Terminator Salvation*, Marcus voluntarily enhanced his body and became a hybrid, even though he did not remember it at the beginning of the film. He maintained his human will and integrity, while Terminator John Connor in the latest film lost himself and instead became part of the Skynet network. Finally, the film references several science-fiction and time-travel films, including *Blade Runner*, as Chris Knight accurately observes, demonstrating that intertextuality — a postmodern characteristic that will be examined in the next chapters — is becoming increasingly popular even among mainstream genres.[13]

Another example that moves from the scary, uncanny humanoid to the friendly robot with human emotions is the latest Channel 4 series *Humans*.[14] It takes place in the same familiar, science-fiction universe where humans use human-like robots called 'synths' in their everyday lives for a wide range of functions: from hard manual labour to the sex industry and health-care. In that universe, a scientist has managed to instil into some special robots the ability to think and feel like humans. These special robots are considered a threat and are marginalised, but at the end of the first season they manage to form special bonds with some humans and are partially accepted. Even though the plot presents nothing extraordinary for the genre, it is significant that the series was a big success and reached very large audiences, something that no series dealing with a similar topic has ever achieved before, as science fiction is usually targeted at a specific fan base of viewers.[15] The series has multiple references to the three case studies in this chapter, as they are considered classics of the genre. Even the casting choices for the actors resonate these references with the best example being actor William Hurt, who in *A.I.* played Professor Hobby. In *Humans*, he is Dr George Millican, a retired scientist who played a vital role in the creation of sentient synths or humanoids. Portrayed as an old man in the series, he is losing his memory and relies on his Pinocchio-esque synth for some moments of nostalgic comfort, as his robot companion has stored all the memories of Dr Millican with his dead wife, almost like an artificial son. The constant allusions and visual references to all three case studies of this chapter give the impression that the series continues the narrative of an open-ended topic — in this case the shared life between humans and humanoid robots. As mentioned in the beginning of this part, in reference to Vivian Sobchack's theory, this shows clearly that the cyborg is a type of image in science-fiction film that exists as a separate, parallel universe in the viewer's imagination. As such, it carries on the symbolism and ideological context it is loaded with from film to film. Every new film that uses this type of image cannot but refer to all its forerunners.

This part has focused on three different examples of posthuman retellings of the myth of Pinocchio. All three are now considered classics of the genre and they showcase how the general attitude towards posthumanism and transhumanism has shifted towards more tolerant views in recent decades. As was shown in the analysis of the case studies, the motif of the cyborg desiring humanity does not only reflect the change of attitude towards technological progress throughout the years, but is also intertwined with existential questions regarding humanity and the self, and it belongs to the literary tradition of the animate/ inanimate archetype. As such, it entails the concept of desire which functions as a driving force and is also connected to the concept of free will, as explained throughout this part. Analysis of how the confrontation scene in *Pinocchio* is revisited in the three different retellings demonstrates how the Pinocchio myth has been adapted and perpetuated in posthuman science fiction as the desire of the simulacrum for humanity. As illustrated by the three case studies, questions regarding human nature remain pertinent and are revisited frequently. The most recent example can be found in the television series *Humans* in which the single character who is a true hybrid between human and machine — since he was resurrected with the help of technology after he died — defines humanity not as a state of being, but as a value. In the next chapters, this idealistic approach towards humanity will be challenged and the myth of Pinocchio will be examined from a different angle.

Notes to Chapter 4

1. Giuliana Bruno, 'Ramble City: Postmodernism and "Blade Runner"', *October*, 41 (1987), 64–71 (p. 65).
2. Douglas Kellner, Flo Leibowitz, and Michael Ryan, '*Blade Runner:* A Diagnostic Critique', in *Jump Cut: A Review of Contemporary Media*, 29 (1984), 6–8 <http://www.ejumpcut.org/archive/onlinessays/JC29folder/BladeRunner.html> [accessed 14 September 2021].
3. Ibid.
4. Ibid.
5. Erik Blankinship, 'Pinocchio: A Spielberg Odyssey', film review, *The Tech* (11 July 2001), p. 7. <http://tech.mit.edu/V121/PDF/N29.pdf> [accessed 21 March 2019].
6. Fredric Jameson's original quotation: 'It is easier to imagine the end of the world than to imagine the end of capitalism'. 'Future City', *New Left Review*, 21 (May-June 2003) <https://newleftreview.org/issues/ii21/articles/fredric-jameson-future-city> [accessed 10 October 2021].
7. The phrase is repeated throughout his work. Thomas Ligotti, *The Conspiracy Against the Human Race* (New York: Hippocampus Press, 2010).
8. Ibid., p. 28.
9. Robert Sharp, 'When Machines Get Souls: Nietzsche on the Cylon Uprising', in *Battlestar Galactica and Philosophy: Knowledge Here Begins Out There*, ed. by Jason T. Eberl (Malden, MA: Blackwell, 2008), pp. 15–28 (p. 19).
10. Rosi Braidotti, *Metamorphoses: Towards a Materialist Theory of Becoming* (Cambridge: Polity Press, 2002), p. 217.
11. *Terminator Salvation*, dir. by McGinty Nichol (USA: Halcyon Company, 2009).
12. *Terminator Genisys*, dir. by Alan Taylor (USA: Paramount Pictures, 2015).
13. Chris Knight, 'He's Back From the Future — Again: Terminator Reboot with Ah-nold a Well-crafted Addition to Canon', *Edmonton Journal*, 2 July 2015.
14. *Humans* (UK & USA: Channel 4 & AMC, 2015).
15. Huw Fullerton, 'Humans Series Review: "A surprise success — thriving where Utopia drowned"', *Radio Times* 2 August 2015 <http://www.radiotimes.com/news/2015-08-02/humans-series-review-a-surprise-success---thriving-where-utopia-drowned> [accessed 21 March 2019].

❖

Metafiction
Postmodern Retellings of the Pinocchio Myth

Part II takes ideas developed in Part I and examines them in a different context. More precisely, the myth of Pinocchio in correlation with concepts of identity and the self will be revisited through examples of postmodern fiction. While Part I emphasised the perpetuation of the myth of Pinocchio through the metaphor of the cyborg, in this part the emphasis is on the chronologically parallel deconstruction of the myth. The case studies are Jerome Charyn's *Pinocchio's Nose* (1983) and Robert Coover's *Pinocchio in Venice* (1991).

In the present part the confrontation scene, analysed in Part I as an important feature of the Pinocchio myth, is revisited from a different perspective. Now the focus shifts from Pinocchio's realisation of his corporeality, seen in Part I, to the Blue Fairy and her role as the instigator of Pinocchio's desire to become human. While in previous chapters the core of the Pinocchio myth was the desire to become human, now this element is reversed, as both Pinocchios in the two different texts under consideration are human and visiting, or revisiting, their wooden bodies. Both case studies illuminate the reasons why Pinocchio desired humanity and, by exposing these reasons, I intend to put the Pinocchio myth under further scrutiny.

This part explores both how the Blue Fairy is inseparable from Pinocchio's desire for humanity and the complex relationship between the two characters. Both Charyn and Coover make extensive use of Freudian psychoanalysis in revisiting Collodi's original text and in their own narratives. The Blue Fairy and her oedipal relationship with Pinocchio is emphasised as the driving force behind Pinocchio's desire for humanity. Moreover, the Blue Fairy has her own motivations for keeping Pinocchio close to her, other than acting for his benefit. This reverses the good role of the Fairy as it has been adapted in most retellings, and invites a different reading of Collodi's text. There are many examples throughout this part in which the authors deconstruct the Pinocchio myth by presenting aspects of it which contrast with the one mostly adapted in the corpus of Pinocchio retellings.

This repeated reversal of themes brings a carnivalesque element to both retellings. As Brian McHale suggests, it is characteristic of postmodernist fiction to incorporate carnival elements. (Brian McHale, *Postmodernist Fiction* (London: Methuen, 1987), p. 71.) Both these case studies are examples of postmodernist fiction and metafiction.

Coover's text in particular not only has metaphorical references to carnival through parody and the world turned upside down, but it also includes real carnival scenes from the Venetian carnival and the marionettes of the *commedia dell'arte*. Through carnivalesque references, the myth of Pinocchio is also reversed, piece by piece. Another element whose analysis serves to deconstruct the Pinocchio myth is the colour blue, an inherent characteristic of the Blue Fairy: whether she has blue hair as in the original or a blue dress, as in Disney's and other versions, the colour blue is what distinguishes her from all other fairy literature as the archetypal fairy godmother, the protector of Pinocchio. Blue is also used extensively as a reference to the Fairy and her nature both by Charyn and Coover. I therefore analyse the sociohistorical context of the colour blue — including the particular references of the *turchino* hue — in Collodi's time and as the background of the Pinocchio myth.

Another frequently-found theme in numerous retellings and adaptations of Collodi's novel is Pinocchio's growing nose. As a major theme of both the case studies under consideration in this part, it will be examined in detail below. Both works use the nose satirically and psychoanalytically; it is used extensively as a sexual metaphor. However, it is not the only reference to psychoanalytic theory and Freudian interpretation in these retellings. A major theme in the two novels is writing and the psychological effect it has on the authors — therapeutic and self-destructive at the same time. Psychoanalysis is used to explain and occasionally mock the condition of the authors/ protagonists. The rich intertextuality and self-referentiality of the texts, both as the *mise-en-abyme* of the author writing and because of the numerous autobiographical elements the texts share, make them very representative examples of postmodernist fiction and its challenging of existing realities and values, which in turn contributes to the breaking down of the Pinocchio myth.

Charyn's *Pinocchio's Nose* is the story of Jerome Copernicus Charyn, a Jewish American author who grows up in the Bronx during the 1940s. Struggling between his writing and teaching career and trying to overcome his troubled relationship with his mother, he escapes into the world of his novel, *Pinocchio 1945*, by entering Pinocchio's wooden body and thus becoming the protagonist he invents: Pinocchio in Mussolini's Italy. Coover's *Pinocchio in Venice* is the story of Professor Pinenut, who is Collodi's centenarian Pinocchio, having grown up after his magical transformation into a boy and become an Emeritus Professor at an American university and twice a Nobel laureate. He returns to Italy in order to write 'Mamma', the last chapter of his autobiography. As soon as he arrives in Venice, he goes through a series of adventures, encountering old friends and enemies, until he finally meets the Blue Fairy, his inspiration and tormentor, in her true form.

In the next chapters, my analysis will focus on three thematic areas common to the two books, all of which serve to deconstruct the Pinocchio myth. Chapter 5 will examine the relationship the protagonists have with themselves and with writing, together with the psychological effects writing has on the authors/ protagonists and how this relates to the concept of humanity. Chapter 6 will focus on the Blue Fairy and her relationship with Pinocchio and Chapter 7 will focus on Pinocchio's nose.

❖

Pinocchio the Author

Writing, Mythopsychosis, and the Theory of 'I-ness'

In *Pinocchio's Nose*, young Jerome's mother narrates to him her own version of the original story of Pinocchio and this is how his love for literature begins. The very first time we encounter Pinocchio in the text, it is via Bathsheba's version:

> Long ago there lived a piece of wood that knew how to talk; this piece of wood was dying to have arms and legs, so he crept along as quietly as a piece of wood can creep and shouted into the window of an old baker, 'Geppetto, my dear, will you put me in your oven and make a nice pie out of me?' (*PN*, p. 20)

Bathsheba's version alludes to 'The Gingerbread Boy' or 'Pinto Smalto', versions of the animate/ inanimate archetype discussed in Part I, in which the creator is female and bakes a creature that comes alive. As seen earlier, such examples of female creativity simultaneously invoke the fear of female destructive power and the woman-devourer. This is very relevant to Charyn's text, as Bathsheba has catastrophic effects on Jerome's life. She takes on the role of the Blue Fairy as Jerome takes on that of Pinocchio when he narrates the story to his younger relatives after he has grown up to be an author and also works as a teacher: 'I grew up, graduated from Pinocchio to James Joyce, and taught at the Bronx High School of Science. I talked to Herman Melville's ghost' (*PN*, p. 20). In family meetings he narrates his own version of Pinocchio to his younger cousins, embellished with episodes from his childhood in the Bronx: 'I began the story of a Bronx Pinocchio, sprung from the ribs of a baby carriage. No puppet could have thrived on Crotona Park, so I went into flesh right away' (*PN*, p. 29). However, the children grow bored with his story and so he spices up the metaphor of Pinocchio's nose that grows when he is lying, to keep them interested:

> The children's eyes were closing and I had to dice up the story. *Housewives admired Pinocchio's nose. A group of them plotted to capture him and waltz his nose under a pillow. Pinocchio had to dodge these housewives and pray that his nose would shrink.* My little cousins laughed at the smut I had introduced. They weren't interested in character or plot. (*PN*, p. 30)

His duty, as a storyteller, to keep his audience engaged is what makes Jerome focus on the sexual metaphor of Pinocchio's nose, an artistic invention, yet not one that satisfies him. When his uncle's wife, Marie-Pierre, asks him to help her son, Edgar, to learn how to read by telling him stories, he is not happy to undertake the task mainly because he wants to keep away from his uncle's family and business:

> I'd end up a nanny to Edgar and Marie's indentured servant, no better than a wooden boy. I was Moby Dick in shiny pants, octopus and city whale, sixteen arms searching for stories and a ride out of uncle's tower sanctuary. [...] I had to feel my way down the rough steps like a whore whose services were done. Madam Pinocchia. (*PN*, p. 38)

For him the role of the storyteller resembles that of the prostitute when he has to make compromises in order to please the audience; and the title *Pinocchio's Nose* referring to the smut that Jerome the protagonist invents to please his listeners, suggests the book is a text about writing and storytelling and the compromises this involves.

This is further emphasised when, during one of the free meals offered to poor artists by Lemuel Rice, a preacher with extensive knowledge of literature, Jerome hears him condemn writing as 'the work of Satan':

> Brothers, Satan is in that pen. He guides the hand that inks the page. He's in the bowels of your Olivetti, your word processor, your copying machine. [...] He's the whore that lay with a blind man, Homer, and while the blind man was asleep, Satan dipped Homer's pizzle in octopus ink and wrote about that philandering sailor, Odysseus, who took the devil's own time returning to his wife. And that, my brothers, was the beginning of this nasty business, the novel. (*PN*, p. 47)

Even though Jerome does not agree with Lemuel, he reflects upon his words. Once more Charyn provocatively links writing to prostitution, this time presenting the Muse as a whore who gives an author the inspiration to write what will please audiences and so make him famous.

Charyn's narrative moves in two parallel directions throughout the first seven chapters: that of the fictional author, Jerome, and that of the story Jerome is writing for Edgar, 'Pinocchio in Mussolini's Time'. In Chapter 8, the merging of the two story arcs intensifies and Jerome is aware of this shift: 'I began drifting towards Pinocchio. I wasn't writing, mind you. Just drifting. I could feel myself in Rome' (*PN*, p. 151). This happens at a point when Jerome's adventures in Paris become more dangerous than he can deal with, as he is informed that his uncle may be plotting to kill him. As the two narrative lines merge, the fonts no longer change to indicate that the narrative of Pinocchio is a story within a story; now it has all become one. Jerome acknowledges that this is a condition he suffers from:

> Time had dropped me in a cradle that swung here and there. I was warped. It never would have happened if I'd been bar mitzvahed like everybody else. One of these years I'll climb out of Bathsheba's baby carriage. I was determined to cure myself of Pinocchio. (*PN*, p. 151).

In a desperate visit to a library, where he consults a book called *The ABCs of Sigmund Freud*, Jerome finds out that he is suffering from a disease called 'mythopsychosis':

> Buzzed through Freud's *ABC's*, looking for the term that would save me from having to exist as two people. All the stuff about id and alter ego didn't apply to Pinocchio Jérôme. And then I lit upon a definition that told my story.

> Mythopsychosis, the terrifying need to mythologize one's existence at
> the expense of all other things. The sufferer of mythopsychosis seeks
> narratives everywhere, inside and outside of himself. He cannot take a
> move and not narratize it. This is a common affliction among writers.
> [...] There is even a severer form of disease, mytholepsy, in which the
> sufferer cannot escape from his own dream. He falls into the text, lives
> there, and dies, much like Marcel Proust. Medical science has not yet
> discovered a cure for mytholepsy. Once the disease begins, the single
> remedy is his or her own death. For mythopsychosis we have a little
> more hope. The sufferer can decide never to narratize again. He takes
> himself out of the text. This requires a long process of denarratization.

> Freud was practicing foreplay in his *ABC's*. How was I supposed to denarratize
> my life? I'd been scribbling Pinocchio without putting down a word. How do
> you keep a story from jumping in your head? I told myself, I'm not Pinocchio,
> I'm not Pinocchio, I'm not Pinocchio.
> I was instantly in the Quirinale. (*PN*, pp. 152–53)

This is one of the most important passages in the book, as Jerome's condition,
so-called 'mythopsychosis', is the key to understanding the different shifts in the
narrative that otherwise would not easily make sense. Charyn's fictional book
by Freud, *The ABC's of Sigmund Freud*, refers to the *abecedario*, the reading book
Geppetto buys for Pinocchio in Collodi's novel. In Collodi, even though Geppetto
sells his coat to buy this book so that Pinocchio can go to school, it is not at school
but through his adventures that Pinocchio finally learns to obey the Blue Fairy and
work hard — and so become a real boy. In Charyn's novel, the *ABC* plays a similar
role in its uselessness. Jerome hopes to find a cure in it, yet when he repeats three
times, as in a fairy-tale magic ritual, 'I'm not Pinocchio', this creates the opposite of
the desired effect: the author is swallowed up into his own story. Unlike Dorothy
in *The Wizard of Oz* who, after clicking her heels three times, is transported back
home to Kansas, Jerome is taken away from home. This contrast works as an ironic
commentary on Freudian psychoanalysis, which, even though it is widely used
by the author to interpret Jerome's relationship with his mother, here, when the
protagonist turns to it for a treatment to his condition, it fails him.

Jerome's Oedipus complex is intertwined with writing, and Pinocchio is the
connecting element which is, at the same time, both disease and cure. In an attempt
to cure his Oedipus complex and the traumatic experiences of his childhood,
Jerome uses Pinocchio to narratise his life. This creates another problem, that of
mythopsychosis, a form of dissociation, which sends him into the story he creates.
He therefore inhabits a different body — that of Pinocchio — and turns from flesh
to wood. By being in two bodies, he does not fully experience either of the two,
which has complicated consequences. During his time in fascist Italy, he becomes
Mussolini's protégé until they are both hanged. He does not really die, though, as
Brunhilde, his fairy godmother, transports him back to Jerome's life and body ten
years later (in real life) when he has become famous for the book he has written
about Pinocchio in Mussolini's Italy. In the same way that the cylons transferred
their memories into their new bodies, Jerome brings all the memories of the
wooden body back to his human one after he dies as puppet Pinocchio. We can

therefore assume that the writing process was his refuge; a place that absorbed him for ten years to the extent that he experienced it, because of his mythopsychosis condition, as having been absent from his actual life as an author and only present in the one he was writing about. Famous for his Pinocchio book, back in 1993 Jerome refers to the time that passed while he was in Pinocchio's body:

> I must have dreamt through the life of Jerome while I was hiding in Pinocchio. [...] It hadn't been easy. I'd starved for seven years, scribbling away at a novel. And then I turned to my children's book, finished it in five weeks, and now I was on a safari to France. (PN, p. 287)

This could also mean that for the whole period that Jerome was 'away' in fictional Rome, he was suffering from writer's block, as he never managed to finish the book he had been writing for seven years. He was absorbed in it, but not in a rewarding way, and that is why he had to escape into Pinocchio's body. This is an autobiographical reference to Charyn, who for years was trying to write another book while he was writing his Isaac novels — a book, which he eventually never completed.[1] Moreover, while in 1943 Rome, Jerome is not aware of what the puppet Pinocchio has been doing before he 'fell into his body'. As a consequence, he tries to correct fascist Pinocchio without realising that Pinocchio was pretending to be fascist in order to help the Jews. Therefore, by trying to correct that fascist behaviour, Jerome-in-Pinocchio's-body harms the Jewish population of Rome.

Since a substantial part of the novel refers to writing as a refuge, therapy, escape, or disease, the reader's attention is directed towards the metafictitious nature of Charyn's book. One reason for this is that he shares many autobiographical elements with his protagonist — including, of course, his name. *Pinocchio's Nose* is a postmodern novel, rich in intertextuality and metafictional elements. The book is a retelling of *Pinocchio*, as it incorporates the name of Pinocchio in its title and also the character of Collodi's Pinocchio in new adventures. In *The Postmodern Fairytale*, Kevin Paul Smith distinguishes between eight elements of the intertextual use of fairy tales.[2] As Pinocchio often appears among other fairy-tale characters — particularly in contemporary texts — and the influences of Collodi when writing *Pinocchio* included a wide range of fairy tales, Smith's text is relevant to the exploration of the different modes of intertextuality in Charyn's text. In that respect, there are two distinctive intertextual references in *Pinocchio's Nose*. The first is the explicit reference in the title. This 'sets up a whole set of mechanisms whereby the reader automatically assumes that this intertextual reference is somehow relevant to the following text'.[3] It is indeed relevant, since the fictional character of Pinocchio, already known from Collodi's text and from its previous retellings, merges with the character of the author.

The second main intertextual characteristic of Charyn's novel is the allusion to historical figures such as Benito Mussolini and James Joyce, who are, however, presented in a new context. This is what Linda Hutcheon refers to as 'historiographic metafiction', texts that are 'both intensely self-reflexive and yet paradoxically also lay claim to historical events and personages'.[4] In *A Poetics of Postmodernism*, she argues that historiographic metafiction is a main characteristic of postmodernist fiction. Moreover, according to McHale, a novel is by definition postmodernist when it uses what he refers to as 'transworld characters', a term borrowed from Umberto Eco to describe fictional characters from other texts that appear in a new text.[5] As McHale goes on to argue, 'there are a number of ways of foregrounding this intertextual space and integrating it in the text's structure, but none is more effective than the device of "borrowing" a character from another text'.[6] This can be applied both to fictional characters, such as Pinocchio, and to historical ones, such as Mussolini, as in the present case. Smith points out that the 'borrowing' of such historical characters causes the reader to question the boundaries between fiction and reality: 'The names operate as an intertext which forces the reader to question the nature of reality (did this event really happen?) and the nature of representation (which discourses are considered 'authoritative' and why?)'.[7] Intertextuality is one of the most common elements in postmodernist fiction according to McHale, and it is very prominent in *Pinocchio's Nose*. Charyn is influenced by James Joyce and Herman Melville and this is apparent throughout the text, not only because his protagonist shares these influences, but also because of the numerous direct and indirect references, including the appearance of Joyce as a character in the story.

Finally, another element that categorises Charyn's novel as postmodernist fiction is its metafictive intertextuality, as defined by Smith. The constant merging of personalities between the author, Jerome Charyn, his protagonist and narrator, Jerome Copernicus Charyn, and Pinocchio keeps the reader in a constant state of alertness to the text.

> The storyteller, by defamiliarising narrative as we are used to experiencing it and re-familiarising the reader with storytelling in an oral context, causes the reader to think about such commonplaces as the relation of the author to the work and the work to the life, as well as larger-scale issues such as the problem of epistemology and the effect of writing upon consciousness. By drawing attention to the devices that we generally ignore when thinking about fiction and portraying the act of fiction-making in such depth, we can identify the storyteller as a metafictive device.[8]

Moreover, the fact that Charyn the author and Charyn his protagonist have the same name and many biographical elements in common gives an autobiographical flavour to the text and ensures that *Pinocchio's Nose* is a novel that incorporates 'the postmodernist *topos* of the writer at his desk'.[9] McHale explains further how introducing the author *into the fiction* creates another ontological paradox, common in postmodernist fiction:

> Behind the 'truth of the page' — the reality of the writer at his desk — lies the superior reality of the writing itself; but behind the reality of the writing must lie the superior reality of the *act* of writing that has produced it! An uncomfortable circularity, and one that hinges on the strangely amphibious ontological status, the presence/absence, of the author.[10]

As I pointed out earlier, the reader's attention is focused on writing throughout Charyn's novel, both because of the numerous autobiographical elements and because of the protagonist's escapist condition of mythopsychosis. Moreover,

Charyn refers to writing throughout the novel, making it a text that is as much about the story the narrative follows as it is about the writing process itself. The narrator of *Pinocchio's Nose* is Jerome Copernicus Charyn, Pinocchio, an unreliable narrator as he suffers from mythopsychosis and this influences his perception of himself and of time. In addition, due to a traumatic childhood, he has false or constructed memories, a fact that is only revealed towards the end of the book. At the beginning of the novel, Charyn starts with an 'Author's Affidavit' in which he states: 'I, Jerome Copernicus Charyn, solemnly swear that I am sound in the head' (*PN*, p. 7). This already creates suspicion in the reader, as normally an author does not need to confirm his or her mental soundness. This suspicion, together with the metafictive intertextuality described above, leads the reader to be directly involved in piecing together the jigsaw of the narrative. Charyn used autobiographical elements in previous novels as well. Police detective Manfred Coen, in his novel *Blue Eyes* (1974) is a ping-pong fanatic, as is Charyn himself; and as he describes in the Introduction to *The Isaac Quartet*, most of the elements he uses in his detective novels are gleaned from his police detective brother.[11] *Pinocchio's Nose* has many such references, both to autobiographical elements and to Charyn's previous novels, as the crooks and criminals of his detective novels are revisited in the underworld of the Bronx and Paris.

The last four chapters of *Pinocchio's Nose* are set in the future, between 1993 and 2017, as Charyn envisaged it at the time. With regard to speculation about the future, Charyn's novel has similarities with the three filmic examples analysed in Part I, all of which expressed a certain anxiety about technological progress. Yet this is one aspect that does not trouble the author of *Pinocchio's Nose*; the way he writes about the future in his book expresses a more political than technological anxiety: for instance, the US goes bankrupt in 2002 and Texas becomes independent in exchange for bailing the US out. Bulgaria becomes a superpower after finding bauxite in its soil and conquers Europe. This imagining of the future, with the communist Bulgarian Republic of the People representing the Soviet Union, can be seen as Charyn's response to the Cold War and the Reagan doctrine.

Another anxiety about the future relates to publishing and literary criticism: Charyn imagines his near-future world, that of 1993, with the *New York Review of Books* having become a super literary power, able to condemn authors to oblivion or raise them to literary heroes with a single review. As the famous author of *Pinocchio 1945*, Jerome is invited to a literary conference in Texas. Even though he has become very rich and successful from his book, Jerome is not respected by the Literary Guild because he is only an author of children's literature. This is Charyn's critical commentary on the snobbery that exists within the critical literary milieu regarding literary genres. What Jerome wrote before *Pinocchio 1945*, the novel *Blue Eyes Over Miami*, did not sell and so could not support him, even though he considered it to be his masterpiece. *Blue Eyes Over Miami* refers back to the detective novel that Charyn wrote in real life, *Blue Eyes*, but it also references the Blue Fairy, who is very closely related to fictional Jerome's writing and life as an author. It is no coincidence, then, that she also appears as Marvela Ming, a top literary critic at the *New York Review of*

Books who is attending the conference. 'It's then that I noticed the bluish tint of her hair under the cupola. Was Brunhilde out migrating again?' (*PN*, p. 317). Marvela Ming, a power-greedy, manipulative woman, confirms the dark nature of the Fairy that Charyn emphasises.

At this point in the book, the postmodern elements are prominent as the author talks about writing with frequent self-referential comments. His protagonist, Jerome, introduced sexual content into the Pinocchio story because that is what his readers, especially his young cousin, wanted. In a parallel reference it seems as though the author Charyn hopes to become more successful by listening to his audience's needs. It is therefore implied that the reason why he uses the sexual metaphor of Pinocchio's nose is to please his audience, assuming that this is what the audience of the time expected to read, together with some possible future scenarios of communist threat. If we assume that the parallel between the author and his protagonist extends to their opinions about their work, Charyn appears to denounce his book as not his best piece of work, even before it is published.

The reason why both Charyn and his protagonist choose Pinocchio is because, for many male authors, as can be seen from the *Pinocchio* retellings in this book, Pinocchio is a figure they easily identify with. He signifies the naughty disobedient boy, which brings nostalgic memories of boyhood. During the conference, the famous author George Mills accuses Jerome of abandoning his talent to go 'for the quick buck' with Pinocchio:

> 'What's so bad about Pinocchio, George?'
> 'You copped the story, smoothed it out, peppered it with Mussolini and his mistress. I grew up on Pinocchio. I didn't want it tampered with.'
> 'But Pinocchio is the story of my life.'
> 'Ah,' said George Mills. 'Aint we all bad boys. You didn't have to steal him from us.' (*PN*, p. 307)

As Jerome says, the story of Pinocchio is that of his life, and so of the life of Charyn too. As Robert L. Patten points out, '*Pinocchio's Nose* is autobiography *as* metafiction and metafiction *because* autobiography'.[12] Charyn's protagonist identifies with Pinocchio but not because Pinocchio is a bad boy, as George Mills suggests. Jerome's identification with Pinocchio is linked instead with his losing and finding, and then losing himself again, through his writing, his mythopsychosis, and his dysfunctional relationships with almost all the women in his life. Moreover, Mills represents the purists and traditionalists who might not favour retellings of classic literature and who Charyn thinks might object to his novel, yet another example of the story's metafiction that keeps the reader alert to the narrative.

Coover's novel, *Pinocchio in Venice*, is a retelling of *Pinocchio* in the form of a sequel that shares many formalistic elements with *Pinocchio's Nose*. It is a densely written text with numerous intertextual references, not only to Collodi's text but also to Venetian painting and architecture, Thomas Mann's *Death in Venice*, and many other texts. The novel's very dense intertextuality, and elaborate, witty language and parody, demand a very well-read and knowledgeable reader who is persistently alert. It is written in a carnivalesque style with long sentences that express different characters' continuous streams of consciousness with incorporated puns and nonsense jokes. Sentences stream like rivers, overloaded with carefully chosen words and references, challenging the capacity of the reader to follow this intellectual verbal delirium which reflects the characters' personalities and emotions but also the author's wit and sarcasm.

Similarly to Charyn's *Pinocchio's Nose*, Coover's text has many autobiographical elements. The main character, Professor Pinenut, is Pinocchio as a grown-up professor emeritus and Nobel Prize winner, a version of the puppet who has followed the Fairy's instructions closely throughout his life. One of the many levels of narration in this novel is the frequently sarcastic commentary on academia, drawn from the author's personal experience (Robert Coover, like Pinenut, is an emeritus professor, having been a professor at Brown University for ten years). Such comments are to be found dispersed through the text: 'Not even the day I got my PhD was as wonderful!', or 'trampling each other in their desperate search for an exit, it's worse than registration day back at the university' (*PV*, pp. 99, 149). These references are not just witty metaphors but also a commentary on the central theme of the Pinocchio myth, the tension between human and puppet nature: 'All the dense airless lecture halls of his endlessly protracted career have blurred into one, his innumerable pupils into a vast, shapeless, faceless mass. Waiting outside his office door. Waiting to have their little strings pulled. Day after day' (*PV*, p. 125). And like Coover, Professor Pinenut is the author of several prize-winning books. The main purpose of his journey to Venice is to finish his magnum opus and he feels he can only do so if he is close to his roots. To an extent, the text is also about writing (similarly to *Pinocchio's Nose*), but Coover's text, as a parody of itself, takes itself less seriously.

Intertextuality and autobiography are not the only characteristics that define Coover's novel as a postmodernist text. Metafictional elements, frequent self-referentiality, and also the carnivalesque character of the entire novel — all these equally carry the weight of such a definition. In his book *Robert Coover & the Generosity of the Page*, Stéphane Vanderhaeghe argues that even though *Pinocchio in Venice* is a text 'entirely built on intertextuality', it also redefines intertextuality 'in terms radically opposed to the "memory of literature" that the notion is usually linked with'.[13] He goes on to explain:

> Undoubtedly, the text (*Pinocchio in Venice*) writes and reads with the memory of what it was or used to be (*Adventures of Pinocchio*); diverse means are carried out to repeat, quote, rewrite its previous version, progressively brought to the surface as the text's privileged intertext. As such, as is often thought, literature is able to constitute itself into a virtual sum or 'library' through which it imaginarily moves. Yet this view is inseparable from some hermeneutics as it leads one to retrace the intertext in order to see and understand what the text proceeds from, that is, to seize its meaningful origin. However, the more you reflect upon it — or, rather, the more the text reflects upon you... — you 'sense' that the *inter-textual* practice of a novel like *Pinocchio in Venice* revokes all hermeneutic possibility, stressing the very futility of all such labours.[14]

To add to Vanderhaeghe's point, Coover stretches the limits of intertextuality through ongoing references to other texts, both real and imaginary, mocking the concept and function of intertextuality. He exaggerates to the extent that the very idea of intertextuality is rendered obsolete, as even the most well-read readers would not be able to follow his imaginary references. Thus, he uses the carnivalesque element of turning everything upside down, even reversing the literary devices that he uses. Reading Coover's text is an entertaining challenge for the reader, as Coover cannot feel comfortable with the subversive literary devices of postmodernist fiction unless he subverts them too. However, despite his playful approach to intertextuality, it is important to consider that Coover's numerous intertextual references reflect Collodi's numerous sources of inspiration for *Pinocchio*, as described earlier. Coover exaggerates by referring to a multitude of real and imaginary sources to emphasise his questioning of literary ownership or propriety further, as Vanderhaeghe argues.

Another similarity to Charyn's text regarding the novel's content is that Pinenut resorts to writing as an effect of his relationship with the Blue Fairy. He puts into words what he perceives to be her life philosophy and he makes it his own, a missionary of her supposed dogma. He interprets the Fairy's tricks as a desperate effort to alert him to the fact that goodness could die in the world unless everyone exercised it, an almost Christian approach:

> It gave me a mission. Her power was really *my* power, I had but to exercise it. 'I-ness,' I called it in a famous essay: the magical force of good character. My virtue, I felt, my decency, my civility, my faithfulness, might save the world! (*PV*, p. 75).

Elsewhere he describes his theory of 'I-ness' as 'a masterpiece whose single message (other than learning not to be naughty and helping one's parents when they are sick and poor) was that each man makes himself and thus the world' (*PV*, p. 33). This refers ironically to the American dream of the self-made man with a bloated sense of entitlement. The irony is clear, as the reader watches the ridiculous and often senile adventures of this self-made man.

Writing brings Pinenut closer to the Fairy, both when he writes about his theory of I-ness and also through his autobiographical work-in-progress. He needs to be closer to the place where he first met her in order to write his last chapter, 'Mamma', which is all about her. His journey home also proves to be the last chapter of his life. Yet even that is portrayed meta-fictitiously, as at the end Pinocchio, i.e. Professor Pinenut, becomes the book that the reader is holding in their hands. As he is dying in the Fairy's arms, she considers what to do with his decomposing, wooden body:

> 'I'm afraid there's nothing left to do but send you to the pulping mills to help ease the world paper shortage'. She leans down, little more than a loving shadow to him now, to kiss his eyes closed, whispering down the long receding tunnel of his earhole: 'We'll make a book out of you!'
> 'Ah!' he replies with his vanishing voice, grateful for the line she has, in her wisdom, thrown him. 'But a talking book, mamma! *A talking book...!*' (*PV*, p. 329)

So Pinocchio ends up where he started: an inanimate yet sentient object.

Humanity — From Flesh to Wood

The desire for humanity is challenged in these novels in numerous ways. First of all, the protagonists are human, therefore humanity is already a given. In both novels, Pinocchio turns from flesh to wood, a reversal of the original story. In Charyn's novel, Jerome-Pinocchio is physically absorbed in his own invented narrative and lives as puppet Pinocchio in fascist Italy. As explained in the previous section, this is an effect of the condition he suffers from, mythopsychosis. Charyn does not focus on Pinocchio's wooden body, apart from the very special nature of his nose, which will be examined in Chapter 7. Where he focuses on more is Jerome's desire to become a man through the Jewish ritual of bar mitzvah; this is the most direct reference to Pinocchio's desire to become a man. This time, however, manhood does not come through being human, but through a religious ritual.

Jerome Copernicus Charyn never had a bar mitzvah, as his mother could not afford one and did not care enough to do this for him. Bar mitzvah, the Jewish coming-of-age ritual, marks the moment when a boy becomes a man, at the age of thirteen years, approximately the same age as Pinocchio in Collodi's novel. Without the bar mitzvah, according to his religion and cultural heritage, Jerome never passed the threshold of adulthood. He stayed a child for a long time, eager like Pinocchio to grow up and become a man. He had been asking his mother for his bar mitzvah since the age of thirteen, in a similar way as Pinocchio tells the Blue Fairy that he wants to grow up and be a man in Chapter xxv of Collodi's novel. This is the same scene that I described in Part I as the 'confrontation scene', which is so crucial to the Pinocchio myth and Pinocchio's desire to become a man/human. Charyn uses the names Jerome and Pinocchio alternately, to emphasise the identification of Jerome with Pinocchio: 'It was about time I launched myself into manhood. Pinocchio had never been bar mitzvahed' (*PN*, p. 53).

Pinocchio in Venice opens with Professor Pinenut arriving in Venice in the middle of a snowstorm, staying faithful to Collodi's original, which also starts in the middle of winter. If winter is a metaphor for old age, it works very well in this case as it introduces the reader to one of the main elements that will reappear throughout the book, that of old age, at times combined with senility. Old age, however, is a natural stage of Pinocchio's longed-for humanity. Coover's novel does not focus on the experiences or achievements of Pinenut's long life; instead, the emphasis is on the last part of his life and the side-effects of Pinocchio's wish to become a man — old age, sickness, death. By satirically portraying all the disadvantages of the human condition, Coover deconstructs the element of the Pinocchio myth that glorified humanity and was used extensively in the case studies of Part I. Coover uses irony, parody, and grotesque elements, thus returning to the carnivalesque, which repeatedly subvert the Pinocchio myth. According to Mikhail Bakhtin, parody and ritual spectacles of the carnival, as well as foul language, which Coover uses quite frequently, are closely related as manifestations of the same culture, that of folk carnival humour.[15] All three elements constantly alternate in Coover's text. Moreover, Bakhtin emphasises that 'the contents of the carnival-grotesque element, its artistic, heuristic, and unifying forces were preserved in all essential manifestations [...] in the *commedia dell'arte*', characters of which are present both in Collodi's text and in even more detail in that of Coover.[16]

Professor Pinenut suffers from the disease of turning back into wood, which might at first sound as if it would guarantee his immortality. This is an ironic subversion of the wish the Blue Fairy granted him: first of all, because the magic seems to wear out as he returns to his former nature, and secondly, because the much-desired humanity takes its toll on him and bequeaths on him its destiny: death. Even when he goes back to his wooden state, he is still rotting, as if humanity had infected him like a disease. This is the opposite to the optimism and self-enhancement of transhumanist philosophy and it reflects Ligotti's pessimistic philosophy of human nature as mentioned in Part I. Whereas in Part I the posthuman was reflected as the possibility of an enhanced living experience, transcending the human body's limitations through technological progress and advancements, Coover's protagonist finds that what is beyond his human nature (i.e. his post-humanity) is a rotten version of his old self. Humanity has corrupted him; the posthuman for Pinenut is his transformation after being human and it will be the last one. Throughout the book, he loses different parts of his body, as his skin dries and falls off, until at the end of the novel he is unable to walk anymore and has to be carried like a puppet. It is therefore suggested that for him humanity was only a disguise, his true self never having changed. 'Ah yes, I see, your skin is, after all, as one might have supposed, nothing more than a cheap veneer' (*PV*, pp. 79–80). This has an additional significance in the context of the novel, where masks and appearances play a prominent role.

Apart from Pinocchio, who has lived more than a hundred years in this sequel of Collodi's text, there are other characters from *Pinocchio* who appear in *Pinocchio in Venice*. The Fox and the Cat, Alidoro the dog, and Colombo the pigeon are some of them, and they are all affected by old age. Apart from his clearly stated sickness of turning back to wood, Pinenut appears at times to behave like a senile old man as, for example, when leaving his friend Arlecchino to die in order to run after a former student of his, hoping she will share her bed with him. Coover involves his protagonist in several scenes that hover between the grotesque and the ridiculous, only to emphasise the powerful and negative effect of time on a human body, even if that includes the mind of a professor emeritus and twice Nobel laureate. It is also no coincidence that the many intertextual references in *Pinocchio in Venice* include Petrarch's cautionary *Epistolae seniles* (Letters of Old Age), which are mentioned more than once.

The theme of old age is prominent in *Pinocchio's Nose* as well. One of the main characters in the second half of the novel is Pedersen, a thirteen-year-old child who is ill with progeria. He is a close friend of Pinocchio-Jerome, who suffers to see Pedersen die prematurely. The Fairy offers Jerome eternal life and youth as long as he stays with her. Even though he refuses, it appears that she grants him longevity (or eternal life) which is more of a punishment, as he witnesses the death of almost everyone he loves. Placing the theme of ageing within the context of the Pinocchio myth highlights even more the cost of Pinocchio's wish for humanity.

This chapter has investigated how these two postmodern texts challenge the myth of Pinocchio by twisting parts and specific themes of the narrative that lead back to Collodi's text and invite a reading of it that differs from the more popular retellings and adaptations. More specifically, by portraying the consequences of Pinocchio's transformation into a human boy, ageing and sickness, they invite the reader to re-examine why Pinocchio wished for it in the first place. This leads to investigation of the role the Blue Fairy played in influencing his desire. The next chapter will focus on the ambiguous nature and agency of the Fairy, both in the original and in these two retellings.

Notes to Chapter 5

1. Jerome Charyn, 'Introduction', in *The Isaac Quartet* (London: Zomba Books,1984), pp. v–x.
2. Kevin Paul Smith, *The Postmodern Fairytale: Folkloric Intertexts in Contemporary Fiction* (New York: Palgrave Macmillan, 2007).
3. Ibid., p. 14.
4. Linda Hutcheon, *A Poetics of Postmodernism: History, Theory, Fiction* (New York & London: Routledge, 1988), p. 5.
5. Umberto Eco, '*Lector in fabula*: Pragmatic Strategy in a Metanarrative Text', in *The Role of the Reader: Explorations in the Semiotics of Texts* (Bloomington & London: Indiana University Press, 1979), pp. 200–60.
6. McHale, *Postmodernist Fiction*, p. 57.
7. Smith, *The Postmodern Fairytale*, p. 22.
8. Ibid., p. 112.
9. McHale, *Postmodernist Fiction*, p. 198.
10. Ibid., pp. 198–99.
11. Charyn, 'Introduction', in *The Isaac Quartet*, p. vi.
12. Robert L. Patten, 'Pinocchio through the Looking Glass: Jerome Charyn's Portrait of the Artist as a Mytholept', *Novel: A Forum on Fiction*, 17.1 (1983), 67–76 (p. 69).
13. Stéphane Vanderhaeghe, *Robert Coover & the Generosity of the Page* (London: Dalkey Archive Press, 2013), pp. 79, 111.
14. Ibid.
15. Mikhail Bakhtin, *Rabelais and His World*, trans. by Helene Iswolsky (Cambridge, MA, & London: M.I.T. Press, 1968), pp. 4–5.
16. Ibid., p. 34.

CHAPTER 6

❖

The Blue Fairy

In Charyn's and Coover's texts, Pinocchio's oedipal relationship with the Blue Fairy influences the whole life of the protagonist. In this chapter I will explain exactly how this relationship works or malfunctions in each novel. The Oedipus complex, on which Sigmund Freud worked and wrote throughout his life, can be briefly summarised as a phase that children go through when developing sexually and which defines the formation of their psyche. Referring to the Greek mythical hero Oedipus, who unknowingly killed his father and married his mother, Freud emphasises that the sexual desire the child feels towards his mother plays a vital role in the distinction of the id, ego, and super-ego in the individual's psyche while developing and adjusting to society. An ongoing obsession with the mother or neurotic behaviour associated with one or other parent beyond childhood is often caused by a traumatic event during the child's developmental phase.

In *Pinocchio's Nose*, Copernicus Charyn's troubled upbringing in the poor neighbourhoods of the Bronx reappears frequently throughout the novel. His father abandoned his mother, Bathsheba, because she could not give up her habit of stealing. Jerome Copernicus grows up together with his Uncle Lionel (his mother's younger brother) and competes with him for her love and attention throughout his life. The fact that Jerome-Pinocchio cannot become a man because of his missed bar mitzvah represents the trauma of the neglected childhood he experienced because of Bathsheba. This becomes clearer later in the narrative when, at crucial moments, he recalls unpleasant details of his childhood in the Bronx. The relationship with his mother and the competition with his young uncle to win her attention are what mark every step of his later life, including the escapist mythopsychosis he experiences whenever he faces serious trouble. The world he is escaping to (that of Pinocchio) is a world that his mother introduced to him. He is therefore creating the illusion of running away to a different world without really escaping from her.

Revisiting the confrontation scene, as the missed bar mitzvah, emphasises the contrast to the case studies discussed in Part I. The myth of Pinocchio is not perpetuated, but deconstructed. Moreover, the different approach to the confrontation scene positions the Blue Fairy in a different perspective. Throughout Charyn's novel, the Blue Fairy appears in the form of different women but there is always an emphasis on her unkind and dark nature, which was already hinted at by Collodi. Jerome's mother is the main representation of the Fairy, but so is every other woman that has a strong impact on him. To make that even more explicit, there are numerous references to the colour blue when the author refers to his mother or to other women who have a strong influence over him. Bathsheba dyes her hair blue: 'I climbed out of Lionel's crib and recognised my mother's blue hair. What happened to her own strong color, Odessa gray? [...] The blue hair made her look like a peahen in Louis Quatorze's circus' (*PN*, p. 37). His disturbed relationship with Bathsheba is made explicit in the dreams he has of her: 'And I had dreams of stuffing Bathsheba's mouth with strands of blue hair. Because I'm sure my mother used to bribe me with her milk. When I was bad, she took me off the tit' (*PN*, p. 40). His stuffing hair into his mother's mouth can be interpreted as an act both violent and sexual, as 'stuffing the mouth' can be a suppressed metaphor for the sexual act. Everything is subverted and opposed to its original meaning. Similarly, his mother's milk, a symbol of life and of the strong bond between a child and its mother-nurturer is presented as a means of punishment and bribe. In another instance, Jerome even presents it as lethal: 'What did I care if the devil wrote *Ulysses*? The music in that novel was like my mother's milk. Something deadly and accurate, that could lull a boy to sleep' (*PN*, p. 48).

In Montegrumo, where the fictional Pinocchio of the parallel story is born, the Blue Fairy is Brunhilde, the prostitute of the village, who is trusted by Geppetto after he turned her into a socialist. After she dies, her ghost comes back and haunts Pinocchio in the form of his fairy godmother. She is referred to as the Blue Fairy directly and not implicitly, as in the case of other influential women in Jerome's life. It is no coincidence that Brunhilde takes the Fairy's role, as she is the woman whom Geppetto chose to be Pinocchio's mother. In the fictional world, Jerome materialises his suppressed fantasies, as Brunhilde, his 'mother', is the one who initiates him in the discovery of the sexual nature of his nose. Brunhilde also fails in her maternal role, as Bathsheba apparently failed with Jerome. In both *Pinocchio's Nose* and *Pinocchio in Venice* the Blue Fairy in all her manifestations is the negative force that torments the protagonist and represents his Oedipus complex. What Disney tried to sanitise in his adaptation of Collodi's novel is magnified in Charyn's and Coover's retellings.

While in Pinocchio's wooden body, Jerome still suffers from his Oedipus complex as he is fully aware of his previous (human) life. He still desires to be bar-mitzvahed; he finds a rabbi who refuses his persistent requests:

> I asked him for Torah lessons. The rabbi refused. He could teach me Torah, yes, but as a 'senseless decoration'. A puppet wasn't Jewish in God's eyes. I was a golem, a twisted thing, brought to life by other men. (*PN*, p. 237).

In the wooden skin of Pinocchio, Jerome is doubly stuck in childhood. He is still obsessed with being bar-mitzvahed and it is still not possible. Before, he was obstructed by Bathsheba, and now he is obstructed by his material body, a result of trying to escape from Bathsheba's influence. In short, he is worse off than where he started, being unable to grow, either physically or psychologically, in his puppet state. His corporeality intensifies his identity conflict, reminiscent of the confrontation scene in *Pinocchio* when Pinocchio realises that he is not what he thought he was. It is not, however, the only instance in Collodi's novel where he experiences a distance from his own body. At the end of the book, after he has been transformed into a real boy, Pinocchio looks at his old puppet body with bewilderment and possibly contempt: 'How funny I was when I was a puppet!' (*AP*, p. 461). It is at this stage that Pinocchio finally enters the symbolic order, in Lacanian terms, a state he is unable to achieve as Jerome-in-Pinocchio. According to Lacan's theory, an individual's entry into the symbolic order happens when one accepts the Law of the Father, i.e. when one conforms to the generally accepted social order. In Collodi's story, these terms are reversed, since the Law of the Father is defined by the Blue Fairy; therefore the symbolic order is achieved when Pinocchio accepts the Law of the Mother. As with Collodi's Pinocchio, Jerome's self-conflict begins with a woman, the same strict mother who oppresses him throughout Charyn's novel.

As in *Pinocchio's Nose,* the Blue Fairy has different manifestations in *Pinocchio in Venice,* where her role is straightforward: she is a dark force that has manipulated Pinocchio and put him into strings. Their ambiguous relationship is explored throughout the novel and frequently alluded to by references to the colour blue. Another similarity with *Pinocchio's Nose* is that Pinocchio's nose did not grow because of his lying, but because Geppetto misplaced Pinocchio's penis and put it on his face instead.

Apart from these points, there are two recurrent motifs which are interwoven with the above themes: the carnivalesque and the city of Venice. The carnival is used both as a stylistic element and also as a theme of the narrative. Carnivalesque situations and language exemplify Coover's intention to empty Pinocchio's myth of its meaning, creating the space to reinvent and redefine it within that frame. As Bakhtin emphasises, the function of the carnival-grotesque is 'to consecrate inventive freedom, [...] to liberate from the prevailing point of view of the world, from conventions and established truths, [...] from all that is universally accepted'.[1] At the same time, the Carnival as event and circumstance is used extensively throughout the novel, visually through masques and marionettes of the *commedia dell'arte* and narratively as a diegetic frame to emphasise Pinocchio's connection with the world of puppets and masques. This connection is established not only through the critical scene in Collodi's novel where the marionettes recognise him as 'brother', but also historically, as it has been argued that Pinocchio's origins are indeed in the *commedia dell'arte*. According to Federico Pacchioni, Pinocchio dates back to a character of the *commedia dell'arte* called 'Burattino' who had ceased to be popular but was probably a source of inspiration for Collodi.[2] I will return to Pinocchio's origin later on.

Since the Blue Fairy is the co-protagonist and second most important character in *Pinocchio,* the next section explores Collodi's sources of inspiration for her creation. Most of the section is devoted to her blue hair, which distinguishes her from any other fairies in literary history, beginning with a look at the history of the colour blue, as well as the associations made with this colour in Collodi's time. However, since *Pinocchio* was originally conceived as the 'storia di un burattino' and initially finished at Chapter xv (before the appearance of the Blue Fairy), I will first look at the character of the 'bambina coi capelli turchini' [the little girl with blue hair] separately.

According to Paola Giovetti, there is a legend associated with the castle of Montebello which refers to a little girl with blue hair, who died mysteriously and whose ghost has been seen or heard in the castle ever since.[3] The legend of 'Azzurrina' — as the little girl was called because of the blue hair dye that her mother used to hide her daughter's albinism from the superstitious environment of the time — dates back to 1375, but it was popular even after Collodi's time as seen in Tommaso Molari's 1934 publication *Memorie sul castello di Montebello di Romagna*.[4] Moreover, as the castle of Montebello is not far from the region where Collodi lived, it is very possible that he knew of the legend and incorporated it into his story, with the likely expectation that his readers would recognise the reference.

Even if it is true that Collodi was originally inspired by the legend of Azzurrina for the creation of the little girl with the blue hair, a more detailed analysis is needed with regard to the colour blue, as the role of the Blue Fairy in the second part of *Pinocchio* is prominent. In the next section, I will explore the reasons behind Collodi's choice for the Fairy's famous blue hair and the connotations the colour had when Collodi used it.

According to Michel Pastoureau's extensive history of the colour, blue enjoyed a highly prestigious status in the nineteenth century, after it had been used to demonstrate opulence between the twelfth and sixteenth centuries. Pastoureau asserts that 'in the eighteenth century the vogue for new blue tones in dyes and paintings helped establish blue definitively as the favorite color throughout Europe'.[5] He goes on to explain how this popularity was reflected in the increase of words for blue in many languages, and explains how, during the twelfth century, the rarity and high value of lapis lazuli, from which the pigment of ultramarine was extracted, contributed to the exclusive use of blue to depict the Virgin Mary, since its high material value was also reflected symbolically in the portrayal of higher moral values. In Coover's retelling, the connection between the Blue Fairy and the Virgin Mary is made several times. This creates an association between the two female figures, which suggests that Collodi was inspired by artistic depictions of the Virgin Mary for the character of the Blue Fairy and also by the Virgin Mary's maternal and ubiquitous presence, elements reflected in the Blue Fairy. Coover, however, challenges the Fairy's maternal character and by associating her with the Virgin Mary creates a bigger contrast. Coover refers to Italian paintings of the Virgin Mary, reflecting the fact that in Italy blue was used more widely than in the rest of Europe. Philip Ball explains that 'the proclivity for lavish use of ultramarine was confined mostly to Italy, mainly for reasons of commerce: its ports were the conduits through which the pigment came west'.[6]

Blue was also used in royal garments for the French and English courts as well as in heraldry to depict royal coats of arms. It was also a dominant colour in the literature of the Enlightenment and early Romantic period and Pastoureau cites the two examples of Goethe and Novalis who both favoured blue and used it extensively in their novels:

> The most notable example of this is Werther's famous blue-and-yellow outfit, which Goethe describes in his epistolary novel *The Sorrows of Young Werther*.

[...] The novel's extraordinary success and the 'Werthermania' that followed launched a fashion for the blue coat 'à la Werther' throughout Europe.[7]

Novalis used a blue flower as a main motif in his novel *Heinrich von Ofterdingen*, and that blue flower was eventually turned into a symbol of the German Romantic movement; and Goethe refers to blue extensively in many of his works. While Pastoureau attributes this to the fashion of the times, one cannot fail to notice the connection between the importance of the colour blue in Freemasonry and the fact that both Goethe and Novalis were outspoken Freemasons.

Blue is the most popular colour in Freemasonry: it was widely used in different shades for masonic regalia, and it was also extensively used by famous Freemason artists and authors who influenced the world and the literary canon. The first documented attempt to explain the connections between colour and Freemasonry to its members was made in 1904 by F. J. W. Crowe, followed by W. J. Chetwode Crawley in 1910. In his paper 'Masonic Blue', the latter explained the exact hues of blue that had been associated with Freemasonry up to his time.[8] Whether Collodi was a Freemason or not, he must have been aware of the major impact the symbolism of the colour had at his time, both in literature and in the visual arts. It stood not only for the exquisite and the rare, but also for the celestial and the sublime. There are serious claims that Collodi was himself a Freemason, in which case he would have been well aware of the wider symbolism of his decision to use that colour. Even though he was never officially registered as a Freemason, he was familiar with Freemason ideas and the Grand Orient of Freemasonry in Italy classifies him among its famous members, as can be seen on its website.[9] There are several studies examining Collodi's Freemason affiliations, such as the transcript of a presentation on a reading of *Pinocchio* as a hidden masonic parable: cultural anthropologist Paolo Pisani connects the choice of Pinocchio's name to its two compounds, as he claims, *pino* [pine] and *occhio* [eye], and sees this as a reference to the pineal gland, which in the esoteric tradition represents the 'third eye'. In short, Pisani sees Collodi's work as a path towards the opening of this 'third eye' and a spiritual awakening.[10] He identifies the Blue Fairy as a representation of Freemasonry without, however, giving any further details. If the claims that Collodi was a Freemason are true, then it is obvious why Collodi would have made this choice of colour for the Fairy. Paolo Aldo Rossi provides evidence that supports the claim that Collodi was a Freemason and he also reads *Pinocchio* as a masonic parable full of symbolism.[11] It is not relevant to this study to go into further detail as to which masonic symbolism is used in Collodi's text, but it is important to emphasise the connection between the colour blue — and consequently the role of the Blue Fairy — and the historical background to its usage, which widely includes Freemasonry. Even if Collodi was not a Freemason, the influence of famous Freemasons in the world of the arts and literature continued to endow the colour blue with both significance and esteem.

Venice, too, plays an ambiguous role in Coover's narrative, as it is frequently seen as a representation of the Blue Fairy — a place of allure and attraction, but one that proves to be deadly. Everything associated with the colour blue in Coover's text is a direct reference to the Blue Fairy's presence or influence. Given that there are various words to express the colour blue in Italian, it is noteworthy that Collodi chose *turchino* to describe the colour of her hair. Coover emphasises this point through Professor Pinenut's contemplations: 'Cassiodorus called this blue the "Venetian color." It was the color of the darkness which came over the sun at the time of the desolation of the Gothic kingdom. The color of his own desolated life' (*PV*, p. 269). Coover's references are frequently misquoted expressly to mock and question the concepts of authorship and scholarship. Yet the reference to Cassiodorus is also found in John Ruskin's Venetian notebooks:

> Respecting the colour of the women's dress, it is noticeable that blue is called 'Venetian colour' by Cassiodorus, translated 'turchino' by Filiasi, vol. v. chap. iv. It was a very pale blue, as the place in which the word occurs is the description by Cassiodorus of the darkness which came over the sun's disk at the time of the Belisarian wars and desolation of the Gothic kingdom.[12]

Ruskin's editors mention that he wondered in a letter to his father whether the turquoise 'stone was called from the colour, or the colour from the stone' — a Persian stone which was imported to Venice through Turkey, from which the name may have originated.[13] What becomes clear from the above is that the colour described by Collodi as *turchino* has very clear associations with the city of Venice. Whether that reference was obvious in Collodi's time is another matter. According to Perella's notes, 'Collodi used *turchino* to translate the French *bleu* in his rendering of Marie-Catherine d'Aulnoy's famous art fairy tale, *L'oiseau bleu*' (*AP*, p. 482, n. 31). This does not prove, however, whether Collodi had the Venetian reference to the colour in mind or not. As mentioned earlier in the Introduction, it shows the connection of *Pinocchio* to the tradition of fairy tales, with which he was very familiar, as well as a preference, I believe, for that shade of blue. It is worth noting that in d'Aulnoy's original fairy tale, the word *bleu*, which Collodi translates as *turchino*, refers to the colour of the sky.[14] What colour that is exactly is debatable, but it also depends on the country of origin, according to Bernard E. Jones: 'the "sky blue" mentioned by the ancient writers of the East must represent the "deep blue" of the Eastern sky — "a colour approaching to black" — and not the "light blue" of the Northern climate'.[15] It is more likely that in using *turchino* Collodi had a darker blue in mind, not least because the first time this colour is mentioned in *Pinocchio* it is to describe Maestro Ciliegia's nose when it turns blue from fear. This can only be a dark blue, and it is also telling that the first time this colour is referred to in the text, it is in association with fear. Finally, according to Maria Grossmann, *turchino* is classified as one of the most intense and darkest of all shades of blue.[16] All this confirms the assumption of Cassiodorus, which connects the origin of the word *turchino* to the city of Venice. Therefore, since Venice and the Fairy are linguistically connected through the shade of blue that they share, by connecting them also thematically and narratively Coover pays tribute to Collodi who was expert at creating stories out of linguistic idioms, as is evident in the growing nose and the talking cricket of *Pinocchio*, as we shall see later. Coover therefore retells *Pinocchio* not only thematically but also stylistically, by revisiting Collodi's style of language and choice of words. He uses the colour blue to connect Venice to the Fairy and hence the city becomes that metaphor for the entire text.

From very early on, Venice seems to have a very strong power over Professor Pinenut, just as the Fairy does: 'Here I am, the city seems to be saying, in all my innocence and beauty. Within my depths lies that final knowledge you seek. Enter me' (*PV*, p. 21). This proves to be the desire of the Fairy all along. In Chapter 7 Pinenut describes the influence she had in his life:

> Men, if lucky, [...] are graced in their lifetime by one intense insight that changes everything. Mine was the discovery that the Blue-Haired Fairy was pretending not to be dead, but to be alive, that in fact it was not she who had given me a place in the world, you see, but *I* who had called *her* into being. (*PV*, p. 66)

Coover chooses parts of Collodi's text carefully and expands on them when re-narrating the story, not unlike Giorgio Manganelli in *Pinocchio: un libro parallelo*. Indeed this concept that the Blue Fairy was dead all along and the powerful magic of Pinocchio brought her back to life was originally suggested by Manganelli. The idea of the Fairy's revival through Pinocchio's death is clearly found in Collodi's text, as she appears like a ghost in the window, pale with closed eyes and hands crossed over her chest, stating with lips that do not move that she is dead 'in a voice that seemed to come from the world beyond' (*AP*, p. 183). In fact, she only regains her powers when Pinocchio is dying on the Great Oak. Then she can clap her hands and summon the animals of the forest who obey her because, as Collodi reveals at this point in the narrative, 'the Little Girl with blue hair was nothing other than a good Fairy who for more than a thousand years had been living near that forest' (*AP*, p. 191). Manganelli argues that it is this power of the forest that connects Pinocchio and the Fairy: through his sacrifice, the 'talking piece of wood' unleashes the power that is needed to break the spell keeping the Fairy weak and dying, and brings back her powers.

Coover re-imagines the Fairy not as a millennial, good-natured force living in the forest and having power over animals, who serve her obediently, but as a witch-like creature, at times playful, at times malevolent, who resembles a trickster goddess. As is shown in the last chapter called 'Mamma', in which her true nature is revealed, the Fairy has tried all along to keep Pinocchio close to her. In a grotesque scene, where she finally tries to convince him to surrender to her, her form changes constantly between the different masks she has worn to attract Pinocchio. Although her form is unstable, some of her true traits appear during her constant changes:

> She seems almost to be crying, but he cannot be sure, her eyes do not stay in one place long enough. Those fleeting traces of the familiar are now blurred by the strange. Claws on her fingertips. An iron tooth. Smoke curling out her nose, which seems to change shape with every breath. He has seen a scar grow, cross her brow, and rip vividly down her cheek and throat, then as quickly fade and vanish. A moment ago, her ears, peeking out from under hair twisting like thin blue snakes, seemed to be pointed, but now they look like his mamma's once more. (*PV*, p. 323)

Appearances play a very important role in *Pinocchio in Venice*, as the whole text questions the concept of masking and unmasking. Nobody is what he/she seems to be and there is often another mask behind a mask or even a lack of meaning, a lack of subject to be disguised. Pinenut proclaims masking as the ultimate defence of sanity:

> 'The important thing about the Carnival,' he wrote recently in a note intended as part of his monograph-then-in-progress, 'is not the masking, but the unmasking, the revelation, the repentance, the reestablishment of sanity,' but, as always in all the days before yesterday, he was wrong. The important thing *is* the masking. What is sanity itself, after all, but terror's sweet foggy disguise? And love the mask that shields us from the abyss, art its compassionate accomplice? (*PV*, p. 258)

Therefore, the revelation of the Fairy's true identity in the end challenges the order and sanity Professor Pinenut longs for, as seen in the previous passage. The truth he is facing is one that is closer to the terror and the abyss he fears: his nature is much closer to the monstrous nature of the Fairy than he had hoped. It is apparent that both of them are extraordinary creatures who have been through many transformations, deaths, and rebirths. The Fairy confirms that the reason why she has been playing her tricks all along was out of a longing to be accepted among humans. They seemed to be scared by her, no matter what she did, so she tried to die in order to win them over:

> Dying seemed to carry a lot of weight with humans, I thought it might help. But it wasn't in my repertoire, really. I gave it all I had, but I just couldn't get the hang of it. Which disheartened me all the more. And then, just when my spirits were lowest, you came along. (*PV*, p. 324)

Coover's version contradicts Manganelli's here, in that he does not see the Fairy as the victim of a spell which kept her powers bound until Pinocchio came along and liberated her. Instead, he suggests that Pinocchio dragged her out of her boredom, as she recognised a fellow being that could appreciate her more than humans did. A thousand-year-old Fairy who suffers from ennui is also the theme of one of Coover's later texts, the novella *Briar Rose*, which was published in 1996, five years after *Pinocchio in Venice*. The image of the ogre-like Fairy who scares humans despite her good intentions is more common today in popular retellings of fairy tales, as seen, for example, in the *Shrek* series of films; however, it was not common at the time Coover wrote *Pinocchio in Venice*. This, in a sense, has a double effect: even though the tension builds up throughout the novel, with every additional proof that the Blue Fairy is an evil force, the ending comes unexpectedly, as Coover's depiction of the Fairy's true nature is almost coy, compared to the sheer monstrosity expected by the reader. This is one more commentary on the theme of masking/ unmasking and one more successful reversal of the reader's expectations. Instead of pure evil, as the whole novel suggested, the Fairy appears to be a trickster. Thus, she returns to one of the first characterisations she used for her relationship with Pinocchio in Collodi, that of *sorellina* [little sister], as Pinocchio is also a manifestation of the trickster archetype. Similarly, Coover takes the same trickster role by playing a trick on his readers, playing with their expectations by weaving together once more stylistics and thematic arc.

Notes to Chapter 6

1. Bakhtin, *Rabelais and His World*, p.34.
2. Federico Pacchioni: 'Forse siamo ora in grado di capire perché i burattini di Mangiafoco riconoscono e riabbracciano Pinocchio con tanto entusiasmo, accogliendolo come un fratello che torna a casa dopo una lunga assenza' [Perhaps we are now able to understand why Mangiafuoco's marionettes recognise and are reunited with Pinocchio so enthusiastically, welcoming him like a brother who returns home after a long absence]. 'La passione di un Burattino: teste di legno ribattezzate all'ombra della Commedia dell'Arte', *Intersezioni: Review of the History of Ideas*, 3 (2009), 339–56 (p. 355).
3. Paola Giovetti, *L'Italia dell'insolito e del mistero: 100 itinerari 'diversi'* (Rome: Edizioni Mediterranee, 2001), p. 76.
4. Tommaso Molari, *Memorie sul castello di Montebello di Romagna* [1934] (Verucchio: Pazzini, 2002).
5. Michel Pastoureau, *Blue: The History of a Color* (Princeton, NJ, & Oxford: Princeton University Press, 2001), p. 134.
6. Philip Ball, *Bright Earth: The Invention of Colour* (London: Vintage, 2008), p. 271.
7. Pastoureau, *Blue*, p. 136.
8. F. J. W. Crowe, 'Colours in Freemasonry', *Ars Quatuor Coronatorum: Transactions of Quatuor Coronati Lodge No. 2076, London*, 17 (1904), 3–11; and W. J. Chetwode Crawley, 'Masonic Blue', *Ars Quatuor Coronatorum:Transactions of Quatuor Coronati Lodge No. 2076, London*, 22 (1910), 309–20.
9. Grande Oriente d'Italia, 'Massoni celebri' <http://www.grandeoriente.it/che-cosa-e-la-massoneria/massoni-celebri/> [accessed 21 March 2019]. Michele Pietrangeli, the Grand Secretary of the Grand Orient of Freemasonry (GOI) in Italy, has confirmed in an email communication of 13 November 2015 that the Grand Librarian of the Grand Orient of Italy has made extensive research in the historical archives of the GOI in response to my query regarding Collodi's official membership. There is no evidence of Collodi's registration, but there are serious claims of his affiliation to freemasonry because Freemason ideas resonate extensively in his work.
10. Paolo Pisano: 'Del resto, il nome stesso scelto dall'autore per battezzare questo "burattino-bambino", altro non è che la derivazione della composizione delle due parole "pino" e "occhio". Quel "pino" che è l'albero i cui frutti i "pinoli", hanno la stessa forma della ghiandola pineale che, nella tradizione esoterica, rappresenta appunto il "terzo occhio". La favola dunque, appare come un percorso verso l'apertura di questo "terzo occhio", quindi verso il risveglio dell'essere.' [Moreover, the name chosen by the author to christen this 'puppet-child', is none other than the composition of the two words 'pine' and 'eye'. The 'pine' is the tree whose fruits, the 'pine nuts', have the same shape as the pineal gland which, in the esoteric tradition, represents the 'third eye'. The fable, therefore, appears as a path towards the opening of this 'third eye', thus a path to awakening]. 'Collodi con il suo "Pinocchio" a 'I Venerdì del Grande Oriente', Grande Oriente d'Italia, 19 April 2013 <http://www.grandeoriente.it/collodi-con-il-suo-pinocchio-a-i-venerdi-del-grande-oriente/> [accessed 21 March 2019].
11. Paolo Aldo Rossi, 'La fata turchina e le metamorfosi di Pinocchio', in *Fate: madri, amanti, streghe*, ed. by Sonia Maura Barillari, L'Immagine Riflessa/ Quaderni Serie Miscellanea, 13 (Alessandria: Edizioni dell'Orso, 2012).
12. John Ruskin, *The Stones of Venice, vol. 2*, in *The Works of John Ruskin*, ed. by E. T. Cook and Alexander Wedderburn, 39 vols (London: George Allen, 1903–12), x (1904), 447 <https://www.gutenberg.org/files/30755/30755-h/30755-h.htm> [accessed 20 October 2021].
13. Ibid.
14. In the fairy tale, the verse 'Oiseau Bleu, couleur du temps, | Vole à moi promptement' is mentioned, which Collodi translates as 'Uccello turchino, color del cielo, | Vola e ritorna subito a me', keeping the reference to the colour as 'sky blue'. See Marie-Catherine d'Aulnoy and Jeanne-Marie Leprince de Beaumont, *Fiabe d'amore*, trans. by Carlo Collodi [1876] (Florence: Giunti, 2011), p. 39.
15. Bernard E. Jones, *Freemasons' Guide and Compendium* (London: George G. Harrap, 1950), p. 471.

16. Maria Grossmann, *Colori e lessico: studi sulla struttura semantica degli aggettivi di colore in catalano, castigliano, italiano, romeno, latino ed ungherese* (Tübingen: G. Narr, 1988), p. 71.

CHAPTER 7

❖

Pinocchio's Misplaced Nose

Coover places the origins of Pinocchio's desire for humanity in a particular scene in Collodi's text, which was also portrayed as an illustration in the original publication (figure 7.1). It is what I referred to in Part I as 'the confrontation scene'. However, Coover's interpretation takes this scene in a specific direction. As examined earlier, Pinocchio recognises the grown-up Fairy and he wants to become like her, a grown-up. In order to do that, she tells him that he has to become a real human boy first and instructs him how to do this. Yet the human form was one of the Fairy's disguises. In truth, Pinocchio was already much closer to the Fairy's real nature in his puppet state.

FIG. 7.1 Original illustration by Enrico Mazzanti for Carlo Collodi, *Le avventure di Pinocchio: storia di un burattino* (Florence: Felice Paggi, 1883), p. 128.

Coover, however, poses a different question: why would Pinocchio want to become like the Fairy? In Pinenut's narration of his past, this question is answered: 'When he recognised her, he knelt and hugged her knees, and she gave him a glimpse of a possible future, more than one: he had to choose' (*PV*, p. 72). It is a sexual motivation that drives the prepubescent Pinocchio to desire humanity. This moment is what he reminisces upon during a cold winter night in Venice when he thinks he might be dying: 'but all that comes to him there under his helmet of iced scarf is what he saw that awesome day when she spread her knees as though to reveal to him his fate' (*PV*, p. 46). The fate he chose, of course, was that of becoming human, as instructed by the Fairy. However, he seems to have suffered all his life, trying to live by the rules she imposed. This is possibly the reason why he suffers from his deadly illness, turning back to wood. It seems as though the human disguise never quite fitted him. He realises this in the end, after the Fairy's revelation:

> You always were the *good* little fairy, weren't you? Society's little helper! Civilization's drill sergeant! But I was free! I was happy! And you, with your terrifying heartbreaking parade of tombstones and canon, put strings on me where there were none. You cheated me! All my life *I have been nothing but a puppet!* (*PV*, p. 320)

Coover replaces the meaning of words and concepts with their opposite, as is shown by this reading of Pinocchio's metamorphosis into human form. Pinenut clearly realises that he has been manipulated after the Fairy had used every trick, from psychological blackmail to sexual allurement, on him. Collodi's text forms part of Pinenut's memories, so he refers to the role of the Fairy both in Collodi's and in Coover's text, where his adventures continue.

The sexual motivation that is implied in the confrontation scene and which confirms Pinocchio's oedipal relationship with his Fairy mother, is also closely linked to the implicit (in Collodi) and explicit (in Coover and Charyn) references to Pinocchio's nose as penis. Before I refer to the ways in which and reasons why the two authors emphasise this element, it is worth mentioning that, as with the dark nature of the Blue Fairy, it is already present in Collodi's text. The sexual reference to the male member in Pinocchio's elongating nose is an allusion that Collodi purposefully and satirically included in his picaresque coming-of-age tale. In addition, it is the story of an early-adolescent boy who, for the first time, encounters a woman and explores his sexual desire towards her. This is consistent with Pinocchio's character throughout the text: it is during early adolescence that children become more restless and independent from their parents; they are eager to try things on their own and are frequently overconfident, misjudging or ignoring possible dangers, as Pinocchio does throughout the book. Pinocchio therefore shows the easily recognisable behaviour of a prepubescent/ early-adolescent boy.

If we consider *La storia di un burattino,* the first part of *Pinocchio,* as the original tale that Collodi had in mind (up to Chapter xv, finishing with Pinocchio's hanging on the Great Oak), there are only two occasions when Pinocchio's nose grows and neither of them is associated with lying. The first one is when Geppetto carves him, and the second is when he is frustrated by the optical illusion of the painted kettle when he is very hungry. On both occasions his nose grows, but not out of proportion. In fact, there is an instance in Chapter VII when Pinocchio lies that the cat ate his feet, yet his nose does not grow.

When Collodi decided to continue the story of Pinocchio and revive the dead puppet, he expanded on themes that he had already introduced in the first part of the story, such as Pinocchio's disobedience and his growing nose. So when Pinocchio has his first encounter with an adult female character, his nose grows disproportionately for the first time in the narrative. We can assume that the sexual connotation of the nose was clear to Collodi for several reasons. First of all, the attribution of one's character traits to physiognomic characteristics was very popular during the eighteenth and nineteenth centuries and there were extended theories as to which part of one's physical appearance corresponded to which trait. The nose had been a metaphor for the penis for many centuries. Giambattista della Porta wrote an encyclopaedia on physiognomy, *De humana physiognomonia* [On Human Physiognomy] (1586), and an Italian translation was published in 1644. He writes that the nose corresponds to the penis and the nostrils to the testicles.[1] This assumption dates back to Ovid, who had the nickname 'Naso'. Sander Gilman refers to it as follows:

> It was not merely that in turn-of-the-century Europe there was an association between the genitalia and the nose; there was, and had long been, a direct relationship drawn in popular and medical thought between the size of the nose and that of the penis. Ovid wrote: 'Noscitur ex naso quanta sit hasta viro'.[2]

However, Don Harrán notes that while this is a popular attribution to Ovid because of his nickname, it is not one that can be traced to his writings.[3] Regardless of the phrase's origin, what is interesting here is that Collodi could have been exposed to such information and therefore his puppet with the big nose and with its numerous transformations could be an indirect tribute to Ovid 'Naso' and his *Metamorphoses*. It is, in fact, almost impossible for Collodi not to have been exposed to such details, including physiognomy and popular references, as the nose was one of his interests as an author: the same year that the first instalments of *Storia di un Burattino* appeared in the children's magazine *Giornale per i bambini*, he published a collection of stories entitled *Occhi e nasi* [Eyes and Noses].[4] The collection of stories does not refer explicitly to eyes and noses. The phrase is used to broadly mean 'bits and pieces'. Collodi wrote an introductory note to explain his choice of words for the title, suggesting that the stories are left open ended, the details to be filled in by the readers' imaginations. However, the fact that he considers the eyes and the nose the most important parts of the face, enough to give a first description of one's character or, in this case, of a story, is reflecting his keen interest in the topic.

Collodi was very conscious of linguistic idioms and expressions as he had previously written educational books. In the second part of *Pinocchio*, he uses two Italian proverbs about lying and explores them visually through Pinocchio's story. This indicates both an instructive and a playful approach to language. When Pinocchio lies to the Fairy and his nose grows disproportionately, she tells him, with reference to these two proverbs: 'Lies, my dear boy, are quickly discovered;

because there are two kinds. There are lies with short legs, and lies with long noses. Yours is clearly of the long-nosed variety' (*AP*, p. 211). The first proverb is 'Le bugie hanno le gambe corte' [Lies have short legs]; even though metaphorically this means that one cannot go too far when lying or one will be discovered, it alludes visually to Pinocchio's feet being burned in the first part of the story. The second proverb is 'La bugia corre su pel naso' [The lie runs up your nose]. Both proverbs are mentioned in *Dizionario delle origini, invenzioni e scoperte*, an Italian dictionary of 1828, so both were already in use in Collodi's time.[5] The proverb about the nose is another visual reference already present in the first part of the story, as mentioned earlier. Collodi chooses the imagery of the growing nose to continue the story as it offers the comical elements that his young readers will enjoy and the sexual connotations to amuse his older audiences. The *Dizionario* explains that this second proverb refers to the blushing that occurs when someone is lying, and of course blushing has other causes too, such as shame or sexual arousal.

Furthermore, it was common in Collodi's time to attribute sexual connotations to the nose in literature. One such example is Laurence Sterne's *The Life and Opinions of Tristram Shandy, Gentleman*. The theme of the protagonist's nose in relation to his penis was portrayed in illustrations and on covers of the book, the most famous being the frontispiece of a Dutch edition of 1771 that portrays Tristram Shandy with a penis for a nose.[6] Sterne's book was first translated into Italian in 1842.[7] And it is very likely that Collodi had access to the story, as is apparent from Sterne's influence on Collodi's style, about which Marcheschi writes: 'L'umorismo collodiano in genere privilegia la libera imitazione degli esiti parodici, ironici, satirici dello Sterne, non esclusa la giocosa malizia delle allusioni sessuali' [Generally speaking, Collodi's humour freely draws on Sterne's parodic, ironic and satirical style, without excluding the playful malice of sexual innuendos].[8] Given Collodi's knowledge of Sterne's work and the popularity of physiognomy during his time, it is highly likely that Collodi was perfectly familiar with the sexual connotation of the nose.

As mentioned earlier, Pacchioni argues that Collodi was inspired by the plays of the *commedia dell'arte* for the character of Pinocchio. In particular, he refers to plays in which Burattino was cheated by two thieves — this similarity with *Pinocchio* being as telling as that of the title of the play *Le disgrazie di Burattino* [The Misfortunes of Burattino] by Francesco Gattici.[9] Apart from that, Burattino was a type of Zani, as Flaminio Scala points out, and one of their characteristics was that 'they were [...] obsessively hungry', a vivid image of how Pinocchio appears in Collodi's text.[10] Finally, apart from the plays Pacchioni mentions, in *La fortunata Isabella*, one of Scala's plays, Burattino is Isabella's servant.[11] When he thinks she has been abducted, he weeps over her loss, only for it to be revealed later that she was safe after all, a narrative strongly reminiscent of Pinocchio's lament over the Fairy's grave. Besides, the title of the first part of Collodi's story was *Storia di un Burattino*, and it is in this part that Pinocchio is recognised and cheered by his brothers and sisters, Mangiafuoco's marionettes. The recognition refers therefore not only to their wooden nature, but also to their common past as stock characters in the *commedia dell'arte* tradition. Coover emphasises this connection, both by including the marionettes of Mangiafuoco in his retelling and also through the setting and stylistics of his text, with frequent reminders or direct references to settings and situations of the Italian comedic form:

> He hadn't expected to see so many masks this long before Carnival, but he has read about the recent enthusiasm for this ancient custom, and, for all its vulgarity and promiscuous connotations, he is secretly pleased, for it recalls for him quite piercingly that long-ago time of his own beginnings' (*PV*, p. 27).

Even though Collodi drew largely on the *commedia dell'arte*'s 'Burattino' for his character of Pinocchio, the element of his elongating nose is not a feature of the earlier character. As shown previously, Collodi added this as a response to Pinocchio's encounter with a woman when he decided to continue the story of Pinocchio and elaborated on themes introduced during the first part of the story. In Coover's text, this is emphasised even more, as is shown by a revisiting of the confrontation scene in *Pinocchio in Venice*:

> He'd been cast up by a storm and was begging at the edge of town when she found him. She offered him a supper of bread, cauliflower, and liquor-filled sweets in exchange for carrying a jug of water home for her. He'd last seen her as a little girl, and moreover presumed her dead, so he didn't recognize this woman, old enough to be his mother, until she took her shawl off and he saw her blue hair. Whereupon he threw himself at her feet and, sobbing uncontrollably, hugged her knees. 'Oh, why can't we go home again, Fairy?' he wept. 'Why can't we go back to the little white house in the woods?' Her knees spread a bit in his impassioned embrace, and the fragrant warmth between them drew him in under her skirts. He wasn't sure he should be in here, but in his simple puppetish way he thought perhaps she didn't notice. He felt terribly sleepy, and yet terribly awake, his eyes open but filled with tears. (*PV*, p. 116)

So far, this remains true to Collodi's original, yet spiced up with Coover's details. However, the following part of the confrontation scene reflects Coover's Freudian interpretation:

> 'Let me tell you a story, my little illiterate woodenknob,' she said above his tented head, 'about the pretty little white house and the nasty little brown house — do you see them there?' He rubbed his eyes and running nose against her stocking tops and peered blearily down her long white thighs. Yes, there was the dense blue forest, there the valley, and there (he drew closer) the little house, just hidden away, more pink than white really, and gleaming like alabaster. But the other — ? 'A little lower...' She pushed on his head, sinking him deeper between the thighs, until he saw it: dark and primitive, more like a cave than a house, a dank and airless place ringed about by indigo weeds, dreary as a tomb. She pushed his nose in it. 'That is the house of laziness and disobedience and vagrancy,' she said. 'Little boys who don't go to school and so can only follow their noses come here, thinking it's the circus, and disappear forever.' He was suffocating and thought he might be disappearing, too. She let him out but, even as he gasped for breath, stuffed his nose into the little white house: 'And here is the house for good little boys who study and work hard and do as they are told. Here, life is rosy and sweet, and they can play in the garden and come and go as they please. Isn't that much better?'

'Yes, Mamma!' he said, and it *was* better, but he was still having trouble breathing. He tried to back out but he was clamped in her thighs. (*PV*, pp. 116–17)

Coover interprets the Fairy's doctrine as one of a heteronormative society that demands its members be functional and rewards production with reproduction, as shown by the reward she promises him if he works hard: the little white house, a metaphor for the vagina. He can have access to it and reproduce only as a hard-working man and not as a puppet. The confrontation scene, portrayed as a sexual encounter, is what instils in Pinocchio the desire for humanity and defines his relationship to the Fairy as one of obedience and reward. Professor Pinenut tries to live by the Fairy's rules all his life and this is what seems to be the cause of his back-to-wood sickness. He forms his theories and writes about them according to the morals and principles that the Fairy has directed.

Pinenut's sexual desire for the Fairy is the driving force behind his decisions and, like the neurosis of his Oedipus complex, it follows him in every step of his life. In the end, the complex is resolved as he succumbs to the Fairy's true nature and she fulfils his Oedipal desires. It is resolved through annihilation, though, as in return Pinenut asks her to undo her magic, as though he had never been transformed into a human. His desire to become human was triggered by his desire for her but now that they can be united anyway, humanity is no longer necessary for Coover's Pinocchio.

Charyn's Pinocchio, on the other hand, does not resolve his Oedipus complex so easily. His neurosis is stronger, as the main manifestation of the Blue Fairy in *Pinocchio's Nose* is his real mother, Bathsheba. The use of his nose as penis is only explored in the parallel story in which Jerome inhabits Pinocchio's body. Brunhilde, the prostitute, who is also Pinocchio's substitute mother, teaches him the function of his nose after she discovers that he has no genitals. She finds out that the sexual function of a penis has been transferred to his nose instead, so she teaches him how to 'tickle' her with it. Even though Jerome fulfils his Oedipal fantasies through Brunhilde, it is Bathsheba's attention that he has never succeeded in earning and her neglect haunts him throughout his life. It is because of her that he invents the story of Pinocchio, the fictional space he disappears into in order to escape from his upsetting reality.

Part II has focused on two postmodern retellings of Pinocchio that deconstruct the Pinocchio myth of becoming by revisiting specific themes already present in Collodi's text and invite a different reading of it. Both protagonists turn from flesh to wood and both narratives expose the true motives behind their original wish for humanity: the Blue Fairy. She is the puppeteer manipulating Pinocchio in both retellings, as well as in Collodi's text, and this part has focused on her in order to explore the various aspects of the desire to become human.

Notes to Chapter 7

1. Giambattista della Porta: 'E degno d'annotarsi esser proportione tra le parti della faccia con quelle di tutto il corpo, e da loro vicendevolmente si corrispondono, ò nella misura, ò nella

quantità, ò ne' tempi. Il naso risponde alla verga, che havendo alcuno lungo, e grosso, outro acuto & gioffo, ò breve, il medesimo si giudica di lui, così le nari rispondono a i testicoli. Nasuti apresso Lampridio si dicono quelli, che più maschi sono' [It is worth noting that there is a proportion between the parts of the face with those of the whole body, and they mutually correspond to each other, either in measure, in quantity, or in age. The nose corresponds to the penis, which some have long, and thick, others pointed or short, and we think the same of them, and so the nostrils correspond to the testicles. Those with big noses, according to Lampridio, are those who are considered to be more masculine]. *Della fisionomia dell'huomo* (Venice: C. Tomasini, 1644), p. 83.

2. Sander Gilman, *The Jew's Body* (Routledge: New York, 1991), p. 188.

3. Don Harrán, 'The Jewish Nose in Early Modern Art and Music', *Renaissance Studies*, 28.1 (2014), 50–70 (p. 59, n. 26).

4. Carlo Collodi, *Occhi e nasi: (ricordi dal vero)* (Florence: F. Paggi, 1881).

5. *Dizionario delle origini, invenzioni e scoperte nelle arti, nelle scienze, nella geografia, nel commercio, nell'agricoltura*, 4 vols (Milan: A. Bonfanti, 1828), I, 469.

6. Laurence Sterne, *The Life and Opinions of Tristram Shandy, Gentleman. Including the Sentimental Journey.* (Amsterdam: printed for P. van Slaukenberg, 1771).

7. For the records of the Italian translation in 1842, see <shorturl.at/enyHo> [accessed 17 October 2021].

8. Marcheschi, 'Introduzione', in Collodi, *Opere*, p. xxii.

9. Francesco Gattici, *Le disgratie di Burattino: commedia ridicolosa, e buffonesca* (Venice: Battista Combi, 1624). Pacchioni argues: 'Oltre alla somiglianza tra i titoli (si provi a sostituire *disgrazie* con *avventure*) e a una certa affinità col legno e con i pesci già presente nel Burattino secentesco, la scena del cesto, considerando le versioni dello Scala e del Gattici, si presenta come evidente archetipo dell'inganno del Gatto e la Volpe ai danni di Pinocchio. Come Burattino, anche Pinocchio è scoraggiato dal lavoro, come Burattino è attratto dalle meraviglie illusorie di un paese di godimenti, sedotto da promesse di amicizia e ricchezza, e alla fine derubato'. [In addition to the similarity between the titles (try to replace misfortunes with adventures) and an affinity with wood and fish already present in the Burattino of the seventeenth century, the scene of the basket, according to Scala's and Gattici's versions, looks like an obvious archetype for the deception of Pinocchio by the Cat and the Fox. Like Burattino, Pinocchio is discouraged from working; like Burattino, he is attracted by the illusory wonders of a land of pleasures, seduced by promises of friendship and wealth, and is eventually robbed]. 'La passione di un Burattino', p. 16.

10. Richard Andrews, 'Introduction', in *The Commedia dell'Arte of Flaminio Scala: A Translation and Analysis of 30 Scenarios*, ed. and trans. by Richard Andrews (Lanham, MD, Toronto & Plymouth: Scarecrow Press, 2008), pp. ix–lvi (p. xxiv).

11. A synopsis of the scenario of Flaminio Scala's *La fortunata Isabella* can be found at <https://sites.google.com/site/italiancommedia/plays-and-scenari/scenari/la-fortunata-isabella> [accessed 21 March 2019].

PART III

❖

Graphic Novel

Posthuman and Postmodern Retellings of the Pinocchio Myth

The first part of this book focused on the character of Pinocchio and the perpetuation of the myth of becoming, examined through the perspective of posthuman retellings of the Pinocchio myth. Part II deconstructed the myth of Pinocchio by inviting a different reading of the original text by Collodi through the examples of two postmodern texts that used autobiographic elements and metafiction extensively. These texts reversed the themes and concepts of the Pinocchio myth by using parody, irony, and the carnivalesque, thus breaking the myth down into its components and challenging it. This part will follow a similar trajectory in exposing the Pinocchio myth. The two case studies I examine are contemporary graphic novels; the focus, therefore, is on how the Pinocchio myth is deconstructed in a different medium from the ones referred to so far and within a more recent socio-political context.

The texts examined are *Pinocchio* by Ausonia, published in Italy and France (2006), and *Pinocchio* by Winshluss (2008). The following chapters place these works within their contexts, both stylistic and theoretical, examining how the authors challenge the norms of their genres, to what extent they use postmodern and posthuman elements, and how this relates to the Pinocchio myth. They then highlight the postmodern elements in both texts and how they both approach Pinocchio's posthumanity. By the end, my analysis will have shown how both texts form a critique of consumerist values and, having deconstructed the myth of becoming, how both are very reluctant to propose solutions, contrary to the optimistic conclusions that were examined in Part I.

This part's retellings are both graphic novels: a medium that combines the two previous media, that of image (in Part I) and of word (in Part II), just as it is a combination of the previous parts' approaches (i.e. posthumanism and postmodernism). The two graphic novels were published two years apart in Italy and France and, as I will show further on, there are many similarities between them, both stylistically and thematically.

Ausonia is the artistic name of Italian cartoonist, illustrator, and painter Francesco Ciampi. *Pinocchio*, his first graphic novel, was nominated for the Premio

Micheluzzi in 2007. He received the Micheluzzi award in 2011 for the third volume of his trilogy *Interni*, to which I refer at the end of Chapter 9. He teaches the art of comics and illustration at the Scuola Internazionale di Comics in Florence. In *Pinocchio* (2006), Pinocchio is an animated bag of meat sewn together by the butcher Geppetto, who is a marionette, as is everyone else in his world. In the same way that Collodi's Pinocchio is extraordinary because he is a live marionette among humans, so Ausonia's Pinocchio is a live, flesh creature among marionettes. His adventures lack the playfulness of Collodi's text, as they are made up of a series of bleak incidents, in which Pinocchio is almost always sexually abused: by Mangiafuoco, by Madame Turchina's brothel customers, and also in prison. In the world of the marionettes, lying is a virtue and truth is abominable. The marionettes are at war with the crickets, who support the truth. By entering and inhabiting a marionette's body, the crickets can win them over to their side and these 'turned' marionettes form the resistance in the war. Pinocchio has been infested by a cricket, too, and this proves to be the cause of his suffering, as is revealed at the end of the novel, when his body is torn into pieces until the cause of his honesty is found.

Winshluss is the artistic name of French comic artist and filmmaker Vincent Paronnaud. Most famous for co-directing *Persepolis* with Marjane Satrapi (a film which won the Prix du Jury at the Cannes festival in 2007), he published *Pinocchio* the following year. This graphic novel was awarded the Fauve d'or prize in 2009 at the prestigious Festival international de la bande dessinée d'Angoulême. Winshluss's *Pinocchio* is the story of a killer robot that Geppetto has invented to sell to the military and become rich. The co-protagonist in the story is a cockroach with the name Jiminy Cafard, who, shortly after Pinocchio comes to life with the help of electricity, takes up residence in some compartment of Pinocchio's metal head. Jiminy, a direct reference to Disney's Jiminy Cricket, is a writer with writer's block and his actions in his new apartment affect Pinocchio's actions too. Pinocchio's adventures consist mainly of wanderings and encounters with different characters. His wishes are never expressed and his killer instinct is mostly dormant. At the end of the story, he is adopted by a childless couple.

Pinocchio has appeared in numerous graphic novels internationally. This book, however, focuses on the two aforementioned examples because of their subversive nature and the inclusion of posthuman elements. This part is divided into two chapters. Both chapters deconstruct the Pinocchio myth by subverting expectations or existing values: Chapter 8 focuses on the visual representation of Pinocchio in the two texts, followed by a section dedicated to the theme of Funland. Chapter 9 analyses the role of the cricket.

❖

Challenging the Pinocchio Myth

Pinocchio, Deconstructed

The history of visual representations of Pinocchio is a study of its own that spans countries, time and media. What is relevant to this book is an exploration of the visual techniques that are used in the two case studies in this part, in order to examine how they expose the Pinocchio myth.

Ausonia's Pinocchio starts with a subversion that is both visual and narrative. Visually, the first encounter with Pinocchio on the cover is shocking, as his appearance is the exact opposite of the familiar amiable (if naughty) wooden boy: Ausonia depicts Pinocchio as a frightening monster (see figure 8.1).

The novel's universe consists of marionettes and Pinocchio is a boy made of minced meat sewn into a pig's skin. Pinocchio's posthumanity is shocking both narratively and visually. The cover already suggests that this will be a horror story, yet the reader's expectations are subverted, as the only horrors that Pinocchio faces are those of humanity and of everyday life. This is shown early on in the narrative when Pinocchio is called to give evidence before a court. He looks very different from the previous panels in the book, as can be seen by comparing figures 8.2 and 8.3 with figure 8.4.

When asked by the judge what has happened to his body, Pinocchio answers, 'Life, your Honour'. The consequences of ageing on his fleshy body have a shocking effect on the marionettes, who call him 'monster', and on the reader as well. The visual effect of the drawings is disquieting, as they allude to the theme of ageing, as was discussed in Part II. The resemblance of Pinocchio's body to a human one is very strong and, as Geppetto uses a saw to cut off Pinocchio's maggot-infested legs (figure 8.3), this resemblance enhances the impression of abuse rather than parental care. This is significant, as it is only the first of a series of abuses that Pinocchio suffers and which manifest themselves visually on his ageing body which strongly resembles an ageing human body (figure 8.4).

The image of his maggot-infested legs is additionally shocking in its allusion to a dead, decomposing human body. On the inside cover, there is a close-up illustration of minced meat, which resembles maggots. This dual visual reference points to the nature of Pinocchio's body, which is later explained in Ausonia's text,

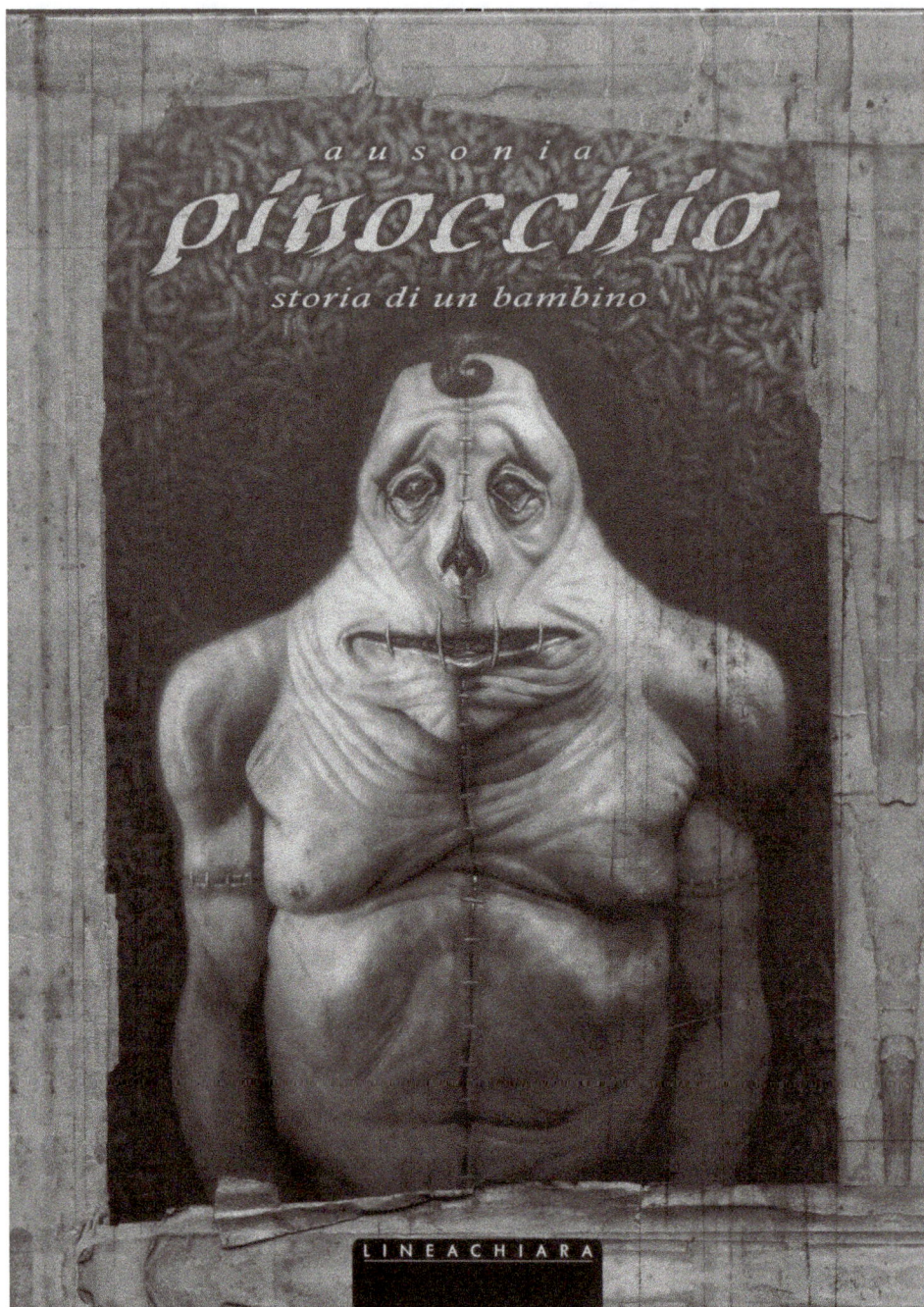

FIG. 8.1. Ausonia, *Pinocchio* (Trent: Lineachiara, 2014),
front cover © 2014 Lineachiara.[1]

Fig. 8.2. Ausonia, *Pinocchio* (Trent: Lineachiara, 2014), p. 11. © 2014 Lineachiara.

Fig. 8.3. Ausonia, *Pinocchio* (Trent: Lineachiara, 2014), p. 12. © 2014 Lineachiara.

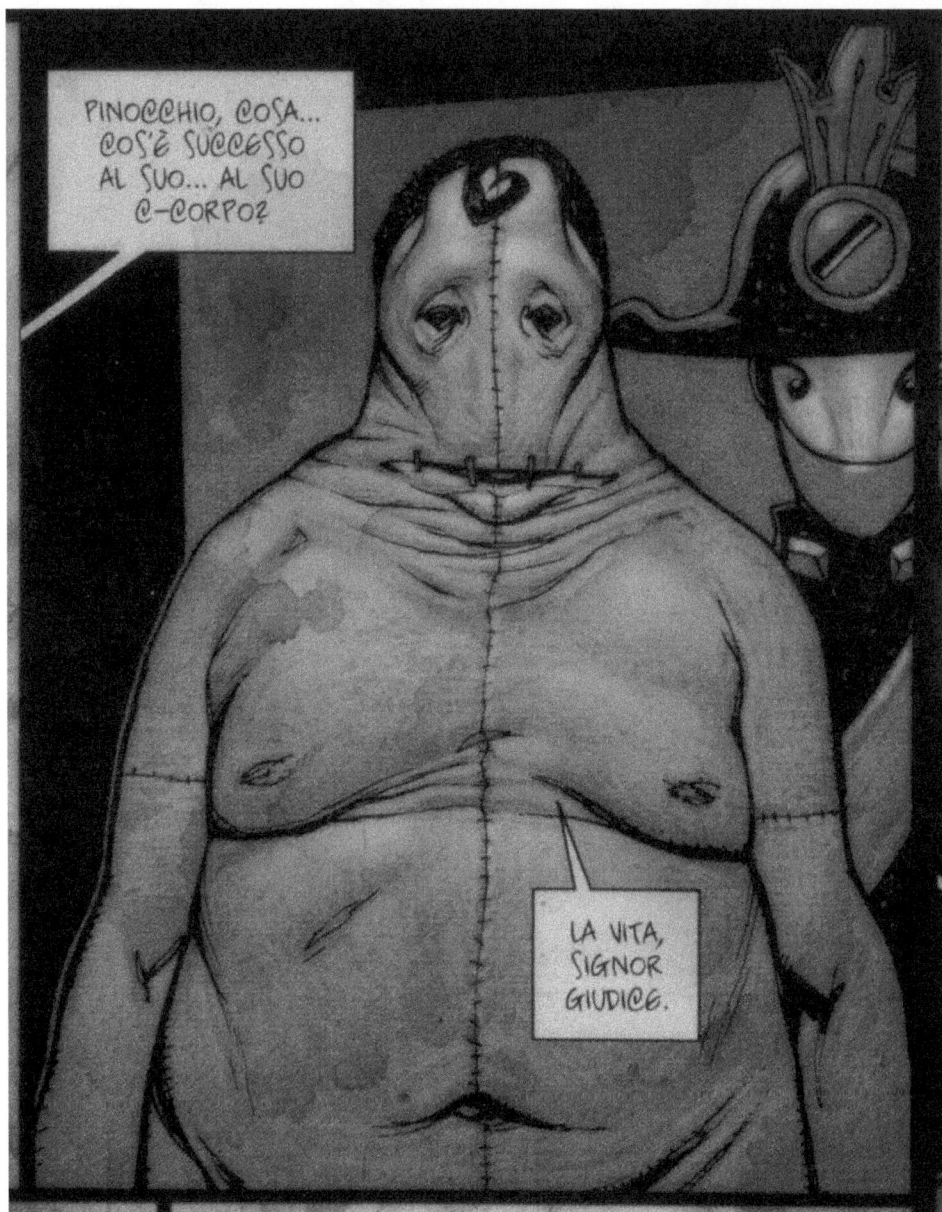

FIG. 8.4. Ausonia, *Pinocchio* (Trent: Lineachiara, 2014), p. 16. © 2014 Lineachiara.

and at the same time to human mortality, through the reference to a decomposing body. Finally, Ausonia's portrayal of Pinocchio makes reference to Frankenstein's creature as well, especially since the marionettes explicitly call him 'monster', as the creature is popularly called in *Frankenstein* — an echo of Pinocchio's inherent relationship with Frankenstein's creature through the animate/ inanimate archetype connection, as described in Part I.

The second subversion that occurs in Ausonia's narrative is that Pinocchio's nose grows when he is telling the truth, which is the exact opposite of what happens in Collodi's text. As the narrative continues, one element after another of the original text is reversed, subverted, or distorted. Mangiafuoco is not hungry for food but for sex. He does not give Pinocchio the golden coins out of charity, but as payment after he has raped him. The Blue Fairy, Madame Turchina, is a brothel owner; she saves Pinocchio only to force him into her employment and exploit him. She teaches him how to lie so that his nose does not grow. Even the Italian proverbs that Collodi used in reference to lying are reversed: 'La sera, Madame Turchina, mi insegnava a mentire. Diceva... che nella società di burattini, non avrei fatto molta strada... dicendo sempre la verità' [In the evening Madame Turchina taught me how to lie. She said that in the society of the marionettes I wouldn't get very far by telling the truth].[2] Madame Turchina overworks him in order to make money and improve her body by plastic surgery, as marionettes are willing to pay a lot for a night with a boy made of flesh.

Ausonia uses the fictional world of marionettes as a metaphor to denounce child trafficking and prostitution; and Winshluss, children working in a toy factory to condemn child labour. In Ausonia's story Pinocchio's body very soon starts sagging from the abuse, a metaphor that somatises the effects of abuse in a child's psyche. After the doctors admit that they cannot mend him, Madame Turchina throws him out, as he is of no further use to her. Pinocchio's adventures continue after he is imprisoned for telling the truth, as in Collodi's text. Only, in Ausonia's version, his cellmate rapes him and adds to the abuse that Pinocchio has already experienced.

Just as the reader's expectations are reversed by Ausonia's constant subversion of Collodi's original symbolism and narrative, the main postmodern element of Ausonia's text, so is his Pinocchio's posthuman condition reversed. Ausonia's is a different kind of posthumanism from what has been seen so far: Pinocchio has a carnal nature that differentiates him from the world of marionettes; and his values also differ from those of the marionette world — while the marionettes' corrupt and vile society represents the decline of human civilisation, Pinocchio's character and actions are closer to the Enlightenment's values and vision of human nature. By the end of the novel, however, Pinocchio has rejected these values, and his humanity along with them. In that sense, he becomes post-human, but in a negative way, as he discards the good side of his humanity: the part of himself that he discards is in accordance with the goal that Collodi's Pinocchio is trying to achieve, an idealised version of humanity, in which truth and hard work conquer all.

Winshluss's *Pinocchio* is a highly intertextual and 'intervisual' graphic novel. In order to achieve the pleasure of the text in Barthes's sense, the reader has to be constantly aware of the multiple references (mostly visual but also textual) on which the story is built, quite like Robert Coover's *Pinocchio in Venice* as discussed in Part II.[3] It is the intertextuality and self-consciousness of Winshluss's *Pinocchio*, which in its turn 'produces a self-conscious reading', that makes it a postmodern text.[4]

The text consists of different storylines, which are distinguished by different drawing styles varying from soft pastels to dark colours or black and white ink, but all the stories are intertwined and linked to the single narrative that portrays Pinocchio's world. Laurence Grove's description of the cover (figure 8.5) gives a very representative view of the whole work:

> At first glance the book has the trappings of a childhood favourite: a large volume, sturdily bound, with a front cover whose bright colours, silver sparkle and plethora of details dance around the central Pinocchio figure. It is the closer look that underlines the disturbing details: Pinocchio is a confused robot whose name is aflame, he is surrounded by roses, but roses with prominent thorns, with a background of machinery that suggests inevitability and from whose cogs rise wailing ghosts. Further motifs point to the fickleness of fate, be it the double one on the dice, the sword marked 'deus ex machina' (next to dollar-laden flowers), or the plummeting eight-balls. This is no book for children.[5]

Grove's description is a good example of the art of deduction in which the reader is invited to participate in the medium of graphic novels. Winshluss's *Pinocchio* is even more inviting in terms of reader participation, since it has almost no text at all: the only storylines with speech bubbles are those of Jiminy Cafard, Pinocchio's conscience, and Police Inspector Javer talking to his cat. Since the rest of the book has no speech bubbles, it is left to the reader to guess or decide what really happens. What the characters may be saying, as well as what Pinocchio and the rest may be thinking or feeling, is based on the reader's perception of the visual narration. As Amélie Junqua emphasises, 'when the narrative thread is yielded to the reader, the mute graphic story enables a process of appropriation — a simultaneous creation and translation — that opens up the reader's imagination to the extent that several levels of interpretation may coexist'.[6] Comics traditionally require the reader's participation in the narrative process, as the reader can always imagine in his/her own way what happens between the gutters.[7] In this case, the reader's participation is intensified by the absence of textual narrative.

Winshluss follows both Collodi's text and Disney's film adaptation. He states on the first page: 'L'histoire qui suit est très librement adaptée du roman éponyme de Carlo Collodi' [The following story is very freely adapted from the eponymous novel by Carlo Collodi]; but he also mentions in an interview that he is strongly influenced by Disney, as *Pinocchio* was one of the first films he saw as a child and it fascinated him.[8] The main twist he gives to the Pinocchio myth involves questioning Pinocchio's desire to become real. Collodi and Disney deal quite differently with this topic. I analysed Collodi's approach in Part II, in which the ambiguous role of the Blue Fairy was also discussed. For Disney, American audiences were not ready to face the double nature of the female character that Collodi illustrated; therefore, the Fairy with the blue hair becomes the Blue Fairy, who is the personification of a star. The little girl no longer exists, the Fairy is only a protector, educator, and

FIG. 8.5. Winshluss, *Pinocchio* (Albi: Les Requins Marteaux, 2008), cover.
© 2008 Les Requins Marteaux.

helper, and a very stereotypically blonde one at that. In Disney, Pinocchio owes his existence to Geppetto's 'wish upon a star' to have a child. That is how the Blue Star-Fairy makes the wooden, lifeless puppet alive and informs him that if he behaves well, he will become real. Thus, this becomes Pinocchio's purpose from the beginning of the story, unlike what happens in Collodi's text.

With his ambiguous silence, Winshluss's robot Pinocchio prompts a further rereading of Collodi's original text, with a focus on what would have happened had the Blue Fairy not existed. Indeed, the absence of the Fairy in Winshluss's text is very telling. Pinocchio's absence of will and stoic *apatheia* and acceptance of whatever occurs to him is contrasted with the Aristotelian thought of personal development that leads to *eudaimonia*, as presented in Collodi's text.[9] Winshluss's Pinocchio has reached freedom by eradicating desire, indifferent to the *eudaimonia* that Collodi's Pinocchio reaches when he is able to look at the wooden puppet that used to be himself and completely renounce that part of his past. Interestingly enough, as was shown in Part I, this kind of statement is made by a robot, which falls into the same category as cyborgs and clones and therefore signifies human progress and self-enhancement; and is indeed an inversion of the preconceptions the reader would have about Pinocchio, or to use Barthes's term of 'mythology', his meaning is in contrast to itself.[10]

In *Mythologies*, Barthes explains that words are not 'innocent' of meaning: though the relationship between the signifier and the signified in a linguistic unit of signification is arbitrary, this is not the case at a semiotic level. Words are charged with ideological connotations and meaning; the normalisation of this process in everyday discourse is what creates semiological and ideological myths and mythologies. Myths become attached to words or images and are therefore part of the cultural discourse. As Andrew Leak explains:

> The function of myth (as a semiological system) is to impose cultural messages under a cover, or alibi, of naturalness. [...] This, of course, is precisely what ideology seeks to accomplish, and myth is therefore the perfect instrument for the job.[11]

Winshluss tackles ideology by recreating a Pinocchio who is focused on *being* rather than *becoming*. Becoming is part of the capitalist ideology and petit bourgeois 'dream' of personal (and consequently social) transformation of the individual, an illusion that Winshluss rejects. As he explains in an interview:

> Pinocchio a une action réduite, c'est le reste de la société qu'on voit en train de merder à cause du fric, du pouvoir, du cul. Mais, attention, si c'est une fable morale, je ne suis absolument pas moraliste. J'expose ma vision du monde, mais je n'ai pas non plus de solution.[12]

> [Pinocchio's effect is limited. It is the rest of society that is fucking up for money, power, sex. But beware: this might be a moral story, but don't expect me to be a moralist. I show the way I see the world, but I don't have a solution.]

As he states, it is very important for him to show how he sees contemporary society; it is important to him that people are aware and do not conform to whatever is presented as normal. As he remarks elsewhere, 'Baudrillard voyait naître cette société qu'il critiquait. Moi, je suis né dedans: elle est plus dure à démonter quand on en voit le côté ludique' [Baudrillard witnessed the birth of the society he criticised. But I was born into it: it is more difficult to dismantle when you see its fun side].[13]

Winshluss deconstructs certain myths by reversing the reader's expectations, as we have seen, and in so doing questions the discourse that reflects current ideology. This is what has formed the metalanguage of the different signs, whether they are linguistic or visual. In Pinocchio's example, the signified [non-human child with mechanical body who wants to become real] reinforces the current ideology of the 'necessity' of social mobility — improving oneself and moving upwards in terms of class or financial status. This semantic field could represent anyone, child or adult. Collodi's Pinocchio is made to perform as a puppet and bring Geppetto money; when later he awakens Geppetto's fatherly instincts, he is urged to go to school and even to work in order to be rewarded with the desired change in himself, an imposed desire, as I explained earlier. Winshluss's text reminds us that the educational system aims, among other things, to produce a functional labour force that will secure future pensions and the sustainability of the current ideology.[14] Consequently, certain things *are* expected from children and, in order for this to happen, society infiltrates them with wishes and desires that are presented as though they were their own (capitalist dreams of wealth, success, and social mobility). In Winshluss's work, Pinocchio is made to earn Geppetto money as a killer robot which will be sold to the military. Instead of following the expected narrative of the puppet/ robot's efforts to become something else, Winshluss suggests that all Pinocchio desires is to be left alone. He is not interested in the expectations of his maker: this is in opposition to the previous Pinocchios (those of Collodi and Disney) who struggled with the conflict between their own nature and social demands until they became 'domesticated', that is turned into 'real' simulacra — 'puppets' with invisible strings controlled by society and its demands. Roberto Benigni's film adaptation of the Collodian text portrays this very successfully, as we see Pinocchio, having surrendered himself to the social demands of work, being exploited by his father, who drinks all the milk Pinocchio brings and leaves nothing for Pinocchio, urging him to work all night, until he reaches a state of complete exhaustion.[15] It is no coincidence that the film was a big commercial failure in the US, as American viewers, too familiar with and attached to the Disney version, failed to understand and appreciate the references to Collodi in Benigni's adaptation. Moreover, as Cristina Bacchilega points out, they would not have been familiar with the other Italian film adaptations of Pinocchio that Benigni's film refers to.[16]

Snow White and the Seven Dwarfs

Another example of the deconstruction of a unit of signification is Winshluss's retelling of Snow White, in one of the storylines that are intertwined with the main narrative line of Pinocchio. After being persecuted by the seven perverse dwarfs (in Winshluss's retelling) and falling off a cliff in order to escape, Snow White ends up at the bottom of a river and is carried away unconscious by the stream, through a barrier towards the sea. A woman who has been introduced earlier in the story is surfing on the coast when she notices Snow White's unconscious body; she then swims to her and saves her. On the beach, she gives first aid and Snow White comes round. Back at her flat, the woman is taking care of Snow White when she notices a scar, a sign of her earlier abuse by the dwarfs; she points at it and her hand slips towards her breast. The two women start kissing and then passionately make love. While the reader might expect Snow White to be saved by the prince, she is instead rescued by a woman with whom she falls in love.

In Winshluss's text, the mythologised signs under consideration here are not only linguistic or visual, but also narrative, as well as a combination of the three, as is evident in the above example. Words, images, and narratives are all charged with ideological connotations often produced or reproduced by the cultural industry and the media. The example of the seven dwarfs is very significant. In the chapter 'Les Sept Salopards dans "Jingle Balls"', the seven dwarfs miss Snow White after her escape and watch videos of the 'good old days', when they gang raped her while she was lying comatose in her glass coffin. To cure their nostalgia they capture a pizza delivery girl, dress her in Snow White's clothes and put her in the glass coffin. When Inspector Bob Javer arrives to arrest them, he finds them naked as they have been torturing her for some time. Visually, they are not the cute Disney dwarfs one would expect in a fairy tale — quite the opposite, as this is not a fairy tale any more. Winshluss calls them the 'sept salopards' [seven bastards]. Gone are Disney's seven amiable dwarfs who live in the forest and help Snow White, replaced by Winshluss's seven perverse dwarfs who live in the forest and abuse Snow White and others. By reversing the metalanguage of Barthes's mythological signification, Winshluss invites the reader to question any concept that reflects the dominant ideology, such as the Disneyfied version of the world that does not allow space for social critique. In short, in the original tale of Snow White the refuge in the seven dwarfs' house symbolises the pre-adolescent stage of innocence that protects Snow White from the dangers of her awakening womanhood. The dwarfs in their anonymity are reminiscent of children before they discover their individuality: 'Dwarfs in symbology represent the underdeveloped and the unformed. They are pre-adolescent and not developed sexually. They live an immature and pre-individualistic form of existence that Snow White must transcend'.[17] This symbolism is abandoned by Disney, who gives a strong individual personality to each dwarf, but in this visual representation of amiable little bearded dwarfs, something does not fit: the possible allusion to them being children has gone and Snow White lives in a house with seven men, no matter that they are small in size. It is rather difficult to place in context a story where a woman lives in a house with seven single men, whom she

FIG. 8.6. Winshluss, *Pinocchio* (Albi: Les Requins Marteaux, 2008), p. 45.
© 2008 Les Requins Marteaux.

takes care of, and with no sexuality involved.[18] Winshluss's version of a woman being captured by seven perverse men is perhaps more realistic, even though it might destroy the Disney dream. In Bill Willingham's *Fables*, a series of graphic novels in which fairy-tale characters are reimagined, Snow White has also been abused by the seven dwarfs and she takes revenge by killing them one by one.[19] Pinocchio is one of the fairy-tale characters in *Fables*, too; here, however, Geppetto has a more prominent role than Pinocchio, as he creates an army of wooden soldiers to take over the world. As explained in the Introduction, Pinocchio's inherent relationship to fairy tales is frequently reflected in its retellings, both traditional and postmodern. In Winshluss's postmodern text Pinocchio's wanderings also allude to another postmodern Pinocchio amidst fairy-tale characters, Luigi Malerba's *Pinocchio con gli stivali* [Pinocchio-in-Boots].[20] Malerba's text of 1977, though, is an early questioning of the form of the fairy-tale genre, while Winshluss's focus is on questioning consumerist values and the Establishment.

Another example of the visual and narrative deconstruction of familiar units of signification is Winshluss's depiction of the Disney-like animals that watch what is happening in the dwarfs' house. In *Snow White and the Seven Dwarfs*, Disney introduced the element of cute talking animals that help the hero or the princess, a typical characteristic throughout Disney's animated films ever since.[21] Winshluss places the easily-recognisable animals from the Disney films, such as the deer, the birds, the rabbit, the owl, etc., in the role of spectators. The first time they appear

FIG. 8.7. Winshluss, 'Les Sept Salopards dans Jingle Balls',
in *Pinocchio* (Albi: Les Requins Marteaux, 2008), p. 112. © 2008 Les Requins Marteaux.

in the narrative, they watch shocked through the window the open-heart surgery that the dwarfs perform on Snow White in order to revive her — the owl vomits because of the horrifying spectacle (figure 8.6). But when the dwarfs torture the pizza delivery girl, the animals watch again through the window, completely absorbed; and when Inspector Javer arrives and arrests the dwarfs, the animals are portrayed with an irritated expression, as if their late-night show has been interrupted. Though they do not sympathise with the dwarfs and do not intervene by helping either the dwarfs or the girls, they seem to enjoy watching the girls' torture. Whether they do enjoy what they see or not, they are certainly addicted to watching it, an allusion to the culture of spectacle and violence offered daily by the modern media (figure 8.7). Despite its comical and satirical nature, Winshluss's style is fiercely critical: it forces its readers to consider whether they are spectators of the violence that surrounds them and to what extent their passivity makes them complicit.

These animals are an example of Winshluss's visual intertextuality and self-referentiality. They first appear in his work *Mr Ferraille*, a compilation of stories about a robot that corrupts everyone he meets with the vices of contemporary consumerist culture in their worst possible form.[22] The animals are a direct reference to the robot, as they appear on the front and back covers of the book. This links Pinocchio with Mr Ferraille in different ways, as I will show later.

Mr Ferraille is Winshluss's response to the superhero comics genre, replicating some of its elements and mocking it at the same time: instead of saving the world, Mr Ferraille is a super robot who encourages violence and has no moral boundaries. He is an opportunist, co-operating with anyone, such as Hitler and the USSR, according to the time period in question. He personifies the amorality of consumerism and capitalist values, having a direct influence on the individual by addressing the base needs which respond to the id's desire for instant gratification.

On the front cover (figure 8.8), Mr Ferraille arrives in the animals' idyllic world, as the colours and drawing denote. He is talking them into selling their land to him in return for whatever he advertises to them (this is left to the reader's interpretation). Then afterwards, in order for them to be able to stay there, the animals have to work in the worst conditions while Mr Ferraille becomes richer (figure 8.9). Some of the animals have turned to alcoholism and prostitution, as shown on the back cover. The colours are dark, the sky and the lake look polluted, and the innocent Disney animals have turned into thirsty consumers of visual violence. Although Winshluss quite accurately pointed out that he does not provide solutions, he does expose, in vivid colours, the malaise of contemporary culture.

Pinocchio has many elements in common with *Mr Ferraille*: the social critique, the sarcasm, even narrative elements that are revisited and explored further, such as Pinocchio's conscience as a cockroach, which was first introduced in *Mr Ferraille* and which I will analyse in the next chapter.

It is noteworthy that Winshluss links the fairy tale of Snow White to Pinocchio, given that Disney's first animated film was *Snow White and the Seven Dwarfs* in 1937, followed by *Pinocchio* three years later. Filmation Studios retold Pinocchio's story in *Pinocchio and the Emperor of the Night* in 1987, and in 1993 they did the same with the tale of Snow White in *Happily Ever After*, both retellings focusing on what happens after the ending of the stories as we know them from Disney.[23] There is therefore already a tradition of retellings of these two tales, and Winshluss adds to this tradition. There is also a visual link between Snow White and Pinocchio, as the long scar that sews her body together in the middle is reminiscent of the patches all over Pinocchio's body, which link his metallic parts together.

Moreover, Winshluss's Snow White refers visually to Betty Boop, a cartoon character created by Dave Fleischer who, together with his brother Max (Fleischer Studios), was Disney's main competitor. Fleischer's *Snow-White* (1933) was the first animated film adaptation of the famous fairy tale, featuring Betty Boop.[24] Winshluss's text has many references to this film, both visual and narrative. Fleischer's cartoons had a darker sense of humour than Disney's and this is reflected in Winshluss's style. It is also quite playful, or even farcical, of Winshluss to pay visual tribute to both Disney and Fleischer, the two big competitors, uniting in the same story the 'Disney' animals and Snow-White/ Betty Boop.

The tales of Pinocchio and Snow White are also narratively linked: they are both tales of children leaving childhood and facing the fears of adolescence. As mentioned before, Snow White finds temporary refuge in the dwarfs' house, traditionally a safe place. Ian Robinson suggests that:

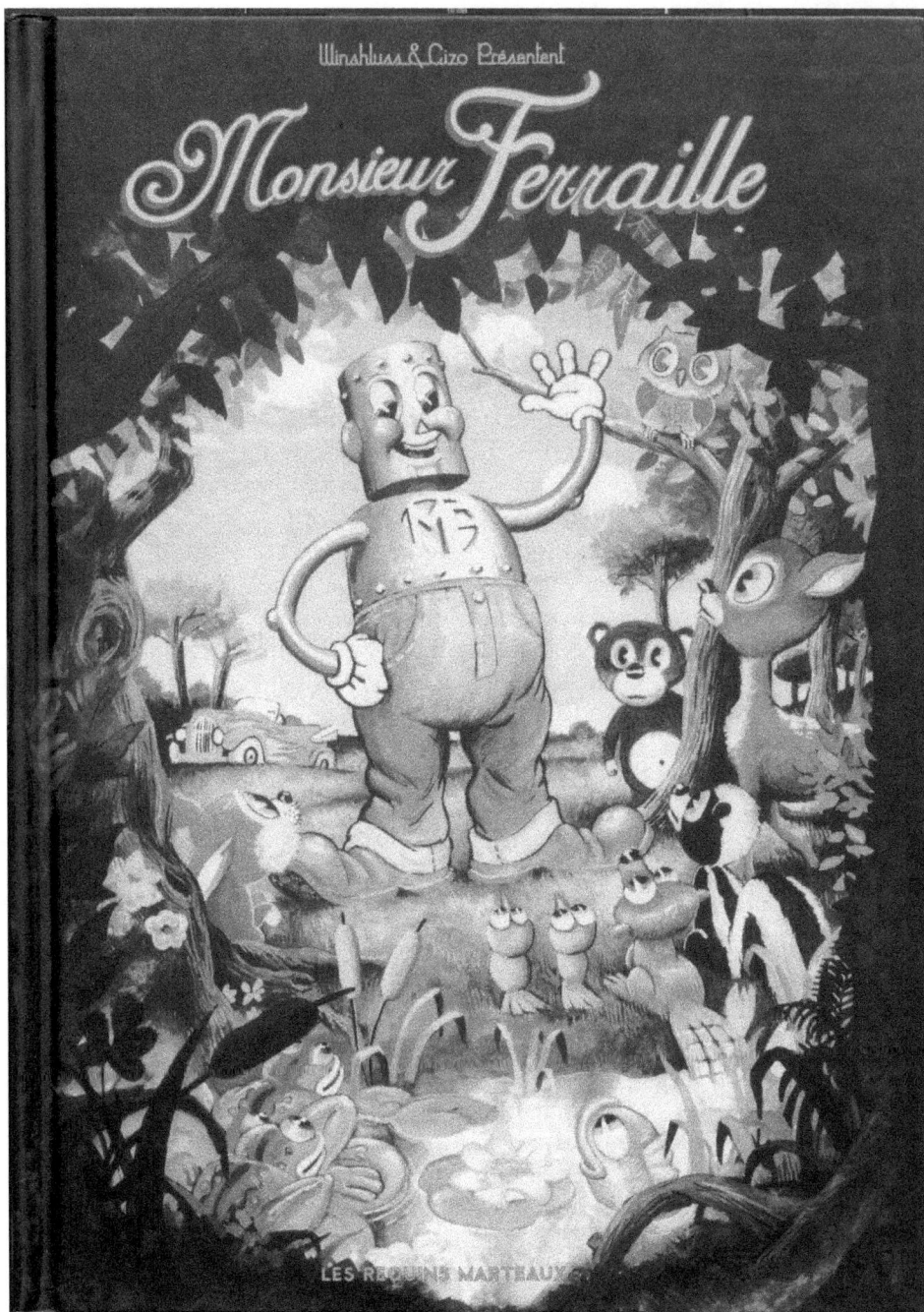

Fig. 8.8. Winshluss, *Monsieur Ferraille* (Albi: Les Requins Marteaux, 2001), front cover.
© 2001 Les Requins Marteaux.

FIG. 8.9. Winshluss, *Monsieur Ferraille* (Albi: Les Requins Marteaux, 2001),
back cover. © 2001 Les Requins Marteaux.

> The period of time Snow White spends with the dwarfs is a period of latency and repressed desire. Snow White learns about the work ethic and is socialised into woman's domestic role, but the question of her womanhood, her sexual desirability as a woman, which was raised by her mother's mirror, has been put aside for a time.[25]

Additionally, Bruno Bettelheim points out that 'the seven dwarfs suggest the seven days of the week — days filled with work. It is this working world Snow White has to make her own if she is to grow up well'.[26] However, not even in the dwarfs' safe house is she able to escape the fears and insecurities of adolescence. And, after being confronted with her budding sexuality (symbols of which are the bodice, the comb, and the apple, the three temptations that the old woman/ evil queen brings to trap her), she falls into a swoon, during which her childhood must die in order for her womanhood to emerge. For this to happen, as Bettelheim's interpretation suggests, male intervention is needed and so (as in other fairy tales such as 'The Sleeping Beauty') a king's son has to kiss her in order to ensure her awakening and rebirth as a woman.[27] Recent fairy-tale revisions have addressed the sexist imagery of classic fairy tales that Disney reproduced. In his version Winshluss makes the prince and his one-dimensional role redundant.

Pinocchio's story has many similarities to that of Snow White. Pinocchio has to learn the work ethic, too, and he is similarly threatened by his budding sexuality. The symbolism of the growing nose that shrinks back to normal with the help of the Fairy is very significant and has been used as a sexual symbol by many, including by Robert Coover and Jerome Charyn, as we saw in Part II. Winshluss also adds to this tradition, at least visually (even though the sexual aspect is not given a central role, as in Coover or Charyn). Pinocchio's desire to become a man awakens when the Fairy becomes a woman. He wants to be able to please her, but becoming a man is as unpleasant and threatening to him as becoming a woman is for Snow White. That is why he decides to escape to the 'Paese dei balocchi' — a children's world — in the same way that Snow White hides in the house of the child-like dwarfs. Finally, Snow White emerges from the glass coffin ready to be a woman and likewise Pinocchio emerges from the whale's belly reborn and ready to be a man. He proves this with the hard work that finally transforms him into a proper boy, which is a necessary step on the path to becoming a man, according to the Fairy's doctrine.

Winshluss deconstructs both stories. In the case of Snow White, the dwarfs' refuge is actually her prison and as she is revived she runs away from the glass coffin and to her (near) death. She is rescued not by a prince, but by a woman, and discovers her sexuality through a woman's love. This is not a children's tale any more, but rather the story of a girl's coming of age, and this Snow White's tale can be seen to allude symbolically to the dangers a woman is exposed to in a patriarchal and misogynist world. As for Pinocchio, Winshluss frustrates the reader's expectations: there is no Fairy who instigates his wish to become a man. There is no desire on Pinocchio's part to change and no transformation in the end. In short, the narrative of the work ethic as a supposed virtue is missing from both retellings. What is more, the two characters have nothing to fear in relation to their inner development: they are both threatened and victimised by the expectations of their surroundings. It is no coincidence that Snow White visually resembles Betty Boop, the 1930s cartoon icon and sex symbol of the Depression Era, suggesting a societal expectation to be feminine and seductive, submissive to male lust, in opposition to her nature. Likewise, Pinocchio is expected to act as a military robot, obeying his owner's every command; this is against his nature, too, as he seems to like company and is playful and peaceful, his only aggressive outbursts being in self-defence, as will be explained later on.

Winshluss illustrates Pinocchio's negation of violence by contrasting him with the setting he finds himself in, which is ultra-violent, a fairy tale not for children, as Grove suggested when describing the cover. Violence is a constant presence in all the storylines. Before Pinocchio is introduced to the reader, Inspector Bob Javer's storyline opens the book, as he plays Russian roulette on his own with his cat, drunk and depressed. The scene ends with the cat's blood everywhere. All the storylines, with the exception of that featuring Pinocchio's foster parents, are full of violence. The dwarfs rape Snow White and the pizza delivery girl; Geppetto cuts his wife into pieces; Stromboli burns child-workers who are not quick enough at their work in his toy factory; Lampwick's father beats his mother; the children of the Enchanted Island undergo a painful transformation into murderous wolf-soldiers; Geppetto is beaten by Bob Javer until the former confesses his guilt — these are just some of the examples of very descriptive and explicit violence in the story. Of course, violence has always been a major element of fairy tales, especially in their oral versions, which were addressed not only to children. Reflecting this tradition, Winshluss weaves his story in a very traditional fairy-tale atmosphere, only this time his aim is to criticise violence and the way it is normalised and consumed as a form of entertainment.

Paese dei Balocchi — Funland

Both Ausonia and Winshluss criticise violence and war and this is evident in their retellings of Collodi's 'Paese dei Balocchi' or 'Funland'. This section focuses on this part of the narration in order to illustrate how the Pinocchio myth is used further to condemn the culture of violence and consumerism.

Before analysing the two versions, it is worth tracing the origins of Collodi's inspiration for the Paese dei Balocchi in *Pinocchio*. In Collodi's text, Pinocchio is talked into escaping to Funland by his friend Lampwick. He is intrigued by Lampwick's descriptions of a place where there are no schools and, instead, children have fun all day long. It appeals to Pinocchio's libidinal nature, which is pleasure-oriented, and which is reflected in his early description of how he would like to spend his life: 'eating, drinking, sleeping, having fun, and living the life of a vagabond from morning to night' (*AP*, p. 109). He is very close to becoming a proper boy, as the Fairy suggests, when he decides to escape to Funland instead; the temptation of instant gratification wins over his motivation to follow the Fairy's rules in order to become like her. However, the paradise of Funland proves to be an illusion, because after five months of fun Pinocchio is transformed into a

donkey and sold to a circus. Apart from its didactic function of giving the message
to young readers that a world without school and work can only lead to illiteracy
and misery, it also has the narrative function of creating suspense by postponing
the resolution of the story. Funland is a significant part of the Pinocchio myth: it
is the last distraction before Pinocchio's transformation into a real boy. If Funland
had not been a trap, Pinocchio would have given up his dream of becoming human.
As a narrative device, it ensures that Pinocchio's adventures are prolonged, but it
is essential that Funland is fake in order for the narrative to reach the climax the
readers have been expecting: Pinocchio's final transformation into a boy. For this
reason, Funland appears frequently in retellings of Collodi's text.

Collodi was inspired to create this fake utopia by the legend of the Land of
Cockaigne, as is evident in his choice of words to describe it: 'questa bella cuccagna
di balocarsi e di divertirsi le giornate intere' [this wonderful life of ease passed in
fun and games all day long] (AP, p. 370). The legend of this land is first encountered
in written form in an Irish manuscript from around 1330 in the poem 'The Land
of Cokaygne', which speaks of a land with an abundance of food, where the geese
fly already cooked and ready to eat and there are rivers of milk and honey.[28] There
are no rules or restrictions and sexuality is overabundant, too. This myth was very
popular during the Renaissance and beyond but, as Denis Rohrer suggests, it was
appropriated by seventeenth-century 'moralists and pedagogues of the bourgeoisie,
making it into a children's story condemning gluttony and laziness'.[29] In their
retellings, the carnival context and topsy-turvy elements of the original text were
reversed and the element of danger incorporated in the story. An example of such
an appropriation is in the fairy tale of Hansel and Gretel, in which the gingerbread
house that alludes to the descriptions of Cockaigne is in fact the house of a cannibal
witch. As emphasised in the Introduction, Collodi was very familiar with the genre
of fairy tales and his Paese dei Balocchi is another illustration of this.

In Ausonia's text, the Paese dei Balocchi is a utopian place that remains untouched
by the war between the marionettes and the crickets. In the midst of war, Pinocchio
finds solace there, together with his friend Lucignolo. They live there happily for
some time. Pinocchio describes it as a beautiful place, as the marionette children
living there are 'not yet corrupted by existence'.[30] However, Lucignolo reveals to
him that she is Lucy, a girl who has been exploited by Madame Turchina. She
escaped and joined the resistance and her mission is to spread thousands of cricket
eggs in the Paese dei Balocchi. However, before she can complete her mission,
she is killed by the authorities and Pinocchio is arrested; this is how he ends up in
prison and in the court, where he narrates his story. This subversion of Lampwick's
character reflects Ausonia's critique of the war. In his text, Funland is untouched
and still utopian. Lucy personifies the danger of Funland's corruption and the
spreading of the war. Even though she fights for the truth, she encapsulates the
danger for this utopian place.

When asked about the war between the marionettes and the crickets, Ausonia
explained that the war in Iraq had influenced him.[31] Lucy functions as a reminder
of the events of the Iraq war. In the name of truth and goodness, she is ready to

sacrifice the peace and happiness of a still-utopian Paese dei Balocchi. Ausonia criticises the position of the Western allies who committed atrocities, hiding behind the excuse that they were fighting for a good cause. His criticism is further intensified by presenting Funland as an ideal place, corrupted from the outside. Unlike Collodi's text and most of its retellings, he does not present Cockaigne as a utopian place that conceals a trap. The threat to this utopia is the will to defend the truth, the side of good in the war between good and evil. He therefore suggests that independently of the reason behind it, any act of war is wrong and to be condemned.

Winshluss's Pinocchio does not choose to go to Funland or The Enchanted Island, as it is called. He finds himself in a zeppelin heading that way; here for the first time he meets Lampwick, a street urchin who had escaped from youth prison. Lampwick shows Pinocchio a brochure for The Enchanted Island where a world of fun and amusement for children is advertised. However, when they reach the island, this has all gone: the sweets are rotten and full of worms, the toys destroyed, and children wander around starving and miserable. A military regime has taken over and the cargo that the zeppelin transported to the island consisted of guns. Posters are seen around with the symbol of two crossed candy canes, a reference to the crossed claw-hammers symbol and therefore alluding to fascism.[32] An uprising follows, led by the man who used to be the clown of the circus. Since this place is without context, it can be considered as a critique of any type of dictatorship and military violence. In a sequence reminiscent of another fairy tale, Winshluss portrays the Clown's general playing the clarinet like a Pied Piper luring the children into the circus tent. The Clown sings and his song has the power to transform the children into violent wolves that he will later use as soldiers to take power from the King. The scene alludes to both the Collodian transformation of the children into donkeys and also, in the brutal way this happens, to the films *Pinocchio and the Emperor of the Night* and *Pinocchio 3000* (mentioned in the Introduction) and, in particular, to Puppetino turning children into puppets with his horrible music.[33]

Pinocchio, however, is the only child who is not transformed, another illustration of his lack of will and purpose. His general *apatheia*, described earlier, seems to protect him from the Clown's spell. Pinocchio is hung from a huge candy cane, one among many which decorate the streets of the Enchanted Island, while the wolf-children army dethrones the King, who is replaced by the Clown. Pinocchio hangs from the candy cane for a long time, until the rope holding him breaks. At this point, the Clown has been dethroned by another rebellion. This passage of time, as one dictatorship follows another, highlights the purposelessness of war. Both Ausonia's and Winshluss's retellings of the Paese dei Balocchi subvert the reader's expectations by presenting these places as destroyed by war. In Ausonia the war reaches Funland in the middle of the narration, but in Winshluss, the reader never sees Funland in its original form. It is already the ghost of a formerly happy place, infected by war and misery.

Collodi's imaginary Paese dei Balocchi has been a source of inspiration for many contemporary artists, even outside the context of the Pinocchio myth. One

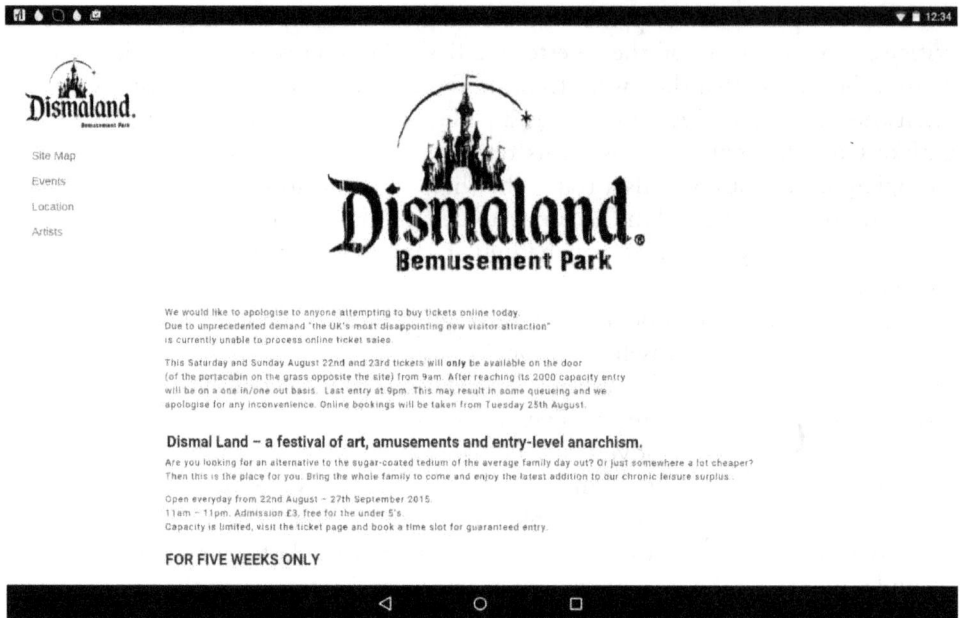

FIG. 8.10. Screenshot of *Dismaland*'s website, 22.12.2015 [© 2015 Banksy]

such example is the animation film *Despicable Me 2*.[34] The famous minions of the franchise are lured by an ice-cream van, which turns into a space ship that kidnaps them. It transports them into an artificial holiday resort, a 'Funland' of sorts, where they spend their time happily on an endless vacation until they are transformed into monsters. The references to Collodi's Funland that run throughout this part of the story are metaphorically significant because in the context of the film, the minions are tireless workers, encapsulating from the employer's point of view a contemporary version of the ideal employee: one who works endlessly and is happy with their employer's success as if it were their own. By portraying them as perfectly happy on holiday, instead of finding happiness in the success of their boss, this image of the tireless worker is challenged. However, it is debatable whether the film raises awareness of contemporary work ethics and employment demands (the model of the stress-resistant multi-tasker with a permanent smile on their face) or whether it ends up normalising this work environment by cutifying the minions and their devotion to their employer. The latter is probably the case, especially since the introduction of the Funland element into the narrative shows that this long, relaxing vacation at the seaside resort turns the devoted workers into monsters.

Another example of a contemporary interpretation of Collodi's Funland is the recent theme park installation 'Dismaland' by British graffiti artist Banksy.[35] The theme park was closer to Winshluss's version of Funland, mainly for two reasons: first, both artists were inspired by Disney and have a common artistic vision of dismantling the values that the Disney corporation represents. They both used visual references to familiar themes found in Disney, only to invert their meaning.

The best example of this is Banksy's choice of name and visual symbol for his theme park, which is in perfect contrast to the content and attractions of the park. 'Dismaland' is a direct reference to 'Disneyland', as is also obvious from the logo Banksy used for the theme park (figure 8.10). However, this is not an amusement, but a bemusement park, as the artist clarifies: nothing a visitor would expect from Disneyland can be found in this park. This is the second and more important way in which Dismaland alludes to Winshluss's Enchanted Island — its bleakness. Among the exhibits are a dead princess, a distorted mermaid, a fairy castle in ruins, and a pond with boats filled with refugees. The staff are deliberately uninterested. The organisers noted that the show would 'offer an escape from mindless escapism'.[36] Banksy's political activism did not stop with his commentary through his art. After the end of the installation, the park was 'relocated to the jungle migrant and refugee camp in Calais and renamed "Dismal-aid", in order to use its materials such as timber and fixtures for providing shelter for refugees'.[37]

Notes to Chapter 8

1. Ausonia's *Pinocchio: storia di un bambino* was originally published by Pavesio in 2006. The images used in this book are from the new revised edition of 2014 published by Lineachiara. The differences between the two editions are minor and mainly stylistic, aiming to create a darker atmosphere as Andrea Antonazzo explains: 'La nuova edizione di *Pinocchio* non sarà molto diversa dalla precedente. Ausonia ha rivisto solo alcuni elementi della grafica e ha sporcato le immagini per rendere l'atsmosfera più cupa. Ha inoltre rifatto il lettering con il suo font, e questa cosa, per quanto minima, a suo dire ha "giovato tantissimo alla coerenza interna delle tavole"' [The new edition of Pinocchio will not be very different from the previous one. Ausonia only revised some elements of the graphics and dirtied the images to make the atmosphere darker. He also redid the lettering with his font, and this, however minimal, in his own words 'greatly helped the internal coherence of the panels']. 'Il ritorno del Pinocchio di Ausonia', *Fumettologica*, 24 October 2014 <http://www.fumettologica.it/2014/10/ritorno-pinocchio-ausonia/> [accessed 18 November 2015].

2. Ausonia, *Pinocchio*, p. 28, panel 4: Collodi often used proverbs in his text. As seen in Part II, the Blue Fairy when referring to the types of lies that exist, i.e. those with short legs and those with long noses, alludes to the Italian proverb 'Le bugie hanno le gambe corte', meaning that one cannot go too far by telling lies. This is what Ausonia reverses by using another expression (*fare strada*) to give the exact opposite of Collodi's message.

3. See Roland Barthes, *The Pleasure of the Text*, trans. by Richard Miller (New York: Hill & Wang, 1975).

4. Bran Nicol, *The Cambridge Introduction to Postmodern Fiction* (Cambridge: Cambridge University Press, 2009), p. 40.

5. Laurence Grove, *Comics in French: The European Bande Dessinée in Context* (New York & Oxford: Berghahn Books, 2010), pp. 175–77.

6. Amélie Junqua, 'Wordless Eloquence — Shaun Tan, The Arrival, and Winshluss, Pinocchio', *Revue de recherche en civilisation américaine*, 5 (2015) <http://rrca.revues.org/685> [accessed 21 March 2019].

7. Ann Miller: 'This term refers to the space visible both outside the *hypercadre* ("hyperframe"), Peeters's term for the (usually) discontinuous frame formed by the outer frames of all the panels (Peeters 1991:38) and between the frames'. *Reading bande dessinée: Critical Approaches to French-language Comic Strip* (Chicago: University of Chicago Press, 2007), p. 86.

8. In Benjamin Roure, 'Winshluss: 'Déconner est une forme d'action''', *BoDoï*, 1 February 2009 <http://www.bodoi.info/winshluss-deconner-est-une-forme-daction/> [accessed 21 March 2019].

9. I refer here to the philosophical conflict between Aristotle and the Stoics over how one reaches the highest state of being. For Aristotle, *eudaimonia*, which can be interpreted as happiness or contentment, can be achieved by finding the golden mean between one's passions and reason. For the Stoics, on the other hand, *apatheia*, the state of mind where all passions and desires are eradicated, was the path to the highest state of being. *Apatheia* in that context refers to composure and equanimity and not to apathy.

10. I use the term 'mythology' in the way that Roland Barthes introduced it in *Mythologies*, trans. by Annette Lavers (St Albans: Paladin, 1973).

11. Andrew Leak, *Barthes: Mythologies* (London: Grant & Cutler, 1994), p. 25.

12. Cited in Vincent Brunner, 'Pinocchio', *Park Mag* (November 2008) <http://lesrequinsmarteaux.over-blog.com/article-25815691.html> [accessed 17 October 2021].

13. Cited in Marion Dumand, 'La Résistance plus que le talent', *Politis* (December 2008) <https://www.politis.fr/articles/2008/12/la-resistance-plus-que-le-talent-5037/> [accessed 17 October 2021].

14. This is the process that Louis Althusser defined as 'Ideological State Apparatuses' (IPAs) in 'Ideology and Ideological State Apparatuses', in *Lenin and Philosophy, and Other Essays* (London: NLB, 1971), pp. 127–86.

15. *Pinocchio*, dir. by Roberto Benigni (Italy & USA: Miramax Films, 2002).

16. Cristina Bacchilega, 'Fairy-tale Films in Italy', in *Fairy-tale Films Beyond Disney: International Perspective,* ed. by Jack Zipes, Pauline Greenhill, and Kendra Magnus-Johnston (London: Routledge, 2015), pp. 94–108.

17. Ian Robinson, 'Annotations for Snow White and the Seven Dwarfs', n. 17, *Sur La Lune Fairytales* <https://www.surlalunefairytales.com/s-z/snow-white-seven-dwarfs/snow-white-seven-dwarfs-annotations.html#SEVENTEEN> [accessed 17 October 2021].

18. See, for example, Donald Barthelme, *Snow White* (New York: Simon & Schuster, 1996), a postmodern retelling of Snow White's tale written in a realistic and often humoristic way.

19. Bill Willingham, *Fables:Rose Red*, illus. By Mark Buckingham and others (New York: Vertigo/DC Comics, 2011), and *1001 Nights of Snowfall* (2006).

20. Luigi Malerba, *Pinocchio con gli stivali* [1977] (Parma: MUP, 2004).

21. *Snow White and the Seven Dwarfs* (USA: Walt Disney Productions, 1937).

22. Winshluss, *Mr Ferraille* (Albi: Requins Marteaux, 2001).

23. *Happily Ever After,* (USA: Filmation Associates, 1993).

24. *Snow-White* (USA: Fleischer Studios, 1933).

25. Robinson, 'Annotations for Snow White and the Seven Dwarfs'.

26. Bruno Bettelheim, *The Uses of Enchantment: The Meaning and Importance of Fairy Tales* [1976] (London: Penguin, 1991), p. 209.

27. Ibid.

28. Anon. 'The Land of Cokaygne', BL Harley 913, ff. 3–6v. See Peter Dronke, 'The Land of Cokaygne: Three Notes on the Latin Background', in *Medieval Latin and Middle English Literature: Essays in Honour of Jill Mann*, ed. by Christopher Cannon and Maura Nolan (Woodbridge: Boydell & Brewer, 2011), pp. 65–75.

29. Denis Rohrer, 'In the Land of Cockaigne', *Alimentarium* <http://www.ealimentarium.ch/en/magazine/pleasure/amazing-feasts/land-cockaigne> [accessed 30 November 2015].

30. Ausonia, *Pinocchio*, p. 43, panel 3.

31. Ausonia: 'Erano gli anni della guerra in Iraq. Il tema delle menzogna nelle motivazioni che spinsero a quella guerra era molto forte' [Those were the years of the Iraq war. The topic of the lies behind the reasons that led to that war was very strongly present]. Email communication, 1 October 2014.

32. Created as a critical commentary on fascism by Pink Floyd for their 1982 film, *Pink Floyd: The Wall*, and used until today by neo-Nazi groups known as Hammerskins.

33. There are more references to *Pinocchio 3000* in Winshluss's text. More specifically, in *Pinocchio 3000*, Pinocchio's conscience is a penguin instead of a cricket; he follows him in a similar manner that Jiminy Cricket does in the Disney version. In Winshluss's version, a penguin lives with Geppetto and keeps him company while he is in the belly of the whale and then follows him also after Geppetto is liberated by Pinocchio.

34. *Despicable Me 2*, dir. by Pierre Coffin and Chris Renaud (USA: Universal Pictures, 2013).
35. Banksy, 'Dismaland' [temporary installation], Weston-super-Mare, 2015.
36. Mark Brown, 'Banksy's Dismaland: "Amusements and Anarchism" in Artist's Biggest Project Yet', *Guardian*, 20 August 2015 <http://www.theguardian.com/artanddesign/2015/aug/20/banksy-dismaland-amusements-anarchism-weston-super-mare> [accessed 21 March 2019].
37. 'Dismal-aid! Banksy Donates Dismaland Attraction to Shelter Calais Migrants', *RT*, 16 October 2015 <https://www.rt.com/uk/318883-dismalaid-banksy-dismaland-calais/> [accessed 21 March 2019].

CHAPTER 9

❖

The Talking Cricket — Conscience

In Part II, Freud's psychoanalytic theory was used to emphasise Pinocchio's oedipal relationship with the Blue Fairy, and in this chapter it is applied again, this time to the Talking Cricket as a metaphor for the super-ego. As the super-ego's function is annulled or reversed in the work of Ausonia and Winshluss, so the Pinocchio myth is further deconstructed.

The Talking Cricket appears three times in Collodi's original story. The nature of its character is that of a moralising adult giving advice to or scolding the restless Pinocchio, a role that resembles that of a person's conscience. As Freud explains in *The Ego and the Id*, the super-ego is the part of the human mind that internalises societal norms and acts as a form of conscience:

> The super-ego retains the character of the father, while the more powerful the Oedipus complex was and the more rapidly it succumbed to repression (under the influence of authority, religious teaching, schooling and reading), the stricter will be the domination of the super-ego over the ego later on — in the form of conscience or perhaps of an unconscious sense of guilt.[1]

It is therefore clear that in Freudian psychoanalysis the super-ego is manifest in the form of conscience. The Talking Cricket has the function of Pinocchio's conscience in Collodi's text and even more obviously in the Disney film adaptation. It is from this adaptation that the cricket became more famous, as its character changed from the repressive and threatening super-ego to a more amiable and forgiving companion, assigned by the Fairy to protect Pinocchio.

Collodi's Pinocchio kills the cricket early on in the story as he reacts violently to its criticism, revealing his early stage of development, when he is unable to control his libidinal instincts and his Oedipus complex is still unresolved. The formation of the super-ego occurs when the individual has internalised the reality principle, yet, as West argues, at this early stage of Collodi's story Pinocchio acts according to the pleasure principle.[2] In Disney, this side of Pinocchio is changed to a meeker and more infantile version instead of the restless adolescent that Collodi created. Disney's Pinocchio does not kill the Talking Cricket, which now has a name — Jiminy Cricket — and is a fully developed character. The role of the cricket-conscience transforms from the threatening and criticising voice to the voice of an advisor and saviour. I shall refer to Disney's version, particularly with reference to the character of the Talking Cricket, as Disney transformed its character significantly and left a strong influence on the Pinocchio myth. Any Pinocchio retelling that dates from after Disney and refers to the Talking Cricket cannot but bear Disney's amiable character in mind. Moreover, Winshluss's text has more references to the Disney adaptation than to the Collodi original. Winshluss confirms this influence on his work:

> Quand j'ai repris Pinocchio, tout le monde pensait que c'était une adaptation du Pinocchio de Collodi. Mais en fait, c'est une adaptation des souvenirs que j'ai du dessin animé de Walt Disney. Très peu de personnes finalement ont lu Collodi.[3]

> [When I took up Pinocchio, everyone thought it was an adaptation of Collodi's Pinocchio. But in fact it is an adaptation of the memories I have of Walt Disney's animations. Very few people have actually read Collodi.]

When referring to the role of conscience in this chapter, I will focus on its nature as defined by Freud's psychoanalytic theory. As Freud describes it, the ego (in this case represented by Pinocchio) 'owes service to three masters and [is] consequently menaced by three dangers: from the external world, from the libido of the id, and from the severity of the super-ego'.[4] If we adopt the image of the ego for Pinocchio, the id with its libidinal forces is clearly manifested in his unresolved oedipal complex, as analysed in Part II. The external forces that threaten Pinocchio are some of the characters he meets in the course of his adventures, such as the Fox and the Cat. Finally, the third master that Pinocchio has to obey is his conscience, or the Talking Cricket, which represents the super-ego. Freud explains that:

> We can tell what is hidden behind the ego's dread of the super-ego, the fear of conscience. The superior being, which turned into the ego ideal, once threatened castration, and this dread of castration is probably the nucleus round which the subsequent fear of conscience has gathered; it is this dread that persists as fear of conscience.[5]

The fear of castration to which Freud refers can be interpreted in our case as the fear of exclusion from society; the fear of isolation, which incorporates the fear of death.

When the super-ego is absent, the ongoing battle between the id and the super-ego, on which the ego balances, is immediately won by the id. The ego is in thrall to its libidinal instincts and seeks immediate gratification. As shown in Part II, the desire to be human is caused by Pinocchio's sexual desire for the Blue Fairy, a theme that was widely elaborated in Coover's text. In other words, Pinocchio's Oedipus complex triggered that desire. By the terms that the Fairy imposes through Pinocchio's super-ego, his Oedipus complex seems to be resolved, as he can postpone the gratification of this desire and move from the pleasure principle to the reality principle. Once he does as he is told, his desire will be fulfilled. What he must do (super-ego) in order to get what he wants (id) is difficult for Pinocchio; this is why in the original text he often relapses until he finally manages to tame his id, and his wish is then fulfilled.

In both retellings, the role of Pinocchio's conscience is very prominent. In Ausonia, the crickets are the enemy in the world of the marionettes. They represent truth, which is despised by the marionettes, and their war tactic is to inhabit the bodies of the marionettes to turn them towards the truth. This is how one such cricket inhabited Pinocchio's body and guided him throughout his life towards the path of truth. This was the reason why Pinocchio suffered as a social misfit and this is why in the end, after enduring long torture to find the cricket in his body, Pinocchio decides to crush it and lead a life of belonging. It doesn't matter if this belonging is to a false world, it is Pinocchio's choice, something he did not have when the cricket in his body was guiding him. Thus Ausonia brings the reader face-to-face with a moral dilemma without taking sides. As corrupt as the world of the marionettes might be, it does not justify the crickets' tactic of 'infecting' the marionettes with a conscience, thereby giving them no chance to choose voluntarily to support the good cause the crickets are fighting for.

After Pinocchio leaves prison, he abandons the city and reaches 'La terra delle api industriose' [The Land of the Busy Bees], a retelling of Collodi's original island of the busy bees. This is a place of child labour where they build arms to be used by child soldiers during the war. The theme of the war, originally referred to in Collodi, has been widely re-narrated in both these graphic novels. The first time Pinocchio meets a talking cricket is in a dream, in which it warns him to wake up before the assassins get him. The first cricket he meets in reality is during the war and the cricket explains to him that this is a war against the truth and Pinocchio is not safe because he does not know how to lie.[6] Pinocchio's adventures continue with Lucignolo, who is in fact Lucy, another child-victim exploited in the brothel of Madame Turchina. As seen earlier, Lucy tries to infest the Paese dei Balocchi with thousands of cricket eggs, but she is killed before she can complete her mission. After Pinocchio is arrested again, as an accomplice to Lucy, he tells his story to the court and then the narration returns from flashbacks to real-time action. The judge decides that they have to find and destroy the cricket inside Pinocchio. Collodi's scene of the four rabbits carrying a coffin is revisited visually in Ausonia's *Pinocchio*, when four rabbits cut through Pinocchio's flesh with scissors and knives in order to 'cure' him of the cricket inside him.

Once they finally find the cricket and remove it from inside him, Pinocchio sees the world with different eyes: he becomes sensible and chooses the way that will grant him acceptance in society, i.e. killing the cricket. The cricket tries to save its life and calls the Judge, the rabbits, and Pinocchio murderers — 'assassini', referring directly to Collodi's Talking Cricket. In Collodi's text, the ghost of the cricket that Pinocchio killed warns him against the *assassini* before Pinocchio knows that they are after him; the cricket is the first to mention that word (*AP*, p. 172). This is not the only reference to Collodi: Ausonia uses the Italian language and its idioms in a similar manner to Collodi by visualising an idiomatic expression, as demonstrated in the last chapter. The expression Ausonia refers to is *avere i grilli per la testa* [to have crickets in the head]: after the cricket is removed from Pinocchio, he can think logically, according to the standards of his society.[7] He repents for his revolutionary acts and kills the cricket with his own hands. 'È stato difficile... provare ad essere libero. È stata un' avventura spaventosa, una vita fatta di sofferenza continua' [It has been difficult... trying to be free. It has been a frightening adventure, a life of constant suffering].[8] The act of killing the cricket is not caused by his temper, as in Collodi. It is his conscious decision after hours of torture and a tormented life; it is the result of his wish to belong and not suffer any more. In order to belong in the society of the marionettes, Pinocchio has to numb his conscience instead of listening to it. This is a metaphor for contemporary society and a critique of morals and values where lying is acceptable, as it goes unpunished in all ranks of society. As mentioned earlier, the author is referring to politicians and their involvement in the Iraq war. He refers in particular to the motivations that led to that war and the lies that were involved. The role of the cricket as Pinocchio's conscience is therefore ambiguous. Even though the crickets served the truth, by entering Pinocchio's body, they violated his personal freedom, thus annulling their original good purpose. The world of the marionettes is a corrupt one, a valid metaphor for our contemporary world, as Ausonia sees it, yet the alternative is not necessarily better. Pinocchio longs to belong and cease his suffering, which is caused by being so different. As the Judge points out, 'Uccidendo il suo grillo, lei potrà essere riammesso nella società dei burattini. [...] Tenga, prenda in mano la causa di tutti i suoi mali... e la distrugga per sempre' [By killing your cricket, you will be readmitted into the society of puppets. [...] There, take in your hand the cause of all your woes... and destroy it forever].[9] Ausonia uses Pinocchio as a metaphor for the modern individual who also longs to belong, since being different causes social isolation. In order to belong to a corrupt society, the individual needs to numb any sensitive aspects of their character that make them different. Consumerism and hypocrisy are accepted values in the world of Ausonia's Pinocchio, which reflects our contemporary world. At the same time, the morality and self-proclaimed righteousness of the opposite values are also put under scrutiny. Like Winshluss, Ausonia does not provide a solution.

In Collodi's novel Pinocchio's desire is to become human in a world of humans. In Ausonia's text, Pinocchio desires to become a marionette in a world of marionettes. The main difference between the two is that in Collodi's Pinocchio that desire stems from his sex drive and natural need to grow up. There is nothing of the sort in Ausonia's Pinocchio and his desire to integrate with the marionettes stems only from his never-ending misfortunes and his wish to belong. His motive is to avoid pain and suffering; it is the choice of a tortured and traumatised Pinocchio, surrendering to his tormentor, as the only way out of his perpetual suffering.

The ending of Ausonia's text is ambiguous. All the hope that was embodied in the cause of the crickets for the truth has been destroyed by Pinocchio's crushing of his own cricket. The only possible future is one of assimilation for the sake of survival. Yet this leaves Pinocchio full of wounds and scars, as he struggles to save whatever is left of him. However, this is his own choice, without the manipulative voice of his conscience inside him.

While the crickets serve the truth in Ausonia's world, they still use children in the war, and fight and kill in the name of truth. It is not entirely clear whether the crickets are the 'good ones', as the author does not seem to support a Manichaean world view. Even those who seem to have a good cause act in a murderous way to defend that cause. Similarly, the marionettes are not necessarily the evil ones, as the author seems to suggest towards the end of the book. During the time that

Pinocchio spends with Lucy/ Lucignolo, Ausonia portrays them lying under a great oak and looking up at the sky. They see the strings of the marionettes disappearing into the sky and Lucy asks Pinocchio: 'Quei fili... Pinocchio, ma dove vano a finire? Tu lo sai?' [Those strings... Pinocchio, where do they go? Do you know?] (figures 9.1 and 9.2).[10] This existential self-reflective manner expressed by Lucy sheds light on a side of the marionettes that has only been hinted at thus far in Ausonia's text.

The ontological questions that are raised and left unanswered refer both thematically and visually to Pasolini's film *Che cosa sono le nuvole?* and, in particular, to its final scene.[11] Iago and Othello, the two puppets that have been discarded in a rubbish dump, see the world outside the theatre for the first time (figure 9.3). As they lie on their backs and look up at the sky, the puppet that was Othello wonders at the beauty of the clouds above them:

> OTELLO   Iiih! E che so' quelle?
> JAGO   Quelle sono... sono le nuvole...
> OTELLO   E che so' ste nuvole?
> JAGO   Mah!
> OTELLO   Quanto so' belle, quanto so' belle... quanto so' belle...
> JAGO   Ah, straziante meravigliosa bellezza del creato!

> [OTHELLO   Ohi! What's up with those?
> IAGO   These are... these are the clouds...
> OTHELLO   And what are these clouds?
> IAGO   Who knows!
> OTELLO   They're so pretty, they're so pretty... they're so pretty...
> IAGO   Oh, wonderful, heartbreaking beauty of creation!]

As Federico Pacchioni remarks, 'i due protagonisti scoprono la loro vera natura e la realtà stessa solo in seguito alla loro fine come personaggi, quando rinascono sotto il cielo della discarica davanti alla "straziante meravigliosa belleza del creato"' [the two protagonists discover their true nature and reality itself only when they die as characters, and are reborn under the sky of the landfill in front of the 'wonderful heartbreaking beauty of creation'].[12] As Pacchioni suggests, this reference to Pasolini and his approach to death as a moment of epiphany generates anticipation in the reader of Pinocchio's final moments. This sequence appears towards the end of the graphic novel, as a flashback that Pinocchio's cricket brings to mind. However, it does not refer to Pinocchio's death, but to his final transformation and the death of the cricket. The visual reference to Pasolini and the 'wonderful, heart-breaking beauty of creation' is consistent with Ausonia's ambiguity: even though Pinocchio decides to conform to a corrupt society, there may still be hope, as he will now be the master of his own self, responsible for his choices and their consequences. This is consistent with the bittersweet feelings that Pasolini's last scene evokes, namely the marionettes experiencing emotions of existential bliss while dying.

The last page of Ausonia's graphic novel (figure 9.5) is a mix of contrasting panels, both with regard to visual effects and to the symbolism of the story this far. The first two panels portray the brutal ending of the cricket at Pinocchio's hand, signifying Pinocchio's moral conversion to the society of the marionettes. Pinocchio denounces truth as a value and his act of killing the cricket is not the

FIG. 9.1. Ausonia, *Pinocchio* (Trent: Lineachiara, 2014), p. 59. © 2014 Lineachiara.

result of an impulsive fit of anger, as in Collodi. He is consciously — even without a conscience — choosing to belong, a choice that his conscience-cricket, as the super-ego, should have directed him towards, yet is reversed in Ausonia, like almost every other aspect of the Collodian text. The final panel refers to the time Pinocchio spent with Lucignolo and the last thought that the readers are left with refers to the existential uncertainty of the marionettes' origin. 'Dove vano a finire, quei fili?' 'Nessuno lo sa' ['Where do these strings go?' 'Nobody knows'].[13] Even though this uncertainty is not necessarily interpreted as hope, it nonetheless leaves

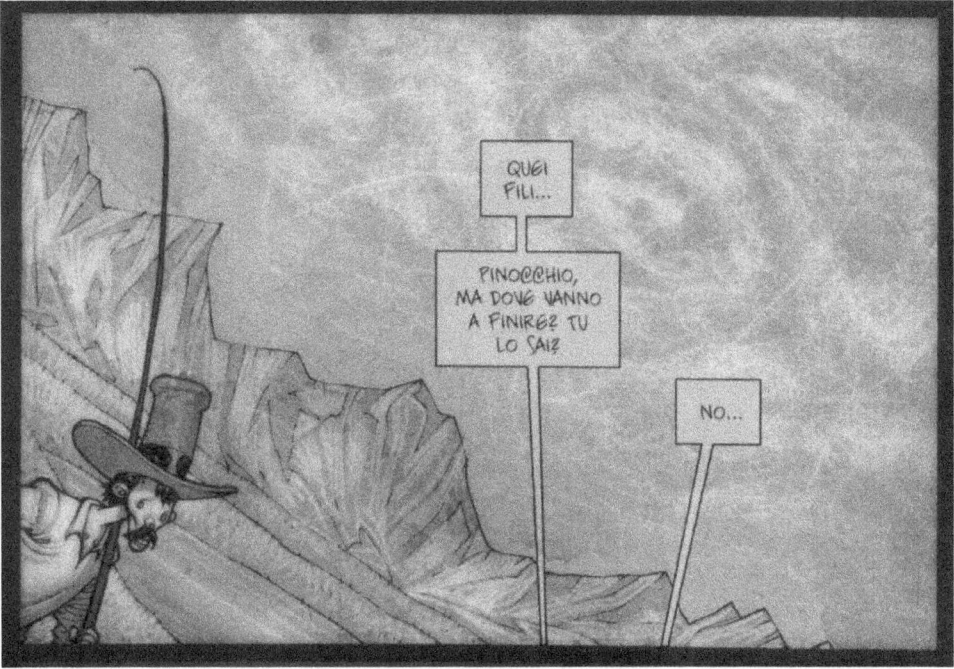

FIG. 9.2. Ausonia, *Pinocchio* (Trent: Lineachiara, 2014), p. 60. © 2014 Lineachiara.

FIG. 9.3. Still from *Che cosa sono le nuvole?*, dir. by Pier Paolo Pasolini, in *Capriccio all'italiana* (Italy: Dino de Laurentiis, 1968).

doubts regarding the evil nature of the marionettes. The visual reference to an open sky, full of possibilities, unanswered questions, and beauty, refers again to the final scenes of Pasolini's film (compare figures 9.4 and 9.5).

FIG. 9.4. Still from *Che cosa sono le nuvole?* 1968, dir. by Pier Paolo Pasolini,
in *Capriccio all'italiana* (Italy: Dino de Laurentiis, 1968).

So far, I have illustrated how the element of the cricket that acts as conscience is subverted. The conscience, or super-ego, reflects the mores of society, to help the individual balance their inner instincts and be accepted in society. However, Ausonia's cricket, which lives in Pinocchio's body and influences his actions as his conscience, does not represent his society's mores, but a higher set of values that do not correspond to an existing society in the world of Ausonia's text. Instead, the crickets are portrayed as 'the other', the enemy in the war of the marionettes, or the 'resistance', depending on who the narrator is. They stand for an imaginary society and their values refer to the humanist values of the post-Enlightenment era. However, the cricket has failed with regard to its conscience function, as it has brought Pinocchio into conflict, and not harmony, with his society. Therefore, the act of killing the cricket results in Pinocchio's harmonising with his corrupt society whereas, in Collodi, killing the cricket allowed Pinocchio an id-oriented behaviour directed at immediate gratification of desire.

There is no optimism or belief in humanity in Ausonia's text. As mentioned earlier, his work is inspired and influenced by his disillusionment with the Iraq war and all that led to it, including the socio-political system, the media, and so on. Ausonia expresses his alienation and mistrust in a capitalist system that endorses consumerist values in numerous ways. One such way is by discrediting the function of conscience: he pinpoints how there is nobody one can trust, not even one's own conscience.

Winshluss's *Pinocchio* has striking similarities to that of Ausonia in terms of the function of the conscience-cricket and more specifically, in its failure to function as super-ego. The cricket in Winshluss is a cockroach, Jiminy Cafard, who lives in Geppetto's kitchen. Through Jiminy's eyes, the reader sees an entire world in that kitchen in which Jiminy is looking for a new place to stay after being kicked

FIG. 9.5. Ausonia, *Pinocchio* (Trent: Lineachiara, 2014), p. 62. © 2014 Lineachiara.

out of his girlfriend's house. He bumps into the newly-made Pinocchio and finds some empty space in Pinocchio's head, in which he makes his new home. The metaphor of a conscience that finds embodiment in a 'newly-born' being, is the perfect example of Winshluss's art of irony and parody, as Jiminy is not exactly a conscience role model. He is a lazy aspiring author with permanent writer's block, living on unemployment benefit and attached to all sorts of material pleasures such as binge-eating, excessive consumption of alcohol and marijuana, and watching television. He is not aware of Pinocchio's existence as a robot since he only sees Pinocchio as a new place to live. He has no interaction with Pinocchio and their two storylines are separate. The only time that he has a direct effect on his host is when Geppetto switches Pinocchio off and Jiminy tries to fix the electricity so that he can continue watching television. However, he messes up the cables and causes a fire in Pinocchio's head; this in turn activates Pinocchio's self-defence instinct and his killer-robot programming is put to use. Pinocchio's death drive is set in motion — so his 'super-ego' controversially functions in triggering his apathetic id. Pinocchio becomes peaceful again when Jiminy manages to put out the fire.

The most significant aspect of Winshluss's retelling is that Pinocchio has no desire to become human — in fact, he has no desire for anything at all. He only responds to what is directly pleasant or irritating to him and in that respect is, in Freudian terms, fixated on the pleasure principle, while he also demonstrates no interest in belonging to his society. This is what the super-ego should have activated in him, had it been functioning properly. The following section will focus on Pinocchio's failed super-ego, Jiminy Cafard, and what his failure signifies. Another factor that is directly linked with Pinocchio's lack of desire to become human is the absence of the Blue Fairy from Winshluss's text. In Part II, I demonstrated how the Blue Fairy was responsible for Pinocchio's desire for humanity. Winshluss confirms this in *Pinocchio*, with the combined absence of the Blue Fairy and Pinocchio's desire to become human. Moreover, a consequence of this double lack is that no transformation occurs to Pinocchio at the end, as such an expectation does not arise from the narrative, as it does in Collodi's text.

One of the main visual references of Winshluss's *Pinocchio* is Disney, but also Winshluss's previous work, *Monsieur Ferraille*, which contains an earlier incarnation of Pinocchio as a three-page retelling of Disney's *Pinocchio* within the larger work, portraying different stories of an immoral robot that corrupts children and youth into the most decadent aspects of consumerist culture. In one of these stories, Monsieur Ferraille, the robot, is Pinocchio. His libidinal urges overtake him the moment the Blue Fairy gives him life. And, unlike Disney's Pinocchio, he kills his conscience as soon as he can. Apart from the motif of Pinocchio as a robot, another element that Winshluss used in both of his texts is that of the conscience as a cockroach. I will discuss the significance of this metaphor later. However, whereas in *Monsieur Ferraille* Pinocchio's id has completely taken over, uncontrollably releasing his death drive and sex drive, in *Pinocchio* Winshluss tries a more effective technique of critiquing and satirising consumerist culture. This time the cockroach-conscience is not killed off, but is instead made dysfunctional: the malaise of his society has affected even Pinocchio's conscience. This parody has the same effect as the shock that the killing of the cockroach had — disillusionment, but this time with added irony.

In *Pinocchio*, the little robot has no quest to become real, as in Collodi or Disney, and therefore he does not need a helper on his heroic journey. He seems purposeless, in a way that resembles his conscience, Jiminy Cafard. The French word *cafard* means both 'hypocrite' and 'depression'. If Pinocchio's conscience/ inner voice is 'depression', then this could be one possible explanation for his *apatheia*. A writer with no inspiration, who cannot deal with his failure and the expectations of his social surroundings, Jiminy daydreams about a future interview he will give when he is a famous writer:

> — Jiminy, à travers votre roman, 'La mécanique du vide', vous avez tenté de cerner le profond mal de vivre qui habite Michel votre héros. Je dois ajouter au passage que votre livre se place d'ores et déjà comme un véritable manifeste générationnel!
> — Merci...
> — Au cours du récit, nous suivons l'errance existentielle de Michel qui au terme de ses pérégrinations réalise qu'il ne fut que le spectateur de sa propre vie...terrible constat! Même sa révolte est vidée de son sens... parce que être en révolte contre la société c'est encore faire partie de cette société... Votre héros le dira lui-même page 178: 'Je suis le fruit de l'union de mon époque et de ses mensonges'. Michel se débat pour mettre un nom sur son malaise... peine perdue!! Définir le vide et sa mécanique, quoi de plus difficile et de plus absurde![14]

> ['Jiminy, throughout your novel, *The Mechanics of the Void*, you have tried to portray the profound unhappiness that possesses your hero, Michel. I should add by the way that your book is already considered a true generational manifesto.'
> 'Thank you...'
> 'As the story unfolds, we follow Michel's existential wanderings, towards the end of which he realises that he has been only the spectator of his own life... what a horrible thing to learn! But even his rebellion is meaningless... because to rebel against society means still being part of this society... Your hero even says it himself on page 178: "I am the product of the union between my time and its lies." Michel struggles to find a name for his discomfort... a waste of time! To define the void and its mechanics — what could be more difficult or more absurd than that!']

In short, Jiminy is trapped within his existential angst, which causes his writer's block and insecurity. Like his imaginary hero, he is trapped in the 'mechanics of the void', as he realises that he is a spectator rather than an actor in his own life. Like his protagonist, he feels immobilised by the fact that even fighting against the system reinforces it since, in order to do so, he uses the discourse into which he is born. In the next chapter where Jiminy appears, called 'Prendre conscience du génie d'un autre permet dans le même temps de prendre la mesure du sien...' [Becoming aware of another person's genius allows one at the same time to take the measure of one's own...], Jiminy, upon finishing Dostoyevsky's *The Idiot* and measuring his own genius against it, smashes his typewriter, giving up.

Jiminy is the funniest character in Winshluss's text. Yet the humour is dark and dry, and that of self-irony.[15] Indeed the whole storyline of Jiminy trying in vain to write a book that expresses his existential angst and social critique is a *mise-en-abyme*, parodying what Winshluss is trying to do with *Pinocchio*. Interestingly enough, in an interview Winshluss uses the words of Michel, the protagonist of Jiminy's unwritten book: 'Mais je ne suis que le fruit de notre époque' [But I am only the product of our time].[16] Michel has many autobiographical characteristics in common with Jiminy, so Winshluss identifies with them both, creating the effect of a *mise-en-abyme* within another *mise-en-abyme*. As Brian McHale suggests:

> *Mise-en-abyme* is another form of short-circuit, another disruption of the logic of narrative hierarchy, every bit as disquieting as a character stepping across the ontological threshold to a different narrative level. The effect of *mise-en-abyme*, Gabriel Josipovici writes, 'is to rob events of their solidity,' and the effect of *this* is to foreground ontological structure.[17]

The effects of the different drawing styles and techniques also highlight this ontological structure. All the other storylines are coloured either in dreamlike fairy-tale pastels, or in the more vivid colours and style of advertisements; they belong to a different realm. Even though all the characters have significant functions in Winshluss's socio-political allegory, they are still fairy-tale or literary characters. Having no written textual narrative, they belong to the 'world before language'.[18] Jiminy's storyline, however, is in black and white, distinguishing it starkly from the rest of the stories. The absence of colour suggests a dull reality that is in contrast with the colourful fairy-tale world. Jiminy's storyline has a written textual narrative as well, emphasising even more strongly the link to the everyday reality of the contemporary world, especially since Jiminy's language is slang.

Cockroaches are known to live in cities together with humans, and to live on human leftovers. Collodi's and Disney's Pinocchios are rural and provincial; Winshluss's Pinocchio is a city boy and therefore needs a city companion, so a cockroach rather than a cricket, which is to be found in the countryside. Cockroaches have often been used to signify culturally or racially oppressed minorities, and the unwanted and misunderstood.[19] Winshluss uses this metaphor of the cockroach to represent Jiminy, a writer who has not yet managed to write his great œuvre, *The Mechanics of the Void*, and does not succeed in forming any type of relationship.

Jiminy Cafard stands for the artist and for Winshluss himself. This metafictional aspect of *Pinocchio* adds one more postmodern characteristic to Winshluss's work. Jiminy can also be seen as a metaphor for any individual who struggles to stand up to consumerist society's demands. Jiminy's life, drawn in black and white, is full of small joys and failures, disappointments and everyday struggles. Pinocchio's storyline, on the other hand, represents the bigger things that happen and influence smaller, everyday people, like Jiminy in his head. In Pinocchio's story, governments and dictatorships change, armies take over and then lose power, horrible crimes are committed and at times uncovered, and all these have an effect on Jiminy, as on the average person, even though he is unaware of all that is happening. However, Jiminy's actions also have an effect on the outside world, through Pinocchio, and this can be seen as an optimistic political comment on Winshluss's part: that the anonymous masses and the average person can each individually influence the system, even if they are considered to be cockroaches.

Ausonia's cricket living inside Pinocchio had a purpose: to keep Pinocchio on the side of the crickets and of truth. Jiminy Cafard's purpose serves only himself: he wants a functioning home in the flat he occupies in Pinocchio's head. He only intervenes in Pinocchio's actions when he is disturbed and has no moral connection to his host. Despite their apparent differences, the main similarity between the two insects is their failure to function as a proper conscience. Both Pinocchios have a dysfunctional super-ego as a result. This changes at the end of Ausonia's novel when Pinocchio kills the cricket. In Winshluss, however, nothing changes in the end between Pinocchio and his conscience. They both live in a state of apathy, activated only when disturbed.

Both Jiminy Cafard's apathy and the absence of the Blue Fairy result in Pinocchio's lack of desire to become human. The only time Pinocchio is portrayed as a real boy by Winshluss is in Geppetto's nightmare (figure 9.6). This is a subversive response to Disney's Geppetto and his wish to have a child, which is what animated Pinocchio. In Geppetto's nightmare, the real Pinocchio attacks him and tears off his face, only to reveal a robot underneath. The first part of the dream shows Geppetto's guilt towards Pinocchio, for having created him only to make money, and possibly also for his complete lack of fatherly instinct towards his creation. In short, Geppetto never wished for Pinocchio to become a real boy yet it happened (with the intervention of a godly hand, reminiscent of Michelangelo's 'Creation of Adam') and now this little boy knows his father's real intentions and is ruthless towards him, no matter how apologetically Geppetto looks at him. The second part of the dream is even more interesting as it reveals Geppetto's insecurity regarding his own identity, and his fear of turning into a robot himself. This touches upon the core of the Pinocchio myth and its part in the literary tradition of the animate/inanimate archetype, as discussed previously. According to Barbara Johnson, as seen in Part I, this archetype can also portray a fear that the reverse may happen, that the animate may turn into the inanimate, life into stillness and death, or, as in Geppetto's dream, human into robot.[20]

Even though Geppetto is an inventor, he does not trust his own creation and is afraid of it — one more link to Frankenstein. This expresses an ongoing technophobia but it contrasts with Pinocchio's decision as a military robot to stay peaceful unless disturbed. Geppetto only sees profit in his creation, but Pinocchio goes on to explore the world, mostly non-violently. Winshluss's ending is as ambiguous as that of Ausonia. Pinocchio stays with his new foster family, seemingly happy. A posthuman future appears possible, yet Winshluss's style is that of irony and parody, neither of which allow for an optimistic ending. Like the whole story, which has been a visual narrative without text (except for Jiminy's story) the ending is also left ambiguous and the reader is invited to interpret what this open ending means. If something goes wrong in Pinocchio's electrical circuits and disturbs Jiminy, he might intervene again, and the happy family the book ends with might

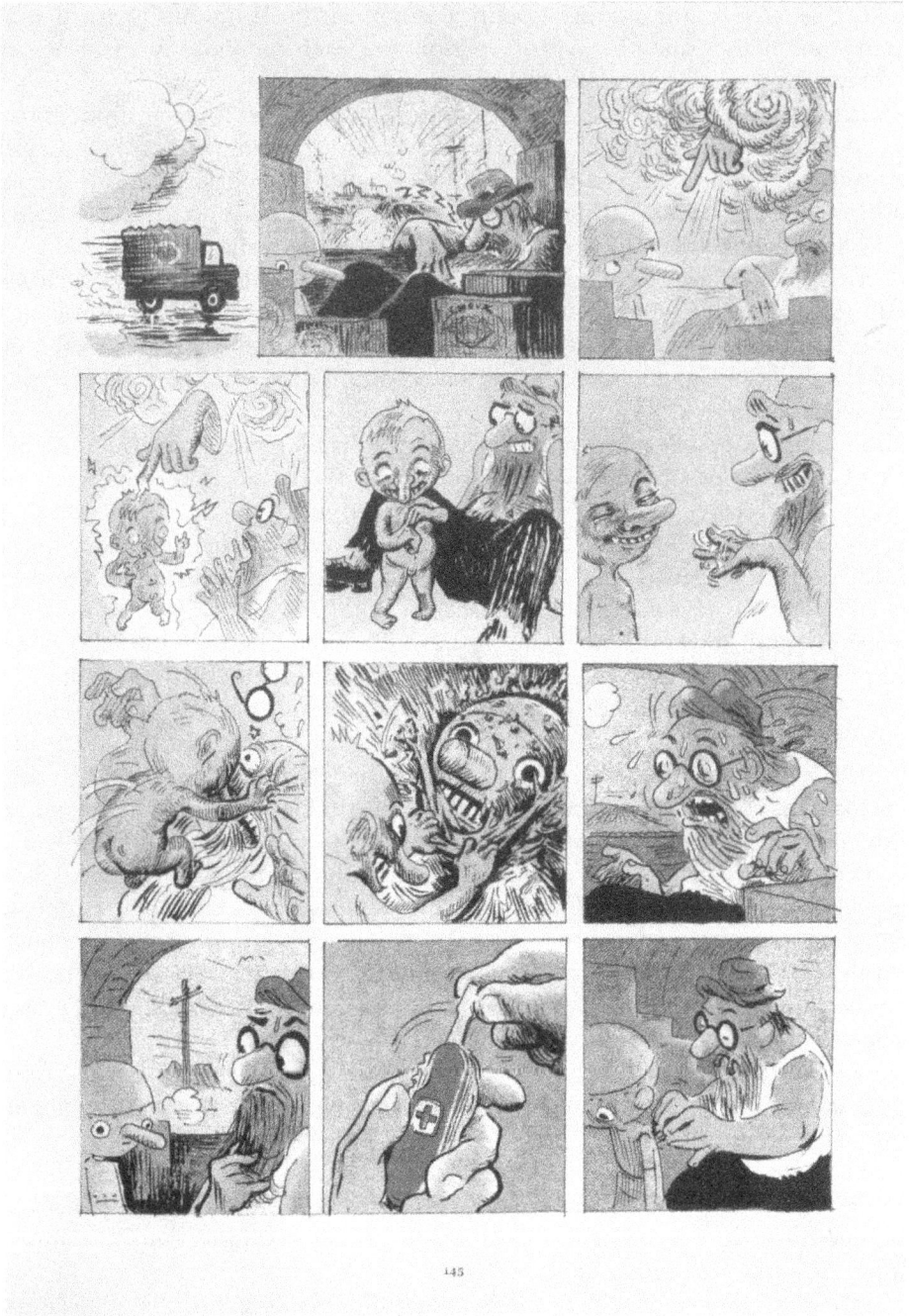

FIG. 9.6. Winshluss, *Pinocchio* (Albi: Les Requins Marteaux, 2008), p. 145.
© 2008 Les Requins Marteaux.

wind up amidst explosions and fire if Pinocchio's violent function is ever activated again.

There are further elements in the works of the two authors that put them in dialogue with each other and with the authors examined in Part II. Ausonia's interests expressed through his works are very relevant to the previous chapters. A year after *Pinocchio*, Ausonia published *P-HPC: Post-human Processing Center.*[21] Differing in style, with large parts resembling a *fotonovela*, but similar to the dark mood of *Pinocchio*, *P-HPC* is a dystopian novel about a future society where plants are dying out for no obvious reason. In that society, Post-human Processing Center is a governmental laboratory that transforms humans into objects. Nobody is forced to go there, but whoever enters it cannot come out again in human form. Advertisements for it proclaim those who volunteer for it as the country's favourite children. Nobody knows what exactly happens to them, but anyone who enters goes through a process of ten stages, starting with body parts being removed and replaced with mechanical ones. The limbs and skin follow and then gradually memories are removed. If the individual manages to reach the tenth level, as not many survive the process, then they become a perfect, obedient executive machine. The mechanical body in *P-HPC* is very different from the attractive cylon models of *Battlestar Galactica* discussed in Part I. Even though the post-humans that are produced in *P-HPC* are the children of humanity, as the cylons were, these robots are as disturbing visually as they are conceptually. *BSG*'s cylons were made similar to the humans, inheriting the entire human emotional spectrum. In *P-HPC* the post-humans are as emotionless as computer software, highly intelligent but not sentient. The fact that they were not created but instead transformed from humans into machines increases the disturbing effect the text has on the reader, intensified by a gradual, visual transformation.

Ausonia's trilogy, *Interni*, published between 2008 and 2011, connects to the material of both Parts II and III.[22] It relates to Winshluss's Jiminy Cafard, as all the protagonists in the trilogy are insects and the main character, a successful author, is a cockroach. Unlike Spiegelman's *Maus*, where the Nazis were portrayed as cats and the Jews as mice, there is no particular distinction in Ausonia between different types of insects.[23] It is in fact quite the opposite as they mix and intermarry; it is rather a reference to different human races, but without drawing any specific parallels. The main emphasis throughout the trilogy is on the process and nature of writing, which is why it resonates strongly with Jiminy Cafard. In its self-referentiality *Interni* is as metafictional and postmodern as Coover's text, if not more so, and pertinent to the questions addressed in Part II: Ausonia is one of the characters and the process of writing, both by Ausonia and his protagonist, are frequently discussed in the text. Throughout *Interni*, Ausonia interrupts the narration to have dialogues with the radical part of his brain, with people-characters who live in his head and with his friends regarding the process of his story and the book we are reading. The same self-observation and self-analysis within the narrative has also been seen in Coover, Charyn, and Winshluss. The fact that the focus of narration shifts so much towards the self demonstrates the influence of psychoanalysis applied to the process of writing. Moreover, the intensified emphasis that this is given by Ausonia, more than in any other example, stretches the genre to its utmost.

Ausonia's explicit analysis of his author's choice to use a specific font or a specific narrative perspective or technique reveals a fear that if he does not mention it in the form of this metafictional meta-analysis of the text, his readers might not notice. It reflects an inner fear of not being understood, even though he makes explicit again that the author we see portrayed is only a fictionalised part of him and not exactly him, and for this reason the fonts in the text are a digitalised version of his handwriting, but not his handwriting. He considers it an approximation of himself, as he believes all autobiographies to be. Yet the efforts he puts into his text in order to make himself clear are telling. The combination of this self-exposure together with his declaration that the reader cannot really know him seems to be a manifestation of his inner fear of being misunderstood, misinterpreted, or even perhaps not interpreted at all. The text therefore becomes a psychoanalytic tool to cure the author's mythopsychosis — as seen in Charyn's text — or existential angst. In other words, the text becomes the author's therapy. This therapeutic effect can also be seen in a dream sequence, artistically equivalent to David Lynch's cinematography applied in *fumetto*, where Ausonia becomes the God of his own creation. With reference to the human desire to become God as discussed in Part I, at a metanarrative level, literature allows Ausonia complete deification, which again helps therapeutically towards his existential angst, something that Jiminy Cafard also suffers from:

> Ogni elemento, ogni segno, ogni parola... tutto qui è parte di me. [...] Le vignette, le fotografie, ogni soluzione drammaturgica, gli inchiostri, i balloon, i dialoghi... ogni personaggio che non sono io è me. E io, come in un mio sogno, sono in ogni cosa.[24]

> [Every element, every sign, every word... everything here is part of me. [...] The vignettes, the photographs, any dramaturgical solution, the inks, the balloons, the dialogues... every character that is not me *is* me. And I, as in a dream of mine, am in everything.]

All the previous examples of Ausonia's collective work and vision as an author and visual artist bring together all the aspects of the Pinocchio myth discussed throughout this book — the posthuman, postmodern, and visual.

Notes to Chapter 9

1. Freud, *The Ego and the Id*, p. 35.
2. Mark I. West, 'Pinocchio's Journey from the Pleasure Principle to the Reality Principle', in Lucy Rollin and Mark I. West, *Psychoanalytic Responses to Children's Literature* (Jefferson, NC, & London: McFarland, 1999), pp. 65–70.
3. Cited in Dorothée Charles, 'Interview de Winshluss', Musée des Arts Décoratifs, Paris, 14 January 2013 <http://www.lesartsdecoratifs.fr/francais/arts-decoratifs/expositions-23/archives-25/winshluss-un-monde-merveilleux/interview-de-winshluss> [accessed 21 March 2019].
4. Freud, *The Ego and the Id*, p. 56.
5. Ibid., p. 57.

6. 'Vattene da questo posto. Qui è dove i burattini combattono la guerra contro i grilli parlanti... Vogliono sterminarci! Per avere un mondo dominato dalle bugie. È per questo che tutti ti odiano... Perché non sai mentire!' [Leave this place. This is where the puppets fight the war against the talking crickets... They want to destroy us! To have a world ruled by lies. That's why everyone hates you ... Because you don't know how to lie!]. Ausonia, *Pinocchio*, p. 39, panels 6–8.

7. The expression 'to have crickets in the head' means roughly to have extravagant ideas and not think logically or sensibly, as if crickets were buzzing in one's head, making it impossible to think clearly: 'Avere idee stravaganti, bizzarre o pretenziose, come se si avesse nella testa una schiera di grilli che con il loro frinire e saltellare incessante impedisse di pensare in maniera logica o sensata', according to the *Dizionario dei modi di dire, Corriere Della Sera* <http://dizionari. corriere.it/dizionario-modi-di-dire/G/grillo.shtml> [accessed 21 March 2019].

8. Ausonia, *Pinocchio*, p. 61, panels 1–3.

9. Ibid., p. 61, panels 7–8.

10. Ibid., p. 60, panel 6.

11. *Che cosa sono le nuvole?*, dir. by Pier Paolo Pasolini, in *Capriccio all'italiana* (Italy: Dino de Laurentiis, 1968).

12. Federico Pacchioni, 'La contaminazione tra teatro di figura e cinema in *Che cosa sono le nuvole?*', in *Contaminazioni culturali: musica, teatro, cinema e letteratura nell' Italia contemporanea*, ed. by Fulvio Orsitto and Simona Wright (Rome: Vecchiarelli, 2014), pp. 233–44 (p. 236).

13. Ausonia, *Pinocchio*, p. 62.

14. Winshluss, *Pinocchio*, p. 99.

15. See Stéphane Beaujean, 'Théâtre des marionnettes', *Les Inrockuptibles*, (9 December 2008) <http://lesrequinsmarteaux.over-blog.com/article-25815691.html > [accessed 18 October 2021].

16. Brunner, 'Pinocchio'.

17. McHale, *Postmodernist Fiction*, p. 125.

18. Romain Brethes, 'Conte ravagé', *Chronic'art* (November 2008) <http://lesrequinsmarteaux. over-blog.com/article-25815691.html > [accessed 18 October 2021].

19. See, for example, Franz Kafka, *The Metamorphosis* (London: Parton Press, 1937); Oscar Zeta Acosta, *The Revolt of the Cockroach People* (New York: Vintage Books, 1989); and Scholastique Mukasonga, *Cockroaches* (Brooklyn, NY: Archipelago, 2016).

20. Johnson, *Persons and Things*, p. 20.

21. Ausonia, *P-HPC: Post-human Processing Center* (Verona: Leopoldo Bloom, 2007).

22. Ausonia, *Interni, o la miserevole vita di uno scrittore di successo*, 3 vols (Florence: Double Shot, 2008–11), III.

23. Art Spiegelman, *Maus* (New York: Pantheon Books, 1991).

24. Ibid., p. 376.

CONCLUSION

❖

This book has focused on the myth of Pinocchio and the different ways in which it has been addressed in posthuman and postmodern retellings. The different types of retelling in the three parts have emphasised the flexibility and adaptability of the myth, which is also reflected by the variety of media examined in each chapter: film, metafictional novel, and graphic novel. As the Introduction explained, the myth of Pinocchio can be summarised simply as the desire of the puppet to become human. It follows the tradition of the animate/ inanimate archetype, and as per Joseph Campbell's definition, it has numerous symbolic, religious, and spiritual connotations that make it a monomyth. The myth of becoming was examined from different perspectives: Part I emphasised the transhumanist interpretation of the Pinocchio myth, while Part II focused on deconstructing the myth by scrutinising each of its components. Part III addressed the myth in the Barthesian sense, criticising the ideology of the establishment and consumerist values.

The comparative analysis of the Pinocchio myth in the variety of media that I have examined in this study offers an interdisciplinary approach to the ever-popular field of retellings of myths and fairy tales. It serves also to show how Collodi's story has acquired an international identity and can be seen from the universal perspective of myth studies. Even though the mythic/ mythological dimension of Pinocchio has been examined before, this is the first systematic study of the Pinocchio myth, its implications, and perpetuation, and the first breakdown of it into its component parts, as it has been retold in the last five decades through different media and literary genres.

One of the challenges of this study has been the limitations imposed by its interdisciplinarity. There are numerous retellings of Pinocchio as well as numerous examples of sentient robots. This study could not cover all these examples, nor all languages. The case studies were chosen as representative examples in order to showcase the plasticity of the Pinocchio myth and its ease of adaptation into different genres. My aim has not been to offer an exhaustive record of examples, but to use very representative ones to highlight the properties of the Pinocchio myth, both when it was perpetuated and when it was exposed.

This study has illustrated, however, how the Pinocchio myth may be seen as a tree branching out into different areas of research, media, and disciplines all worth pursuing in more detail. For example, as the origins of the Pinocchio myth were traced in the animate/ inanimate archetype, a similar connection could be drawn with all trickster characters from ancient mythology to contemporary literature, or all novels that include long-nosed characters. There are many more examples of further comparative paths, as the myth of Pinocchio has an exceptionally rich potential for comparative and interdisciplinary analysis.

There is still a lot to be said about Pinocchio's animist origins, the life force behind the talking wood that Geppetto carves, and which gives Pinocchio his very characteristic liveliness, enthusiasm, and inquisitiveness from early on. Giorgio Manganelli refers to the power of the forest that connects Pinocchio with the Blue Fairy and Bill Willingham in *Fables* traces Pinocchio's origins in the Sacred Grove that the Adversary Geppetto uses to carve a whole army of wooden soldiers. Whether Collodi drew his inspiration from the pool of fairy tales he translated or elsewhere, Pinocchio's pre-puppet existence in the form of a talking piece of wood or a talking tree remains a fascinating mystery.

His naughtiness and tendency for disobedience and mischief connect Pinocchio with archetypal trickster characters, such as the Greek god Hermes, inventor of lying, or the Norse god shape shifter Loki. The original ending of Pinocchio, hanging dead from the Great Oak, and his subsequent resurrection, allude to another Norse god, Odin, who sacrificed himself to himself, hanging from Yggdrasil, the Tree of Life.

Pinocchio's universality transcends national borders and genres. Carrying lightly on his wooden shoulders the weight of numerous religious, mythological, folkloric and archetypal symbolisms, he remains the ultimate representation of childhood and its innocence and a continuous inspiration for endless more retellings and interpretations to come.

APPENDIX

❖

Below is a transcription of Collodi's *Pinocchio* in the chronological order in which the events are narrated. Functions are coded as different letters or symbols. Next to these, in italics, are Vladimir Propp's descriptions of each function, and next to that is a short description of the part of Collodi's novel (with specific chapters mentioned) that corresponds to the aforementioned function.

α. *Future hero introduced.* Ch. I-VIII: Short episodes from Ch. IV-VII which introduce / describe the hero's (Pinocchio's) character.

γ. *Interdiction.* → γ² (*An inverted form of interdiction is represented by an order or a suggestion*). Ch. VIII: Pinocchio volunteers to go to school, knowing this will please Geppetto, i.e. knowing this is expected of him.

β. *Absentation.* → β³ (*Absentation of a member of the younger generation*). Ch. IX: Pinocchio sets off for school.

δ. *Violation (and introduction of the villain).* Ch. IX-XII: Pinocchio sells his spelling-book, he goes to the puppet show, where he has an adventure with the Fire Eater and the marionettes (function: revealing more about his character), and leaves with five golden coins to return to Geppetto, whereupon he meets the Fox and the Cat.

η. *Trickery (the villain attempts to deceive the victim in order to take possession of his belongings).* →η¹ (*Using persuasion*) Ch. XII: The Fox and the Cat try to deceive Pinocchio and get him to plant his coins in the Field of Miracles so that he will get more coins.

θ. *The victim submits to deception.* → θ¹ *The hero agrees to the villain's persuasions.* Ch. XII-XIII: Pinocchio is convinced and as a result follows the Fox and the Cat to the Red Crawfish Inn.

A. *Villainy.* A⁶ → *The villain causes bodily injury.* Ch. XIV-XV: The Fox and the Cat, disguised as the assassins, run after Pinocchio and his coins and hang him from a tree.

F. *Provision or receipt of a magical agent.* → F⁹ (*Various characters place themselves at the disposal of the hero*). Ch. XVI-XVII: The Fairy with the blue hair saves Pinocchio.

From here on a repetition of a series of functions starts, a characteristic feature of fairy tales before they reach resolution.

β³· Ch. XVIII: Pinocchio sets off to meet Geppetto, who is on his way to the Fairy's house.

γ¹. *Interdiction.* Ch. XVIII: The Fairy tells Pinocchio not to go astray and to take the forest path.

δ. Ch. XVIII: Pinocchio gets distracted by the Fox and the Cat.

η^I. Ch. XVIII: The Fox and the Cat trick Pinocchio into going to the Field of Miracles once again.

θ^I. Pinocchio follows them.

A^5 *(Plundering)* A^{15} *(imprisonment)* → A$_5$^{15}. Ch. XVIII-XIX: The Fox and the Cat steal Pinocchio's coins; as a result he gets imprisoned in the town of Catchafool.

D. *The hero is tested by the donor.* → D^I. Ch. XIX: The jailer only lets some people free.

E. *The hero's reaction.* → E^I *(the hero withstands a test)*. Ch. XIX: Pinocchio cunningly responds in a way that satisfies the jailer. The jailer sets Pinocchio free.

↑. *Departure.* Ch. XX: Pinocchio sets off towards the Fairy's house in order to find Geppetto.

D. *The hero is tested by the donor.* → D^I. Ch. XXI: Pinocchio is caught by a peasant who forces him to work as a watchdog for his poultry-yard.

E. *The hero's reaction.* → E^I *(the hero withstands a test)*. Ch. XXII: Pinocchio catches the chicken thieves. The peasant rewards Pinocchio and sets him free.

F^9 *(Various characters place themselves at the disposal of the hero)*. Ch. XXIII: After Pinocchio finds the Fairy's tombstone, a Pigeon finds him and offers to transfer him to Geppetto.

G. *Guidance.* → G^I *(the hero flies through the air)*. Ch. XXIII: Pinocchio flies on the Pigeon to the seashore, where he sees Geppetto in the sea.

γ^2. *(An inverted form of interdiction is represented by an order or a suggestion)*. Ch. XXIV-XXV: After jumping into the water and failing to reach Geppetto, Pinocchio is washed up on the Island of the Busy Bees, where he meets the Fairy again and promises her that he will go to school and be obedient.

δ. *Violation (and introduction of the villain)*. Ch. XXV- XXVIIII: Pinocchio goes to school, but gets distracted by his classmates, gets involved in a fight, is arrested by the *carabinieri*, escapes from them, jumps into the sea, and is then caught by the fisherman.

A^{17}. *(The villain makes a threat of cannibalism)*. Ch. XXVIII: The fisherman puts Pinocchio in the flour together with the fish and prepares to fry and eat him.

F^9. Ch. XXIX: Alidoro, the dog that Pinocchio had saved from drowning, saves Pinocchio from the fisherman.

γ^2. Ch. XXIX: Back with the Fairy, Pinocchio promises once again to be obedient and to go to school and as a reward the Fairy will transform him into a real boy.

δ. Ch. XXX- XXXI: Pinocchio becomes a good student, but just before he is transformed into a real boy, he escapes to Funland with his friend Lampwick.

A^{11}. *(The villain casts a spell upon someone)*. Ch. XXXII- XXXIII: Pinocchio is transformed into a donkey and the little man who brought him to Funland sells him to a circus.

F⁹. Ch. XXXIII-XXXIV: After the Pinocchio-donkey breaks his leg, he is sold to be killed and skinned. He is thrown into the sea to drown, but the Fairy sends fish that eat his donkey skin and he becomes a puppet again.

K. *The initial lack is liquidated.* → KF⁵ *(The receipt of an object of search is accomplished by means of the same forms as the receipt of a magical agent. F⁵ — The agent falls into the hands of the hero by chance).* Ch. XXXIV-XXXV: Pinocchio is swallowed by the Shark and finds Geppetto inside its belly.

↓. *The hero returns.* Ch. XXXV: Pinocchio saves Geppetto from the Shark and carries him safely to the shore.

M. *Difficult task.* Ch. XXXVI: Pinocchio works day and night to provide for his sick father.

T. *Transfiguration.* T¹. *(A new appearance is directly effected by means of the magical action of a helper).* Ch. XXXVI: Pinocchio is transformed by the Fairy into a real boy as a reward for being hardworking and kind.

w°. *(monetary reward).* Ch. XXXVI: Another reward from the Fairy is the transformation of Pinocchio's house into a wealthier one than before.

BIBLIOGRAPHY

❖

Acosta, Oscar Zeta, *The Revolt of the Cockroach People* (New York: Vintage Books, 1989)

Aldiss, Brian, 'Supertoys Last All Summer Long', in *Supertoys Last All Summer Long and Other Stories of Future Time* (New York: St. Martin's Griffin, 2001), pp. 1–11

Althusser, Louis, 'Ideology and Ideological State Apparatuses', in *Lenin and Philosophy, and Other Essays* (London: NLB, 1971), pp. 127–86

Andrews, Richard, ed., *The Commedia Dell'arte of Flaminio Scala: A Translation and Analysis of 30 Scenarios* (Lanham, MD, Toronto & Plymouth: Scarecrow Press, 2008)

Anon., 'The Gingerbread Boy', *St. Nicholas Magazine*, 2.7 (1875), 448–49

——'The Land of Cokaygne', BL Harvey 193

Antonazzo, Andrea, 'Il ritorno del Pinocchio di Ausonia', *Fumettologica*, 24 October 2014 <http://www.fumettologica.it/2014/10/ritorno-pinocchio-ausonia/>

Apollonius of Rhodes, *Argonautica, Book IV*, ed. by Richard Hunter, Cambridge Greek and Latin Classics (Cambridge: Cambridge University Press, 2015)

Apostolidès, Jean-Marie, '*Pinocchio*, or a Masculine Upbringing', *Merveilles & Contes*, 2.2 (1988), 75–86

Apuleius, Lucius, *The Golden Ass or Metamorphoses*, trans. by E. J. Kenney (London: Penguin, 1998)

Aristotle, *Poetics*, trans. by S. H. Butcher <http://classics.mit.edu/Aristotle/poetics.1.1.html#200>

Asor Rosa, Alberto, 'Le avventure di Pinocchio', in *Letteratura italiana: le opere*, ed. by Alberto Asor Rosa, 4 vols (Turin: Einaudi, 1992–95), III, 879–950

Aulnoy, Marie-Catherine, d', and Jeanne-Marie Leprince de Beaumont, *Fiabe d'amore*, trans. by Carlo Collodi (Florence: Giunti, 2011)

Ausonia, *Interni, o la miserevole vita di uno scrittore di successo*, 3 vols (Florence: Double Shot, 2008–11)

——*P-HPC: Post-human Processing Center* (Verona: Leopoldo Bloom, 2007)

——*Pinocchio: storia di un bambino* (Turin: Pavesio, 2006)

——*Pinocchio: storia di un bambino* (Trent: Lineachiara, 2014)

Bacchilega, Cristina, 'Fairy-tale Films in Italy', in *Fairy-tale Films Beyond Disney: International Perspective*, ed. by Jack Zipes, Pauline Greenhill, and Kendra Magnus-Johnston (London: Routledge, 2015), pp. 94–108

——*Postmodern Fairytales: Gender and Narrative Strategies* (Philadelphia: University of Pennsylvania Press, 1997)

Badmington, Neil, 'Theorizing Posthumanism', *Cultural Critique*, 53 (2003), 10–27

Bakhtin, Mikhail, *Rabelais and His World*, trans. by Helene Iswolsky (Cambridge, MA, & London: M.I.T. Press, 1968)

Ball, Philip, *Bright Earth: The Invention of Colour* (London: Vintage, 2008)

Banksy, *Dismaland* [temporary art project], Weston-super-Mare, 2015

Barthelme, Donald, *Snow White* (New York: Simon & Schuster, 1996)

Barthes, Roland, *Mythologies*, trans. by Annette Lavers (St Albans: Paladin, 1973)

——*The Pleasure of the Text*, trans. by Richard Miller (New York: Hill & Wang, 1975)

BASILE, GIAMBATTISTA, 'Pinto Smalto', in *Lo cunto de li cunti* [1674] (Turin: Einaudi, 2002), pp. 838–51

BAUM, FRANK L., *The Wizard of Oz* (New York: Bobbs-Merrill, 1900)

BEAUJEAN, STÉPHANE, 'Théâtre des marionnettes', *Les Inrockuptibles* (9 December 2008) <http://lesrequinsmarteaux.over-blog.com/article-25815691.html >

BERKOWITZ, MICHAEL, 'Rootless Cosmopolitans: The New York Jewish Detectives of Jerome Charyn and Reggie Nadelson', *Transversalités: Revue de l'Institut Catholique de Paris*, 95 (2005), 179–87

BETTELHEIM, BRUNO, *The Uses of Enchantment: The Meaning and Importance of Fairy Tales* [1976] (London: Penguin, 1991)

BIFFI, GIACOMO, *Contro maestro Ciliegia: commento teologico a 'Le avventure di Pinocchio'* (Milan: Jaca Book, 1977)

BLANKINSHIP, ERIK, 'Pinocchio: A Spielberg Odyssey', film reviews, *The Tech*, 11 July 2001, p. 7 <http://tech.mit.edu/V121/PDF/N29.pdf>

BOOKER, M. KEITH, and ANNE-MARIE THOMAS, *The Science Fiction Handbook* (Chicheste & Malden, MA: Wiley-Blackwell, 2009)

BOSETTI, GILBERT, 'Pinocchio, perennità del mito', in *Pinocchio esportazione: il burattino di Collodi nella critica straniera*, ed. by Giorgio Cusatelli (Pescia: Armando, 2002), pp. 117–28

BOSTROM, NICK, 'In Defense of Posthuman Dignity', *Bioethics*, 19.3 (2005), 202–14

BOULD, MARK, and SHERRYL VINT, *The Routledge Concise History of Science Fiction* (New York: Routledge, 2011)

BOWLBY, RACHEL, *Freudian Mythologies: Greek Tragedy and Modern Identities* (Oxford: Oxford University Press, 2007)

BOYLAN, AMY, 'Carving a National Identity: Collodi, Pinocchio, and Post-unification Italy', in Michael Sherberg, ed., *Approaches to Teaching Collodi's Pinocchio and its Adaptations*, ed. by Michael Sherberg (New York: Modern Language Association of America, 2006), pp. 16–20

BRAIDOTTI, ROSI, *Metamorphoses: Towards a Materialist Theory of Becoming* (Cambridge: Polity Press, 2002)

—— *The Posthuman* (Cambridge: Polity Press, 2013)

BRETHES, ROMAIN, 'Conte ravagé', *Chronic'art* (November 2008) <http://lesrequinsmarteaux.over-blog.com/article-25815691.html>

BROWN, MARK, 'Banksy's Dismaland: "Amusements and Anarchism" in Artist's Biggest Project Yet', *Guardian*, 20 August 2015 <http://www.theguardian.com/artanddesign/2015/aug/20/banksy-dismaland-amusements-anarchism-weston-super-mare>

BRUNNER, VINCENT, 'Pinocchio', *Park Mag* (November 2008) <http://lesrequinsmarteaux.over-blog.com/article-25815691.html>

BRUNO, GIULIANA, 'Ramble City. Postmodernism and "Blade Runner"', *October*, 41 (1987), 61–74

BUFANO, REMO, *Pinocchio for the Stage in Four Short Plays* (New York: Alfred Knopf, 1929)

BUSCH, ANITA, '"Pinocchio"-inspired Live-action Film Being Developed at Disney', *Deadline Hollywood*, 8 April 2015 <http://deadline.com/2015/04/pinocchio-inspired-live-action-film-being-developed-at-disney-1201406564/>

CALLUS, IVAN, STEFAN HERBRECHTER, and MANUELA ROSSINI, 'Introduction: Dis/Locating Posthumanism in European Literary and Critical Traditions', *European Journal of English Studies*, 18.2 (2014), 103–20

CAMPBELL, JOSEPH, *The Hero with a Thousand Faces*, Bollingen Series, 17 (Novato, CA: New World Library, 2008)

——*A Skeleton Key to Finnegans Wake* (San Diego: Harcourt Brace, 1944)

CHARLES, DOROTHÉE, 'Interview de Winshluss', Musée des Arts Décoratifs, Paris, 14

January 2013 <http://www.lesartsdecoratifs.fr/francais/arts-decoratifs/expositions-23/archives-25/winshluss-un-monde-merveilleux/interview-de-winshluss>

CHARYN, JEROME, *The Isaac Quartet* (London: Zomba Books, 1984)

—— *The Man Who Grew Younger and Other Stories* (New York: Harper & Row, 1967)

—— *Pinocchio's Nose* (New York: Arbor House, 1983)

CHERUBINI, EUGENIO, *Pinocchio in Africa*, trans. by Angelo Patri (Boston & New York: Ginn, 1911)

CHETWODE CRAWLEY, W. J., 'Masonic Blue', *Ars Quatuor Coronatorum: Transactions of Quatuor Coronati Lodge No. 2076, London*, 22 (1910), 309–20

CHEVRIER, YVES, 'Blade Runner, or the Sociology of Anticipation', *Science Fiction Studies*, 11.1 (1984), 50–60

CLOC, JOE, 'Too Close for Comfort', *New Scientist*, 2899 (12 January 2013)

COLLODI, CARLO, *Le avventure di Pinocchio: storia di un burattino* (Florence: Felice Paggi, 1883)

—— *The Adventures of Pinocchio*, trans. by Nicolas Perella (Berkley & London: University of California Press, 1986)

—— *Pinocchio: The Tale of a Puppet*, trans. by Geoffrey Brock, intro. by Umberto Eco (New York: New York Review, 2008)

—— *Pinocchio: The Story of a Puppet*, trans. by Mary Alice Murray, intro. by David Almond, illus. by Grahame Baker-Smith (London: Folio Society, 2011)

—— *Occhi e nasi: (ricordi dal vero)* (Florence: F. Paggi, 1881)

CONSOLO, SALVATORE, 'The Myth of Pinocchio: Metamorphosis of a Puppet from Collodi's Pages to the Screen', in *Pinocchio, Puppets and Modernity: The Mechanical Body*, ed. by Katia Pizzi (London & New York: Routledge, 2012), pp. 163–74

COOVER, ROBERT, *Pinocchio in Venice* (New York: Linden Press/ Simon & Schuster, 1991)

CREED, BARBARA, *The Monstrous-feminine: Film, Feminism, Psychoanalysis* (London: Routledge, 1993)

CROWE, F. J. W., 'Colours in Freemasonry', *Ars Quatuor Coronatorum: Transactions of Quatuor Coronati Lodge No. 2076, London*, 17 (1904), 3–11

DALTON, STEPHEN, 'Blade Runner: Anatomy of a Classic', BFI homepage, 29 June 2015 <http://www.bfi.org.uk/news-opinion/news-bfi/features/blade-runner>

DE RIJKE, VICTORIA, LENE ØSTERMARK-JOHANSEN, and HELEN THOMAS, eds, *Nose Book: Representations of the Nose in Literature and the Arts* (London: Middlesex University Press, 2000)

DEDOLA, ROSSANA, *Pinocchio e Collodi* (Milan: Bruno Mondadori, 2002)

DICK, PHILIP K., *Do Androids Dream of Electric Sheep?* (New York: Ballantine Books, 1968)

DINE, JIM, 'Walking to Borås' [statue] (2008)

Dizionario dei modi di dire, Corriere Della Sera <http://dizionari.corriere.it/dizionario-modi-di-dire/G/grillo.shtml>

Dizionario delle origini, invenzioni e scoperte nelle arti, nelle scienze, nella geografia, nel commercio, nell'agricoltura, 4 vols (Milan: A. Bonfanti, 1828)

DONÀ, SILVIO, *Pinocchio 2112: romanzo di fantascienza* (Milan: Leone, 2009)

DRONKE, PETER, 'The Land of Cokaygne: Three Notes on the Latin Background' in *Medieval Latin and Middle English Literature: Essays in Honour of Jill Mann*, ed. by Christopher Cannon and Maura Nolan (Woodbridge: Boydell & Brewer, 2011), pp. 65–75

DUMAND, MARION, 'La Résistance plus que le talent', *Politis* (December 2008) <https://www.politis.fr/articles/2008/12/la-resistance-plus-que-le-talent-5037/>

DUNDES, ALAN, 'The Motif-index and the Tale Type Index: A Critique', *Journal of Folklore Research*, 34.3 (1997), 195–202

DUNN, TIMOTHY, '*A.I.: Artificial Intelligence* and the Tragic Sense of Life', in *Steven Spielberg and Philosophy: We're Gonna Need a Bigger Book*, ed. by Dean A. Kowalski (Lexington: University Press of Kentucky, 2008), pp. 82–94

ECO, UMBERTO, 'Introduction', in Carlo Collodi, *Pinocchio: The Tale of a Puppet*, trans. by Geoffrey Brock (New York: New York Review, 2008)

—— *The Role of the Reader: Explorations in the Semiotics of Texts* (Bloomington & London: Indiana University Press, 1979)

ELIADE, MIRCEA, *Myth and Reality* (London: Allen & Unwin, 1964)

FORSDICK, CHARLES, LAURENCE GROVE, and LIBBIE McQUILLAN, eds, *The Francophone Bande Dessinée* (Amsterdam: Rodopi, 2005)

FRANK, YASHA, *Pinocchio (a Musical Legend)* [music score] (New York: Edward B. Marks Music, 1939)

FREUD, SIGMUND, *The Ego and the Id*, in *The Standard Edition of the Complete Psychological Works of Sigmund Freud*, ed. and trans. by James Strachey, 24 vols (London: Hogarth Press, 1953–74), XIX (1961)

FULLERTON, HUW, 'Humans Series Review: "A surprise success — thriving where Utopia drowned"', *Radio Times*, 2 August 2015 <http://www.radiotimes.com/news/2015–08–02/humans-series-review-a-surprise-success---thriving-where-utopia-drowned>

GATTICI, FRANCESCO, *Le disgratie di Burattino: commedia ridicolosa, e buffonesca* (Venice: Battista Combi, 1624)

GILMAN, SANDER, *The Jew's Body* (New York: Routledge, 1991)

GIOVETTI, PAOLA, *L'Italia dell'insolito e del mistero: 100 itinerari 'diversi'* (Rome: Edizioni Mediterranee, 2001)

GRAHAM, ELAINE L., *Representations of the Post/human: Monsters, Aliens and Others in Popular Culture* (Manchester: Manchester University Press, 2002)

GRANDE ORIENTE D'ITALIA, 'Massoni celebri' <http://www.grandeoriente.it/che-cosa-e-la-massoneria/massoni-celebri/>

GRANT, BARRY KEITH, '"Sensuous Elaboration": Reason and the Visible in the Science Fiction Film', in *Liquid Metal: The Science Fiction Film Reader*, ed. by Sean Redmond (London: Wallflower, 2004), pp. 17–23

GRAY, EMILY, *The Adventures of Pinocchio, A Marionette* (Chicago: A. Flannagan, 1912)

GROSSMANN, MARIA, *Colori e lessico: studi sulla struttura semantica degli aggettivi di colore in catalano, castigliano, italiano, romeno, latino ed ungherese* (Tübingen: G. Narr, 1988)

GROVE, LAURENCE, *Comics in French: The European Bande Dessinée in Context* (New York & Oxford: Berghahn Books, 2010)

HARRÁN, DON, 'The Jewish Nose in Early Modern Art and Music', *Renaissance Studies*, 28.1 (2014), 50–70

HAYLES, KATHERINE, *How We Became Posthuman: Virtual Bodies in Cybernetics, Literature, and Informatics* (Chicago & London: University of Chicago Press, 1999)

—— 'Wrestling with Transhumanism', in *H+/-: Transhumanism and its Critics*, ed. by Gregory R. Hansell and William Grassie (Philadelphia, PA: Metanexus, 2011), pp. 215–26

HOBERMAN, J., 'The Dreamlife of Androids', *Sight & Sound*, 11.9 (2001), 16–18

HOELLER, STEPHAN A., 'C. G. Jung and the Alchemical Renewal', *Gnosis: A Journal of Western Inner Traditions*, 8 (1988) <http://gnosis.org/jung_alchemy.htm>

HOFFMANN, E. T. A., 'The Sandman', in *The Golden Pot and Other Tales* [1817] (Oxford: Oxford University Press, 2000), pp. 85–118

HOMER, *The Iliad*, trans. by A. T. Murray <http://www.theoi.com/Text/HomerIliad18.html>

HONEYMAN, SUSAN, *Consuming Agency in Fairy Tales, Childlore, and Folkliterature* (New York: Routledge, 2010)

Humanity+ <http://humanityplus.org/philosophy/transhumanist-faq/#answer_19>

HUTCHEON, LINDA, *A Poetics of Postmodernism: History, Theory, Fiction* (New York & London: Routledge, 1988)

IPSEN, CARL, *Italy in the Age of Pinocchio: Children and Danger in the Liberal Era* (New York: Palgrave Macmillan, 2006)

JAMESON, FREDRIC, 'Future City', *New Left Review*, 21 (May-June 2003) <https://newleftreview.org/issues/ii21/articles/fredric-jameson-future-city>

JEFFERY, SCOTT, *The Silver Age Superhero as Psychedelic Shaman* (2011) <http://stir.academia.edu/ScottJeffery/Papers/1334997/The_Silver_Age_Superhero_as_Psychedelic_Shaman>

JENSEN, VAN, and DUSTIN HIGGINS, *Pinocchio: Vampire Slayer* (San Jose, CA: SLG, 2009)

—— *Pinocchio, Vampire Slayer Vol. 2: The Great Puppet Theater* (San Jose, CA: SLG, 2010)

JOHNSON, BARBARA, *Persons and Things* (Cambridge, MA, & London: Harvard University Press, 2008)

JONES, BERNARD E., *Freemasons' Guide and Compendium* (London: George G. Harrap, 1950)

JUNG, CARL GUSTAV, *The Archetypes and the Collective Unconscious* (London: Routledge, 1968)

—— *Four Archetypes: Mother, Rebirth, Spirit, Trickster*, trans. by R. F. C. Hull (London: Routledge, 2003)

JUNQUA, AMELIE, 'Wordless Eloquence — Shaun Tan, *The Arrival*, and Winshluss, *Pinocchio*', *Revue de recherche en civilisation américaine*, 5 (2015) <http://rrca.revues.org/685>

KAFKA, FRANZ, *The Metamorphosis* (London: Parton Press, 1937)

KALOH VID, NATALIA, 'Translation of Children's Literature in the Soviet Union: How Pinocchio Got a Golden Key', *International Research in Children's Literature*, 6.1 (July 2013), 90–103

KELLNER, DOUGLAS, FLO LEIBOWITZ, and MICHAEL RYAN, '*Blade Runner*: A Diagnostic Critique', *Jump Cut*, 29 (February 1984), 6–8 <http://www.ejumpcut.org/archive/onlinessays/JC29folder/BladeRunner.html>

KIRK, GEOFFREY S., *Myth: Its Meaning and Functions in Ancient and Other Cultures* (London: Cambridge University Press, 1983)

KLOPP, CHARLES, 'Workshops of Creation, Filthy and Not: Collodi's Pinocchio and Shelley's Frankenstein', in *Pinocchio, Puppets and Modernity: The Mechanical Body*, ed. by Katia Pizzi (London & New York: Routledge, 2012)

KNIGHT, CHRIS, 'He's Back From the Future — Again; Terminator Reboot with Ah-nold a Well-crafted Addition to Canon', *Edmonton Journal*, 2 July 2015

KOEPSELL, DAVID, 'Gaius Baltar and the Transhuman Temptation', in *Knowledge Here Begins Out There*, ed. by Jason T. Eberl (Malden, MA: Blackwell, 2008), pp. 241–52

KREIDER, TIM, '*A.I. Artificial Intelligence*', *Film Quarterly*, 56.2 (2002), 32–39

KURZWEIL, RAY, *The Singularity is Near: When Humans Transcend Biology* (London: Gerald Duckworth, 2005)

KUZNETS, LOIS ROSTOW, *Narratives of Animation, Metamorphosis, and Development* (New Haven, CT: Yale University Press, 1994)

LEAK, ANDREW, *Barthes: Mythologies* (London: Grant & Cutler, 1994)

LEEMING, DAVID, *The Oxford Companion to World Mythology* (Oxford: Oxford University Press, 2005)

LIGOTTI, THOMAS, *The Conspiracy Against the Human Race* (New York: Hippocampus Press, 2010)

LORENZINI, PAOLO (Nipote Collodi), *Il cuore di Pinocchio: nuove avventure del celebre burattino* (Florence: Bemporad, 1917)

—— *The Heart of Pinocchio: New Adventures of the Celebrated Little Puppet by Nipote Collodi (Paolo Lorenzini), Adapted From the Italian by Virginia Watson* (New York: Harper & Brothers, 1919)

LUCKHURST, ROGER, *Science Fiction* (Cambridge: Polity Press, 2005)

MALERBA, LUIGI, *Pinocchio con gli stivali* [1977] (Parma: MUP, 2004)

MANGANELLI, GIORGIO, *Pinocchio: un libro parallelo* (Milan: Adelphi, 2002)

MANILA, GABRIEL JANER, 'Tres infancias soñadas: Pinocchio, Alicia y el Pequeño Príncipe', in *Infancia y escolarización en la modernidad tardía*, ed. by J. Carlos González Faraco (Madrid: AKAL, 2002), pp. 201–31

MARCHESCHI, DANIELA, 'Introduzione', in Carlo Collodi, *Opere*, ed. by Daniela Marcheschi (Milan: Arnoldo Mondadori, 1995)

MARINO, JOSEF, *Hi! Ho! Pinocchio* (Chicago: Reilly & Lee, 1940)

MARRONE, GIANFRANCO, 'Parallelismi e traduzione: il caso Manganelli', in *Le avventure di Pinocchio: tra un linguaggio e l'altro*, ed. by Isabella Pezzini and Paolo Fabbri (Roma: Meltemi, 2002), pp. 257–76

McHALE, BRIAN, *Postmodernist Fiction* (New York & London: Methuen, 1987)

MILLER, ANN, *Reading bande dessinée: Critical Approaches to French-language Comic Strip* (Chicago: University of Chicago Press, 2007)

MOLARI, TOMMASO, *Memorie sul castello di Montebello di Romagna* [1934] (Verucchio: Pazzini, 2002)

MONGIARDINI-REMBADI, GEMMA, *Pinocchio Under the Sea* (New York: Macmillan, 1913)

MORE, MAX, 'Transhumanist FAQ' <http://humanityplus.org/philosophy/transhumanist-faq/#answer_19>

MORPURGO, MICHAEL, *Pinocchio, by Pinocchio* (London: Harper Collins, 2013)

MORRIS, NIGEL, *The Cinema of Steven Spielberg: Empire of Light* (London: Wallflower Press, 2007)

MORRISSEY, THOMAS J., and R. WUNDERLICH, 'Death and Rebirth in Pinocchio', *Children's Literature*, 11 (1983), 64–75

MUKASONGA, SCHOLASTIQUE, *Cockroaches* (Brooklyn, NY: Archipelago, 2016)

MULHALL, STEPHEN, 'Picturing the Human (Body and Soul): A Reading of Blade Runner', *Film and Philosophy*, 1 (1994), 87–104

NELSON, VICTORIA, *The Secret Life of Puppets* (Cambridge, MA, & London: Harvard University Press, 2001)

NICOL, BRAN, *The Cambridge Introduction to Postmodern Fiction* (Cambridge: Cambridge University Press, 2009)

OVID, *Metamorphoses* (London: G. Bell & Sons, 1884)

PACCHIONI, FEDERICO, 'La contaminazione tra teatro di figura e cinema in *Che cosa sono le nuvole?*', in *Contaminazioni culturali: musica, teatro, cinema e letteratura nell'Italia contemporanea*, ed. by Fulvio Orsitto and Simona Wright (Rome: Vecchiarelli, 2014), pp. 233–44

——'La passione di un burattino: teste di legno ribattezzate all'ombra della Commedia dell'Arte', *Intersezioni: Review of the History of Ideas*, 3 (2009), 339–56

PANTELI, GEORGIA, 'The Satirical Tradition of Collodi and Pinocchio's Nose', in *The Rhetoric of Topics and Forms*, ed. by Gianna Zocco (Berlin & Boston, MA: Walter de Gruyter, 2021), pp. 381–90

PASTOUREAU, MICHEL, *Blue: The History of a Color* (Princeton, NJ, & Oxford: Princeton University Press, 2001)

PATRI, ANGELO, *Pinocchio in America* (New York: Doubleday Doran 1930)

PATTEN, ROBERT L., 'Pinocchio through the Looking Glass: Jerome Charyn's Portrait of the Artist as a Mytholept', in *Novel: A Forum on Fiction*, 17.1 (1983), 67–76

PERELLA, NICOLAS, 'An Essay on Pinocchio', in *The Adventures of Pinocchio*, trans. by Nicolas Perella (Berkeley: University of California Press, 1986) pp. 1–69

PISANO, PAOLO, 'Collodi con il suo "Pinocchio" a "I Venerdì del Grande Oriente"', *Grande Oriente d'Italia*, 19 April 2013 <http://www.grandeoriente.it/collodi-con-il-suo-pinocchio-a-i-venerdi-del-grande-oriente/>

PORTA, GIAMBATTISTA DELLA, *Della fisionomia dell'huomo* (Venice: C. Tomasini, 1644)

Propp, Vladimir, *Morphology of the Folktale* (Austin: University of Texas Press, 1968)

R. M. P., and Peter Fitting, 'Futurecop: The Neutralization of Revolt in *Blade Runner*', *Science Fiction Studies*, 14.3 (1987), 340–54

Richter, Dieter, *Carlo Collodi und sein Pinocchio: ein weitgereister Holzbengel und seine toskanische Geschichte* (Berlin: Klaus Wagenbach, 2004)

Robinson, Ian, 'Annotations for Snow White and the Seven Dwarfs', *Sur La Lune Fairytales* <https://www.surlalunefairytales.com/s-z/snow-white-seven-dwarfs/snow-white-seven-dwarfs-annotations.html#SEVENTEEN>

Roden, David, *Posthuman Life* (London: Routledge, 2015)

Rohrer, Denis, 'In the Land of Cockaigne', *Alimentarium* <http://www.ealimentarium.ch/en/magazine/pleasure/amazing-feasts/land-cockaigne>

Rollino, Massimo, 'Presentazione', in Giuseppe Garbarino, *Pinocchio svelato: i luoghi, il bestiario e le curiosità nella favola del Collodi.* (Florence: AB, 2014)

Rossi, Paolo Aldo, 'La fata turchina e le metamorfosi di Pinocchio', in *Fate: madri, amanti, streghe*, ed. by Sonia Maura Barillari, L'Immagine Riflessa/ Quaderni Serie Miscellanea, 13 (Alessandria: Edizioni dell'Orso, 2012)

Roure, Benjamin, 'Winshluss: "Déconner est une forme d'action"', *BoDoï*, 1 February 2009 <http://www.bodoi.info/winshluss-deconner-est-une-forme-daction/>

RT, 'Dismal-aid! Banksy Donates Dismaland Attraction to Shelter Calais Migrants', *RT*, 16 October 2015 <https://www.rt.com/uk/318883-dismalaid-banksy-dismaland-calais/>

Ruskin, John, *The Works of John Ruskin*, ed. by E. T. Cook and Alexander Wedderburn, 39 vols (London: George Allen, 1903–12)

Sammon, Paul M., *Future Noir: The Making of 'Blade Runner'* (London: Harper Collins, 1996)

Scala, Flaminio, *La fortunata Isabella* <https://sites.google.com/site/italiancommedia/plays-and-scenari/scenari/la-fortunata-isabella>

Schaefer, Sandy, 'Guillermo Del Toro's Stop-motion Pinocchio Adaptation Still Moving Forward', *Screen Rant*, 2 January 2013 <http://screenrant.com/guillermo-del-toro-pinocchio-not-postponed/>

Segal, Robert A., *Myth: A Very Short Introduction* (Oxford: Oxford University Press, 2004)

Sharp, Robert, 'When Machines Get Souls: Nietzsche on the Cylon Uprising', in *Battlestar Galactica and Philosophy: Knowledge Here Begins Out There*, ed. by Jason T. Eberl (Malden MA: Blackwell, 2008), pp. 15–28

Shelley, Mary, *Frankenstein: or, The Modern Prometheus* [1818] (Oxford & New York: Oxford University Press, 1994)

Shetley, Vernon, and Alissa Ferguson, 'Reflections in a Silver Eye: Lens and Mirror in Blade Runner', *Science Fiction Studies*, 28.1 (2001), 66–76

Smith, Kevin Paul, *The Postmodern Fairytale: Folkloric Intertexts in Contemporary Fiction* (Basingstoke: Palgrave Macmillan, 2007)

Sobchack, Vivian Carol, *Screening Space: The American Science Fiction Film*, 2nd enl. edn (New Brunswick, NJ, & London: Rutgers University Press, 1997)

Spiegelman, Art, *Maus* (New York: Pantheon Books, 1991)

Stambovsky, Phillip, *Myth and the Limits of Reason* (Amsterdam & Atlanta, GA: Rodopi, 1996)

Sterne, Laurence, *The Life and Opinions of Tristram Shandy, Gentleman. Including the Sentimental Journey* (Amsterdam: printed for P. van Slaukenberg, 1771)

Suvin, Darko, 'On the Poetics of the Science Fiction Genre', *College English*, 34.3 (1972), 372–82

Tibbetts, John C., 'Robots Redux: *A.I. Artificial Intelligence* (2001)', *Literature & Film Quarterly*, 29.4 (2001), 256–61

VANDERHAEGHE, STÉPHANE, *Robert Coover & the Generosity of the Page* (London: Dalkey Archive Press, 2013)

WARNER, MARINA, 'Into the Woods', The British Academy Lecture, 11 May 2015, <http://www.britac.ac.uk/events/2015/Into_the_Woods.cfm>

——*Once Upon a Time: A Short History of Fairy Tale* (Oxford: Oxford University Press, 2014)

WATSON, IAN, 'Plumbing Stanley Kubrick', *The New York Review of Science Fiction* (2000) <http://www.ianwatson.info/kubrick.htm>

WAY, BRIAN, *Pinocchio, A New Version of the Story by Carlo Collodi* (London: Dennis Dobson, 1954)

WELLCOME COLLECTION, 'Superhuman' [exhibition], 19 July-16 October, 2012

WEST, MARK I., 'Pinocchio's Journey from the Pleasure Principle to the Reality Principle', in Lucy Rollin and Mark I. West, *Psychoanalytic Responses to Children's Literature* (Jefferson, NC, & London: McFarland, 1999), pp. 65–70

WILLINGHAM, BILL, *Fables* (New York: Vertigo/ DC Comics, 2002–15)

WINSHLUSS, *Mr Ferraille* (Albi: Les Requins Marteaux, 2001)

——*Pinocchio* (Albi: Les Requins Marteaux, 2008)

WOLFE, CARY, *What Is Posthumanism?* (Minneapolis: University of Minnesota Press, 2010)

WUNDERLICH, RICHARD, and THOMAS MORRISSEY, *Pinocchio Goes Postmodern: Perils of a Puppet in the United States* (New York & London: Routledge, 2002)

ZIPES, JACK DAVID, *Breaking the Magic Spell: Radical Theories of Folk and Fairy Tales* (London: Heinemann Educational, 1979)

——*Fairy Tale as Myth — Myth as Fairy Tale* (Lexington: University Press of Kentucky, 1994)

——*Happily Ever After: Fairy Tales, Children, and the Culture Industry* (London: Routledge, 1997)

Films and Television Series

A. I. Artificial Intelligence, dir. by Steven Spielberg (USA: Warner Bros. Pictures, 2001)

Andromeda Stories (released in the USA as *Gemini Prophecies*), dir. by Masamitsu Sasaki (Japan: TOEI, 1982)

Le avventure di Pinocchio, dir. by Luigi Comencini (Italy, France & West Germany: RAI, O.R.T.F., Bavaria Film, Sanpaolofilm, Cinepat, 1972)

Battlestar Galactica, David Eick Productions (USA & UK: British Sky Broadcasting, 2004–09)

Battlestar Galactica: Razor, dir. by Félix Enríquez Alcalá (USA: David Eick Productions, 2007)

Battlestar Galactica: The Plan, dir. by Edward James Olmos (USA: David Eick Productions, 2009)

Blade Runner, dir. by Ridley Scott (USA & Hong Kong: The Ladd Company, 1982)

Caprica, dir. by Michael Nankin & others (Canada & USA: David Eick Productions, 2009–10)

Che cosa sono le nuvole?, dir. by Pier Paolo Pasolini, in *Capriccio all'italiana* (Italy: Dino de Laurentiis, 1968)

Despicable Me 2, dir. by Pierre Coffin and Chris Renaud (USA: Universal Pictures, 2013)

Ghost in the Shell, dir. by Mamoru Oshii (Japan & USA: Bandai Visual, 1995)

Ghost in the Shell 2: Innocence, dir. by Mamoru Oshii (Japan: Bandai Visual, 2004)

Ghost in the Shell: Stand Alone Complex Solid State Society, dir. by Mamoru Oshii (Japan: Production I.G., 2006)

Happily Ever After, dir. by John Howley (USA: Filmation Associates, 1993)

Humans, dir. by China Moo-Young (UK & USA: Channel 4 & AMC, 2015–18)

The Matrix, dir. by the Wachowskis (USA: Warner Bros & others, 1999)

The Matrix Reloaded, dir. by the Wachowskis (USA: Village Roadshow Pictures & others, 2003)

The Matrix Revolutions, dir. by the Wachowskis (USA: Village Roadshow Pictures & others, 2003)

Once Upon a Time (USA: Kitsis/ Horowitz, ABC Studios, 2011–18)

'Past Imperfect', BBC Radio 4, 22 July 2015 <http://www.bbc.co.uk/programmes/b062kx4x>

Pink Floyd: The Wall, dir. by Alan Parker (UK: Metro-Goldwyn-Mayer, 1982)

Pinocchio (USA: Walt Disney Productions, 1940)

Pinocchio, dir. by Roberto Benigni (Italy & USA: Miramax Films, 2002)

Pinocchio (South Korea: Seoul Broadcasting System, 2014–15)

Pinocchio and the Emperor of the Night, dir. by Hal Sutherland (USA: Filmation Associates, 1987)

Pinocchio 3000, or *Pinocchio le Robot* (Canada, France, & Spain: CinéGroupe, Filmax, 2004)

Sense8, dir. by the Wachowskis. (USA: Netflix, 2015)

Shrek, dir. by Andrew Adamson & Vicky Jenson (USA: Dreamworks, 2001)

Shrek 2, dir. by Andrew Adamson & others (USA: Dreamworks, 2004)

Shrek the Third, dir. by Chris Miller & Raman Hui (USA: Dreamworks, 2007)

Shrek Forever After, dir. by Mike Mitchell (USA: Dreamworks, 2010)

Snow-White (USA: Fleischer Studios, 1933)

Snow White and the Seven Dwarfs (USA: Walt Disney Productions, 1937)

The Terminator, dir. by James Cameron (UK & USA: Helmdale Film & others, 1984)

Terminator 2: Judgment Day, dir. by James Cameron (USA & France: Carolco Pictures & others, 1991)

Terminator Salvation, dir. by Joseph McGinty Nichol (USA: Halcyon Company, 2009)

Terminator Genisys, dir. by Alan Taylor (USA: Paramount Pictures, 2015)

The Twilight Zone (USA: CBS Productions, 1985–1989)

INDEX

❖